The Masque of Africa

ALSO BY V. S. NAIPAUL

FICTION

The Mystic Masseur
The Suffrage of Elvira
Miguel Street
A House for Mr Biswas
Mr Stone and the Knights Companion
The Mimic Men
A Flag on the Island
Guerrillas
A Bend in the River
The Enigma of Arrival
A Way in the World
Half a Life
Magic Seeds
In a Free State

NON-FICTION

The Middle Passage
An Area of Darkness
The Loss of El Dorado
The Overcrowded Barracoon
India: A Wounded Civilization
The Return of Eva Perón
Among the Believers: An Islamic Journey
Finding the Centre
A Turn in the South
India: A Million Mutinies Now
Beyond Belief
Letters Between a Father and Son
The Writer and the World: Essays
Literary Occasions
A Writer's People: Ways of Looking and Feeling

The Masque of Africa

GLIMPSES OF AFRICAN BELIEF

V.S.
NAIPAUL

PICADOR

First published 2010 by Picador
an imprint of Pan Macmillan, a division of Macmillan Publishers Limited
Pan Macmillan, 20 New Wharf Road, London N1 9RR
Basingstoke and Oxford
Associated companies throughout the world
www.panmacmillan.com

ISBN 978-0-330-47205-0 HB
ISBN 978-0-330-52658-6 TPB

1 3 5 7 9 8 6 4 2

A CIP catalogue record for this book is available from
the British Library.

Typeset by SetSystems, Saffron Walden, Essex
Printed in the UK by CPI Mackays, Chatham ME5 8TD

Visit www.picador.com to read more about all our books
and to buy them. You will also find features, author interviews and
news of any author events, and you can sign up for e-newsletters
so that you're always first to hear about our new releases.

To the *A team*

N.S., G.C.G., L.F. de R., Ev. de R., T.T., P.E., D.P.J.,

and for Andrew Wylie.

Contents

ONE

The Tomb at Kasubi

I SPENT eight to nine months in East Africa in 1966. A month in Tanzania; six weeks or so in the Kenya Highlands; the rest of the time in Uganda. Some years later I even used a version of Uganda in a piece of fiction; you can do that only when you feel you have a fair idea of a place, or an idea sufficient for your needs. Forty-two years after that first visit I went back to Uganda. I was hoping to get started there on this book about the nature of African belief, and I thought it would be better to ease myself into my subject in a country I knew or half knew. But I found the place eluding me.

I had gone to Uganda in 1966 to be a writer in residence at Makerere University in Kampala, the capital. I lived in a little grey bungalow on the campus, which was spacious and open and well tended, with asphalted roads with kerbstones, and watchmen at the barred entrance. My allowance (provided by an American foundation) was enough to give me a driver and a cook. My duties weren't too well defined, and I was living more or less privately, absorbed in a book I had brought with me, working hard on it every day, and paying less attention to Africa and the students at Makerere than I should have done. When I wanted some relief from the book and the campus, I would drive the fifteen or so miles to Entebbe, where the airport was and where, on the edge of Lake Victoria, which was very grand, the largest lake in Africa, there was also (as there was in other British colonial towns) a Botanical Garden, pleasant to walk in. Sometimes (a reminder of the wildness by which we were surrounded, but from which we were protected) the ground of the Garden was flooded in parts by water from the Lake seeping through.

The drive from Kampala to Entebbe was a drive through country; that was part of its restfulness in 1966. It was different now. You could see from the air, as the plane landed, how Entebbe itself had grown, with more than a scattering of villages or settlements far and wide on the damp green ground below the heavy grey clouds of the rainy season; and you understood that what was once bush in an unimportant area of a small colony had become valuable building land. The shiny new corrugated-iron roofs gave you the feeling that in spite of the bad recent past, forty years as bad as anything in Africa – murderous tyranny followed by war and little wars – there might be a money frenzy down there now.

The drive to the capital was no longer a drive through country. Once you got past the old administrative and residential buildings of colonial Entebbe, still somehow surviving (red corrugated-iron roofs and white-painted bargeboards still in good order), you found yourself in an improvised semi-urban development, flimsy-looking, where many of the buildings that had been put up (groceries, garages, flats) seemed only waiting to be pulled down, and in the meantime were bright, and repetitive, with painted walls advertising mobile phones.

It was like that all the way to the capital. There was no view at some stage of the city and the green hills for which Kampala used to be famous. All those hills were now built over; and many of the spaces between the hills, the dips, were seemingly floored over with the old corrugated iron of poor dwellings. But with all these dwellings there had come money and cars and, for people who didn't have the money, the *boda-bodas*, the bicycles and motorbikes that for a small sum offered you a fast pillion-ride through the stalled traffic, a pillion-ride which in colonial days might have been illegal. The roads couldn't deal with the traffic; even in this rainy season the roads were dusty, scuffed down beyond the asphalt to the fertile red earth of Uganda. I couldn't recognise this Kampala, and even at this early stage it seemed to me that I was in a place where a calamity had occurred.

Later I got the figures for population. They told the story. In 1966 there were about five million people in Uganda. Now – in spite of the rule between 1971 and 1979 of Idi Amin (who was said to have killed a hundred and fifty thousand) and the comparable rule between 1981 and 1985 of the feral Milton Obote, who liked his hair to slope up high from the parting, in a version of the style known here as the English style; in spite of those two, and all the subsequent little wars, still going on after forty years (a million and a half people said to be displaced in the north); and in spite of the Aids epidemic – there were between thirty and thirty-four million people in Uganda. As though Nature, going against logic, wished to outdo itself, to make up for the blood Uganda had lost and didn't want the little country and its great suffering to fade away.

There was a mosque or church at the top of every hill, and major ecclesiastical buildings everywhere else. All the Christian denominations were represented. And in the over-built-up poorer areas there were simpler 'born-again' Christian structures, sometimes fancifully named, with sign-boards: as though religion here was like a business that met a desperate consumer need at all levels. There were competing mosques of various sorts, Sunni, Shia, Ismaili; the Ismaili community, considered heretical by some, was powerful in East Africa. There was even a mosque and a school of the Ahmadiya sect, which honoured a nineteenth-century Indian-born prophet of Islam and was not accepted by all Muslims. To add to the mix, Brother Leader Ghaddafi of Libya was due in a few days, with his stylish clothes and dark glasses, and with his famous female bodyguard (in addition to his two hundred security men), to open a very big Libyan mosque on a prominent hill site in old Kampala. In the commercial area of the town there were two newish Indian stone temples near the Indian places of business. The Indians had been invited back after their expulsion by Amin;

and they had come back to an ambiguous welcome: a local paper was wondering whether they had been compensated twice, and asking its readers to comment. So the red flags flew on the stone temples, to say that the temples were in use.

Until the 1840s Uganda had been isolated, living with itself. Then Arab traders had arrived from the east. They wanted slaves and ivory; in return they gave cheap guns and what in effect were toys. The Kabaka Sunna, known for his great cruelty, had welcomed the Arabs. He liked their toys. He especially liked the mirrors; he had never seen his face before, and couldn't get over it. It was Sunna's son and successor, Mutesa, who in 1861–2 met and entertained and for some months frustrated the explorer John Hanning Speke, who was within days of discovering the source of the Nile.

Mutesa was only twenty-five, almost as cruel as his father, but at the same time outward-looking, a man of intuition and intelligence. He liked the guns he got from Speke; he liked the compass and other instruments he saw Speke using. But Mutesa's Baganda people, with their gift for social organisation, their military discipline, and their elaborate court ritual, evolved over some centuries, had a civilisation of their own. They built roads as straight as Roman roads; they had a high idea of sanitation; they had a fleet on Lake Victoria, with an admiral and naval techniques of their own, and they could launch invasions of Busoga across the Nile. They worked iron and made their own spears and knives; they knew how to make bark-cloth and were beautiful builders of grass houses – with roofs as neatly trimmed as though by a London tailor, Speke thought. Knowing that his people could do all these things, Mutesa arrived, quite marvellously, at the idea that the true difference between himself and Speke, very much a Victorian Christian, always ready to preach to the heathen, was philosophical and religious. Mutesa turned against Islam, which he had partly adopted; he said the Arabs were liars; and thirteen years later, when he met the explorer H. M. Stanley, he asked his help in getting English missionaries to come to Uganda.

The fruit of that decision of a hundred and thirty years before could now be seen in Kampala. Foreign religion, to go by the competing ecclesiastical buildings on the hilltops, was like an applied and contagious illness, curing nothing, giving no final answers, keeping everyone in a state of nerves, fighting wrong battles, narrowing the mind. And it was possible to wonder whether Mutesa himself, if he could come back, mightn't have thought that he had made a mistake, and that Africa, left to itself in this matter, might have arrived at its own more valuable synthesis of old and new.

Why had the foreign-revealed religions wrought such havoc with African belief? These foreign religions had a difficult theology; I didn't think it would have been easy, starting from scratch, to put it across to someone here. I asked Prince Kassim. He was a direct descendant of Mutesa, but on the Islamic side, a family division that reflected Mutesa's early half-conversion to Islam. The prince said I was wrong. Both Christianity and Islam would have been attractive to Africans for a simple reason. They both offered an afterlife; gave people a vision of themselves living on after death. African religion, on the other hand, was more airy, offering only the world of spirits, and the ancestors.

2

I THOUGHT I should go looking for my old bungalow. I had planted a tulip tree (bought at the Entebbe Botanical Garden) in the garden, and at the back of my head at the time was the idea that for one reason or another I might come back to Kampala one day and it might be good then to see how the tree had done. But the Makerere campus was not recognisable. It seemed to me that it had become part of the crowded dusty town. A letter in the local paper saying that university fences had been knocked down and not replaced appeared to confirm what I felt. But then I heard from a lecturer that in spite of the up-and-down history of the place (a vice-chancellor killed in the Idi Amin time, and other senior people jailed and beaten up) certain records, including staff housing, were intact. It was stated there that in 1966 I had lived at 80 Kasubi View.

The name of the road rang a bell, but I wasn't sure about the number; and when I was taken to the bungalow, which was ragged with decay, I felt I hadn't lived there at all. I think that the house might have been selected for me because a big tree in the garden had been cut down a while before and the stump remained. I was taken to look at the stump, but I didn't know what a tulip-tree stump would look like, and no one in my party knew either. But the setting was wrong. My memory of my bungalow and garden was a memory of openness. This was dark and enclosed. The ground fell away at the side, and there was a moraine of garbage where the ground fell away.

There was trouble about garbage in Makerere; it didn't seem to be collected regularly. Here and there on the busy paths or walkways marabout storks, undisturbed by the passage of students, were pecking with their long beaks at broken bundles of garbage. (Speke calls these birds adjutants, and with their big wings folded and their long, thin, yellow legs they did have an official appearance, long-coated and hunched and assessing.) These magnificent birds had become scavengers here, and the garbage they fed on seemed to discolour and deform their faces, giving them ugly, pendent growths. They had now to live with their deformities, for which Nature was not responsible. It was sad to see, and sad, too, for the students: they were crowded together in mildewed halls and dormitories hung with sagging lines of laundry; and, outside, they lived helplessly amid garbage. It would have gone against their instinct. Speke, a hundred and forty years before, wrote with admiration of the Ugandans' concern for sanitation.

It seemed here that everything was working against the university and the idea of learning. And, again, figures told the story. In 1966 there were about four thousand students. Now there were thirty thousand. The main road to where in the old days I remembered a barred entrance was like a busy shopping street. Choked Kampala lay just outside.

There were at least two murders (by outsiders of outsiders) in the Makerere campus while I was in Kampala. In the first incident a young Pakistani car salesman was lured to the campus by bogus customers who said they wanted a trial drive. That would have seemed safe enough to anyone, but as soon as the car was in the campus the salesman was garrotted by a man sitting in the back, and knifed in the neck until he died. In the second incident a security guard, of all people, was killed in the early morning as he tried to rob a *boda-boda* passenger.

Kasubi View, where I was told I had lived, would at some time have given a view of the 1884 tomb of Mutesa I, hill looking to hill across the city. The city was too built up now to give this view. I don't think I had seen it even in 1966. Busy with my book, following the local situation with only half a mind, thinking that I had all the time in the world for local events and local sightseeing, never imagining that in pacific Kampala there would be army trucks on the streets, I had put Kasubi off until it was too late. I had been given a letter of introduction to the Kabaka, Sir Frederick Mutesa, otherwise Mutesa II. But I had not sent it till March. I got a civil reply — amazing in the circumstances — but then it was too late.

Obote, the prime minister, had sent in the army (under Amin) against the almost defenceless palace of the Kabaka. Most people thought that something so sacrilegious — the offering of violence to a man who was more than an African king, was an embodiment of the soul of his people – would never happen. Somehow the Kabaka had managed to get away. He found a terrible kind of pauper's sanctuary in England, painful for a kabaka, and died there three years later in 1969 at the age of forty-five. His tragedy and especially his early death is still mourned by some people in Uganda. (Though Sunna died at forty, and Mutesa I at forty-eight.)

Near the end of my time in East Africa in 1966 I went to see the Kasubi tombs, where (at that time) two Kabakas were buried. I have no memory of going to look at the Kabaka's palace; I suppose it was still out of bounds. And I have only a vague memory of the tombs. I suppose there was still a discouraging army presence. I stayed only a short time, and (I imagine) was not allowed to see inside. But what I saw in those hurried moments stayed with me, becoming more and more magical over the years: a round grass structure, beautifully proportioned, with a high conical roof taller than anything I had seen in grass, the grass very fine, the eaves beautifully trimmed: an African fairy-land.

Now at last I was given the chance to see more.

Kasubi had become a UNESCO heritage site. There was a little office outside the sacred area. We picked up a guide there, or perhaps we were picked up by him. Immediately within the site itself there was a grass gatehouse. It was dark, with wooden pillars in two rows supporting the roof. The pillars were a surprise; I didn't know that pillars below the grass dome were a feature of this architecture. Beyond

the gatehouse, and to the left, was the drum hut. It was full
of drums. Drums were sacred; each had its own sound and
different drums were used for different occasions. But our
guide didn't show us the drums, and though he said he
came from the drum-beating clan that served the Kabaka,
he didn't offer to give us a demonstration. He added that
the Kabaka's drum-beaters had to be castrated, since they
were always about the Kabaka and were likely to gaze on
the Kabaka's women. This was said more to thrill us than
anything else. He himself was not castrated.

From the gatehouse a paved path as straight as a
Buganda road led through the brightness of bare ground to
the main building and the darkness of the entrance there
below the eaves that came down almost to the ground. All
about the edge of this bare area were little huts, some
rectangular, some round. These huts were for attendants
who looked after the place and especially looked after the
fire in the open yard which symbolised the Kabaka's life.
Why was the ground so bare here? Wouldn't grass have
been more welcoming? It was suggested that snakes were
easier to see on bare ground.

Inside the tomb itself, on the left of the entrance, in the
abrupt gloom, and not immediately noticeable, was an old
woman sitting on a purple-striped raffia mat, one of many
raffia mats just beyond the entrance, these raffia mats
providing the only colour in this part of the tomb. The
old woman was bundled up in a long blue-patterned dress
of cotton, a little restless in limb, withdrawn, unseeing, as
became a watcher in the tomb. She was considered a wife

of the dead Kabaka, and as such was privileged. If, as might happen, the spirit of the dead king bestirred itself and wished to be served in any way, she was there for him. She had a collapsed old woman's mouth, and was pale from her life away from light. She did this vigil for a month at a time; she handed over then to another old woman as privileged as herself.

Kabakas did not die. They disappeared, and went to the forest. The 'forest' was just in front, in the inner part of the tomb, screened by brown bark-cloth, hanging down all the way from the top of the dome, like a fire curtain in a theatre. It was absolutely essential, in this kind of building, for everything to come from the local earth. Nothing was to be imported. The religious requirement made for a kind of unity, and a strange beauty. The dome was held up by wooden pillars, trimmed tree boughs, which didn't conceal what they were, and by twenty-two circular beams made from tightly bound reeds. Those twenty-two beams stood for the twenty-two clans of Buganda.

The burial of a kabaka was not straightforward. It was hemmed in by rituals that would have come from the remote past (remote, since people without writing and books cannot remember beyond their grandparents or great-grandparents). The corpse of the king would have been dried over a slow fire for three months. Then the jawbone would have been detached and worked over with beads or cowries; this, together with the umbilical cord, also worked with beads, and the penis and testicles, in a pouch of animal skin, was what would have been buried here. The rest of the body, the unessential man, so to speak, would have been sent somewhere else; but this part of the ritual remained obscure. I could get no direct answer.

On a metal rack in front of the bark-cloth hiding the forest were the fearful spears of the great Mutesa, iron and bronze and brass, some of them truly imperial things, speaking of wealth and murder: gifts from the Arab merchants or obtained from them by barter. They were the only foreign things in the tomb. There was also a reproduction of Mutesa's wide-eyed portrait; it was used everywhere in Kampala, though there was a more interesting and more regal one, based on a photograph by Stanley, in *Through the Dark Continent*. The portrait of Mutesa, used here in the tomb, was unsigned and no one could tell me whether it was done in 1861–2 by Speke or Grant (both of whom were accomplished sketchers) or by someone who had come later. These were the things (though perhaps not the portrait, which might have been placed later) Mutesa wished to be remembered by.

The tomb was still a shrine, and important for that reason, one of the fifty-two shrines of the Baganda people. A shrine wasn't a place for private meditation. It was a place where people could come to ask for boons. There were three baskets on the raffia mat before the spears and Mutesa's portrait. You put money in a particular basket, depending on your need; perhaps then – but I didn't find out – you might have a consultation with a diviner.

While, moved by wonder, I was considering things in the tomb – considering the relics of Mutesa that had been chosen for display, and the way the roof was made, and trying to think myself back to 1884 – a little black-and-white kitten came in and tried to compose itself to sleep in front of the old lady. I thought the kitten might have belonged to the old lady or her family. It cheered me. Cats here are considered familiars of spirits, usually bad ones, and have a rough time. And then a sturdy little boy came from somewhere behind the old lady and began, casually, to kick the kitten, which got up and went somewhere else and tried again to sleep, until his tormentor came. I protested. The guide said something soothing about the boy and the kitten. Perhaps he said they were really friends. I didn't believe him.

Some days later I was looking at a magazine programme on Uganda television. One of the items was about the Kasubi tombs. The woman presenter said – with a degree of ease, like someone only stating a fact about the monument – that nine men had been sacrificed at the time of the building. The guide hadn't thought to tell us that. It cast a retrospective darkness over what I had seen: the bark-cloth screening the mythical forest where great rulers went to die, the pale old lady sitting on the raffia mat on the strangely uneven floor, waiting to be called. I couldn't imagine, though, how the men would have been sacrificed; there was no picture in my head. So the magic survived.

But later, when I heard from Prince Kassim, Mutesa's Muslim descendant, that in the old days human sacrifice was a common practice when they put up the pillars or laid the foundations of a tomb, I remembered the strangely uneven floor of Kasubi, covered by the raffia mats.

3

WHEN SPEKE went to Uganda in 1861 Mutesa was Kabaka, exercising the most despotic kind of power in his court, killing people 'like fowls' (as a visitor said); and once – a difficult story – for no apparent reason taking his spear to his harem and killing women until his blood-lust was sated. But Mutesa at that time had not yet been crowned. Preparations for his crowning took a year, and were going on all the time. Much of the ritual had to be secret. This may explain why Mutesa and his mother, fat and jolly when she was in the mood, gave Speke such a run-around, now friendly and welcoming and hospitable (Speke depended on them for food for his forty-five men), now distant, making him sit in the sun at the palace entrance for many hours.

The most famous part of the crowning ritual was well known, and it concerned Mutesa's mother. She had to get rid of Mutesa's brothers, all but three, to do away with possible claimants to the throne. There were thirty brothers, and the ritual way of destroying them had to be by fire.

How was this done? We have a clue. Twenty-four years later, in 1886, Mutesa's young and headstrong successor, Mwanga, fed up with the troublesome new religions, ordered the burning of his twenty-two Christian pages. A proper martyrdom, it would seem, as good as anything in old Christian iconography, though the church was very young: it was something to be cherished, and the Uganda church has made the most of its early misfortune. There are a number of secondary schools at the site, so the place is always busy. There is also a modern cone-shaped church, architecturally adventurous (in the oil-refinery style), that by its shape suggests a bonfire, and has other symbolism: so many exposed beams on the roof, like sticks on the bonfire, standing for so many martyrs. And, as though this was not enough, a big painted board in front of the church shows passers-by how the pages were burned in 1886.

The pages, in white gowns falling off the right shoulder, were first clubbed or scourged by the palace executioners, and slashed with machetes. Seven executioners are shown, including one who has gone down on one knee and is using a long pole, like a baker's shovel, to keep the fire going. The executioners are all in brown cloth hanging from the left shoulder; this cloth is almost certainly bark-cloth, which is official and religious and correct wear. In the foreground an executioner, wielding a blade, and making room for himself for another blow, pulls hard at the left wrist of a page, whose white gown is already stained with blood spurting from a bad wound on his left arm. The page has his back to us, and he already has both knees on the ground. He turns to look at the executioner, as if in complaint (though as a court page he would have prepared many for brutal execution), and the fingers of his left hand are widely separated: this involuntary gesture is the only sign of pain in the painting.

After their roughing-up the pages would have been wrapped in reed mats from neck to toe – and the painted board (only as good as the artist, after all) for some reason appears to show this as a kind of delicate attention by the executioners, as though the pages were being tucked in for the night – before being thrown into the bonfire with their fellows, where in an unsettling matter-of-fact way, amid the flames and smoke the artist shows an exposed face at the end of each rigid, rolled-up mat.

Mutesa's brothers were princes, sons of Kabaka Sunna. The Buganda tradition was that the blood of princes was not something that could be spilt; this was a religious prohibition; so there could be no clubbing or slashing for them. They could only be burned – in reed mats no doubt. This was their fate; this was what Mutesa's mother had to arrange. In the meantime they went around with Mutesa; they often played music together, flute, lyre, marimba and drum. Once Mutesa took them all up to the top of a hill to show them the extent of his kingdom. Unless you knew what was going to happen you might miss the drama in Speke's pages. This being together with his brothers was Mutesa's way and Mutesa's mother's way of controlling the brothers, potential claimants to the throne, and keeping them away from dangerous intrigue. Speke mentions only once that during a music-playing session half the brothers were manacled.

A good story, though, has come down to us from this part of the grisly ritual. Mutesa and his mother must be imagined discussing who to burn next. Mutesa's mother speaks a name, but then Mutesa says, 'I like that man.' So the man in question is spared: he was the great-grandfather of Prince Kassim, who told this story.

4

THERE WAS another piece of the coronation preparation that Speke witnessed. The woman who cut Mutesa's umbilical cord was now a figure of honour in the court. She was a kind of diviner. For the coronation she had a special mission. She had to go to the tomb of Sunna, Mutesa's father, and study how certain herbs and plants (perhaps planted by her) had grown. According to what she found, Mutesa after his coronation would either stay quiet in his palace or make war on his neighbours. Mutesa made war. It suited his temperament; but at the same time he was in tune with the spirits he served; he would never have been totally free, acting on his own. The Romans, the Roman historian Livy said at the beginning of his great history of Rome, were successful because they were the most religious people in the world; they always acted after consulting the gods. Mutesa could say the same for himself.

Modern Kampala does not always follow the layout of the old city. Sunna's tomb is close to Mutesa's in Kasubi, but it has to be approached in a more roundabout way.

Speke, walking in the neighbourhood of Mutesa's palace one day, came across Sunna's palace. He looked away, because it didn't do to look too closely at the palace even of a dead king. Sunna's tomb would have been near that palace. The place is called Wamala, which means 'far enough'. The story is that was what Sunna exclaimed when he chose the spot for his tomb. And, indeed, today you need to know where to look. The taxi-drivers don't always know; they assume you want Kasubi.

Sunna would have been pained. He was a fearful warrior who built for eternity; he wished his name to go down; he established the pattern for Kasubi. But grass is grass and, only one hundred and fifty years after his death, much of him has disappeared. His tomb is in great disrepair. Prince Kassim thinks it is a disgrace to the Buganda royal family; and other people think it is a loss to the culture of Uganda, where there is already so little.

To go to Wamala you have go down one of the straight Buganda roads to the edge of Kampala, the city that spreads and spreads. The driver says at a certain stage that it is better for us to leave the asphalt road and take a shortcut: this is a red-dirt road, and on this morning it is raining. The dirt of the road is holding, but the water has begun to lodge in the fields of coarse grass on either side. This is a land of water. If the rain doesn't stop, a flood seems likely, and it may wash away the red road. That will be a profitless adventure; but we can only go on, and the driver is game.

We turn off into another red road, narrow and twisting. It seems we are asking for trouble. But, happily, the driver is right. We are near the tomb now, but nothing announces it. There is no barred entrance, no gatehouse, no reed fences, no young men offering their services as guides. The bush begins to seem ordinary: no romance, no history, seems possible in that wet red earth.

And then we are there, driving right up to a tomb which is like a smaller Kasubi, but with a broken roof, great thick sheaves of old grass slipping here and there, and with a bright-green vine threading its way through the grass and looking like moss. We might have come to the abandoned barn of a ruined farm. Magic and wonder might one day be restored; but they are not here now. There is no well-defined yard, no small huts, round or rectangular, for attendants; no attendants; no gatehouse, no drum-house. There is a rectangular grey wooden shed at one side of the lot. It is of modern carpentry, with no religious feel, and out of keeping with the style of the tomb. It must serve some purpose, but there is no one I can ask. I know, without going into the tomb, that there will be no old lady waiting, after a hundred and fifty years, for the spirit of the dead king to request some service. There isn't the money for that now: and it is strange that rituals which would once have seemed necessary and vital, serving what was divine, beyond money, have to be disregarded when there is no money.

Mutesa's tomb at Kasubi was level with the earth. His father's here is on a platform two feet high. Concrete steps take you up and the slipping thatch touches your head. The steps might be modern, but the platform would almost certainly have been created with the foundations and the sacrifices. Inside now, past the thatch, is darkness and desolation, though to the left and right sections of the roof have fallen away and the grey light of the rainy day comes in. It takes a little while to pick out details. There are the two rows of pillars supporting the domed roof, the royal style. To the left, below the missing thatch, is a modern brick wall, no doubt to provide support for the roof and also perhaps, in a remnant of old belief, to hide the 'forest' where Kabakas go when they die. The bricks of the wall, being of local earth, would just have been religiously acceptable; but the mortar, made of imported cement, wouldn't have been right. But ideas of right and wrong, important in 1860, when Sunna died, no longer mattered here, where there was chaos.

For three months after his death (from smallpox) devoted old women would have lovingly dried Kabaka Sunna's body over a slow fire. Where were the precious parts of that body – the umbilical cord, worked over with beads or cowries, the jawbone similarly treated, the penis and testicles in a sack of animal skin? Had they been buried here, as they should have been, to save them from violation, to prevent other people from misusing the extraordinary powers of the Kabaka? Did the brick wall hide the relics, or were they hidden in the grey wooden shed outside?

There was still royal symbolism in what survived of the structure. Tightly wrapped reeds served as circular rafters below the dome, each rafter standing for one of the clans of the Baganda. But below this proud symbolism – the clans:

the Kabaka: the dome of the world – was abject decay. No bark-cloth here, rising from floor to ceiling, theatrical magic, to preserve the mystery of the forest where the spirit of the Kabaka eternally resides. Far to the right of the brick wall, on the other side of the tomb, where the light of the grey day coming through the gap in the roof was like vapour, one piece of bark-cloth hung down, like a rag on a nail, damp from the rain, dark-brown and dirty-looking. The floor was wet. But just in front of the rack with the old Kabaka's short iron spears there was still a raffia mat on the floor and three old raffia baskets for offerings to Sunna's murderous spirit; and perhaps – though it was hard to make out in the gloom – there were a few dark coins in the baskets. The tomb had not been totally abandoned. It was still a shrine; a few people were still prepared to make the journey to ask the difficult Kabaka for a special boon.

Stanley says that Sunna was born in 1820, became Kabaka in 1836, and died in 1860. He was dead when Speke came to Uganda in 1861–2, and Speke, a geographer above everything else, writes about him only tangentially. For living details of Sunna you have to turn to Stanley, though he came to Uganda many years later, in 1875, during his east-to-west crossing of the continent. Many people were still alive then who knew the terrible Sunna, and Stanley, with the newspaperman's relish for a good story, got them to talk.

Sunna had a dog that he loved. He compelled certain villages to grow sweet potatoes to feed the dog (clearly a Ugandan dog); and when the dog died he compelled certain villages to produce bark-cloth for the dog to be buried in. So it was almost certainly Sunna who gave Uganda (and Mutesa in his early days) the heraldic device, so to speak, of the dog, the spear, and the woman.

Sunna was short and powerfully built. He had a habit of looking down. People couldn't see his eyes and were on edge in his presence, since they believed that if Sunna looked up, someone was going to die. It was said that in one day he condemned eight hundred people.

The most famous story about him was his revenge on the people of Busoga. They lived on the eastern side of the Nile. They had broken away from their allegiance to Buganda, and Sunna wished to punish them. There was war. The people of Busoga were great warriors, and resisted Sunna for three months. At length, however, penned up in an island on the lake, they were worn down, and offered to surrender and return to their allegiance. Sunna appeared content; he even gave the impression that he wanted the occasion of the peace-making to be festive. He fed the Wasoga chiefs and warriors generously and gave them much plantain wine. In what looked like a further gesture of forgiveness, he asked the Wasoga to do their war dance during the evening. They were pleased to be asked, but they said they normally did that dance with their spears. He said they shouldn't on this evening; there would be warriors among his own people who would take that unkindly, after the three months of the hard war; better for them, the Wasoga, to use sticks in their dance on this special occasion.

The furious dance began. Thirty thousand Wasoga lost

themselves in the drumming and the stamping, the stick-throwing and the competitive athleticism of their movements. They didn't notice that they, only thirty thousand, were being surrounded by a hundred thousand of Sunna's people. Sunna's people had been provided with cords, the executioners' tools, made from the fibre of the aloe. At a signal they fell on the dancers and bound them, and threw them to Sunna's warriors, who with spears and other edged weapons began to cut the bound Wasoga up into small pieces, and were not concerned to kill their victims first. It had long been Sunna's wish to make a little mountain, a pyramid, of Wasoga flesh and bone, to punish them for their disobedience and their valour and all the anxieties of the three-month war.

This act of terror brought other rebels into line. In the end, though, this reputation for awfulness worked against Sunna. He had a favourite son, physically very big and strong, whom he had trained in his ways. He would have liked this boy to succeed him as Kabaka. But the chiefs of the Baganda, already sufficiently tormented by the extravagance of the father, feared that the wildness of the boy, if given its head, might bring about the ruin of them all. And when, after Sunna's death, the boy declared himself Kabaka, the chiefs didn't allow him to act. They surrounded him and tied him up and very soon had him burnt. It was the fate of nearly all of Sunna's more than thirty sons. Almost as soon as he died, then, almost as soon as his wonderful grave had been built, Sunna's glory began to fade.

It was Mutesa, the wide-eyed son, who came to the

throne and the first thing he did was to behead the chiefs
who had given him power. And it is possible that Mutesa's
style of casual cruelty, before his formal coronation, was
prompted by his wish to show himself as strong as Sunna.

'By my father's grave' was Mutesa's strongest vow. If I
had not seen Mutesa's own grave at Kasubi I would have
thought this grave of his father at Wamala the most splendid
thatched structure I had seen. In Mutesa's time it would
have been perfect in every way, with a relay of religious
old ladies in attendance. Now there were no ladies, no
breath of life, as it were. The dead king was truly widowed,
and his grave, in spite of the sacrifices that would have
attended the laying down of the foundation and the raising
of the pillars, was in ruin. The rain came in, snakes were
said to be in the grass roof, and the sacred relics of umbilical
cord and jaw were not in the place intended for them.

The spears against the iron rack were short and black,
not like the long, burnished imperial spears which the son
was to get from the Arabs and which were to make such a
show at Kasubi. To the right of the short, workaday spears
were Sunna's amazingly narrow shields with a clutch of
black spear heads or arrow heads close to the floor,
seemingly dusty or grimy, and not easy to see in the gloom
without treading on the sacred area.

We had come by such a roundabout way, through what
towards the end looked like real country, I had no idea
where we were. But I saw now, when we had left the tomb,
and had a view through the trees at the end of the yard,
that it was on one of Kampala's many hills, which at one

time might have been thought to give Sunna or his spirit a clear view of the approach of his enemies. But now it was only wretched Kampala, its shacks and garbage ever spreading, that pressed on the king's tomb. Against that ordinariness, which consumed everything, there was no defence.

'Look on my works, ye Mighty, and despair.' Nothing *beside remains . . .*

5

IN 1875, WHEN Stanley passed through Uganda on his east-to-west crossing of the continent, he saw Mutesa, then about thirty-eight, at war against the Wavuma people on the northern shore of Lake Victoria. Mutesa's army was vast. Stanley, doing a rough and ready calculation (and perhaps exaggerating), makes it a hundred and fifty thousand, adding in a hundred thousand followers and women (Mutesa went everywhere with his harem), to make a grand total of two hundred and fifty thousand in Mutesa's camp.

There were musketeers now in Mutesa's army, but this did not give them anything like an overwhelming advantage. The Wavuma, who used only spears, knew about muskets and were not frightened of them. They were also skilled fighters on water. Mutesa's people were better on land; on water they were nervous of tipping over; and for much of the time the advantage seemed to be with the Wavuma. People came out on to the hills above Lake Victoria to see the battle. The engravings in Stanley's book, based many of them on photographs by Stanley, show what the watchers would have seen. They show the beautiful boats lined up, and the formations of the two disciplined armies, though the details of boats and fighting men in the distance are crowded and not always clear. The battle would have been frustrating for the watchers; since the fighters took their time, seeming to retire after every little episode. When Stanley sought Mutesa out to give advice about the battle, Mutesa appeared to have lost interest in it, and wanted to talk only about religion.

War was noise, to frighten the enemy. Mutesa had fifty drummers, as many flute-players, and any number of men ready to shake gourds with pebbles. There were also more than a hundred witchdoctors, men and women, specially selected, fantastically dressed (the Wavuma were no doubt meant to notice), who had brought along their most potent charms, to keep the evil eye off Mutesa and to sink the Wavuma. Before any action they presented their charms to Mutesa who, already half Muslim and half Christian, acknowledged these precious things of Africa – dead lizards, human fingernails and so on – with great style, pointing an index finger at what was presented, not touching it, and then, like a sovereign at a levee, waiting to see what came next.

Protected in this way, Mutesa began to threaten his commanders. He was going to strip the cowards of all their dignity and all the blessings he had given them. They had started life as peasants; they were going to be returned to that state. Some he was going to burn over a slow fire.

(Burning: Mutesa's mind often went back to this punishment, which he had narrowly escaped as a young man.) The chief minister, recognising the passion of his ruler, threw himself on the ground before the Kabaka and said, 'Kabaka, if tomorrow you see my boat retreating from the enemy, you can cut me into small pieces or burn me alive.'

When Stanley next saw Mutesa, Mutesa was in high spirits. His men had managed to seize an old chief of the Wavuma and Mutesa intended to burn the old man alive, to teach the Wavuma a lesson. Stanley talked him out of that, and Stanley also, to everyone's relief, mediated a peace between the parties.

This happened in 1875. In 1884 Mutesa was dead and was being buried in the tomb at Kasubi, which he had modelled on the tomb of his father Sunna at Wamala. He was, indeed, like his father. The country had given him no other model.

So Amin and Obote have a kind of ancestry. The British colonial period, with law and without local wars, has to be seen as an interlude. But how do Africans live with their African history? Perhaps the absence of a script and written records blurs the past; perhaps the oral story gives them only myths.

I HAD GOT to know Susan. She was a poet of merit and a literature teacher at Makerere. She was less than forty and slender and delicate, with a beautiful voice. Her family history could hardly be thought about without pain. She had lost her grandfather and her father. They lived in what was known as the Luweero triangle, north of Kampala. It was a fertile, populous area, and the worst fighting of the civil war or wars had taken place there.

Her grandfather kept cows. He loved these creatures in the African pastoral way. He knew them all by name and temperament; he knew their colour, the shape of their horns. When the fighting started he had to run away. This was in the second period of Obote's rule, after Amin had been overthrown, when the soldiers were vicious and cunning and could only think of finding people they wanted. In his hiding place the old man was worried about his cattle. They couldn't look after themselves; they would soon start to suffer. He thought of them one by one, their needs and habits. At last the idea came to him that he could take a chance and go back to his house and be with his animals for a while. He went back. The soldiers were waiting for him. They killed him with an axe and dismembered the body. They stuffed the pieces into a termite anthill, one of the red anthills of Uganda, and that was where the broken-up body stayed while the war lasted. Afterwards the family recovered the bones and gave them a proper burial.

Her father's fate was worse. He had been taken away before, in the Amin time, and he had never been seen again. No one knew how he had died or where he had died. Not knowing made for a special kind of pain. The subject was never closed; the mind would play always with terrible possibilities. The subject was too painful for Susan's mother; she never talked about it

This was not an exceptional family story, Susan said.

Many people could tell stories like that. The Luweero triangle, where her family came from, had been ravaged by Obote's soldiers.

'They launched a reign of terror that included rape and death. You can see the devastation even today. Luweero is an empty district. You can see unoccupied land. It looks like a ghost district.'

What was it like, living with terror for so long?

'I was very young. I was five then and I only remember there was no sugar. If you asked for sugar it was not there. When Amin was overthrown' – in 1979 – 'I was eight. But when Obote was overthrown I was twelve, and so I was aware of what was happening around me. You feel very insecure for your parents and your neighbours. You cannot get an answer because your parents who would normally give you an answer are suffering too. You start to see the government as a monster. Somebody taking over this place that God has placed you in, and is treating it with impunity. I still don't understand why there are tyrants and why they are allowed to rule.'

Did people feel that the ancestors had let them down?

'I remember people placing their faith in God for a better tomorrow. They had the defiance of despair. That doesn't make you fight with the enemy. You look over him' – she meant focusing on what should be there in the good time – 'and you do not engage with him. I have been brought up to understand God as benevolent. God rescues you from the clutches of evil. I know some friends think we had displeased the ancestors by taking other religions or by denying the existence of the ancestors, and retribution was sure to follow. I was brought up as a Christian so I did not have that traditional religion. But I know that it exists and I respect it. I was born after the colonial period. I find that period traumatic.'

So here, for Susan and people like her, was another cause for disturbance, something before the horrors of Amin and Obote, something that went back to the time of the British protectorate (which Mutesa had wanted). It made now for a full century of disorder.

Susan said, 'It is a case of being aware that there are so many influences vying for my being. I become a melting pot of experiences. I have many parts coming into one another rather than being one holistic whole.'

She worried about her name.

'My first name is Susan. It was given me by my father.' Who had disappeared in the Amin time. 'He had an aunt whom he adored, and she had this name. So it was a sentimental choice for him. Yet I know it is a Judeo-Christian name, and when I came to the university I added my clan's name — Naluguwa, which means "of the sheep clan". I feel it is very much a part of my identity — here you have your own name. I could go as Susan Naluguwa, but I use my father's surname too — Kiguli — because this is how the school registered me.'

And now, though the name was given her by her father, she felt a love-hate for the name Susan.

'I feel that it is so much part of the colonial experience, which was not pleasant. When a person or race comes and imposes on you, it takes away everything, and it is a vicious thing to do. Much as I think the West and modernity is a good thing, it did take away our culture and civilisation, and even if it is gentle it does make us doubt our roots. For example, the missionaries brainwashed you into rejecting the gods, and imposing their own ideas, dogma and doctrines, saying that theirs were the best. There was no two-way dialogue and them trying to understand how our minds and heritage or culture worked. I feel that my people had a civilisation. It was different but it was their own. I taught myself to write in Luganda.' After writing her poems in English. 'I feel humiliated that the school did not teach us our mother tongue.'

Her sister was writing a book on Speke, Grant and the missionaries.

'They took away our land, religion, customs and social structures. Our king, our everything. When the kingdoms were restored' – strangely enough, in a tactical move by Amin, who had led the assault on the palace in 1966 – 'our king asked for the return of "our possessions".' He meant everything associated with the kingship and culture of Buganda. 'The palace was handed back. People suffered great humiliation. They thought what had been done to the palace was sacrilege. It was a great trauma to have the king removed and for him to die in exile. So Amin brought the body back for burial.'

At the beginning Susan had said that she was a Christian; she respected the traditional religion, but did not believe, as some African traditionalists did, that Uganda was going to suffer retribution for adopting other religions and turning away from the ancestors. But there was so much in her quick heart and mind that couldn't be contained in a simple religious definition, so many separate ideas and emotions had tumbled out of her, that she emerged as another person.

I did not, after this, ask her about African history, the oral tradition, and myth. There was obviously no special African way of dealing with, neutralising, a bad history or a bad present. It seemed more likely that it was like dealing with a very long illness. It announced itself one day, and you dreamt then of waking up well one morning. Gradually then you sank into it, and you lost your idea of the quick return of health and wholeness. You made your peace, so to speak, with your illness; and the time began to pass. You began to live in this half-and-half way. It became all you knew; it became life.

6

THE OLD Germanic peoples, according to the first-to-second-century Roman historian Tacitus, thought it was an insult to their gods to imprison them in temples or within the walls of any building. Better for them to be worshipped in the open, in beautiful groves, or glades or rivers: places which then become instinct with the spirit of the god. And there is something like this in the Baganda idea of shrines. The tombs of the Kabakas are obvious shrines. But there are others, and they are all over Buganda – waterfalls, say, or unusual rocks – and even to the visitor who doesn't have the Baganda idea of sanctity, doesn't know how to conduct himself in such places, and cannot respond to the complicated tribal stories, they are at once like a celebration of the natural world and a claim on that world.

The most spectacular of these natural shrines is the Sezibwa waterfall in Mukono district, less than thirty miles from Kampala. Prince Kassim told me later that Mukono was known for sacrifices. I believe he meant human sacrifices. But I didn't know this when I went. It would have given another value to everything if I had known.

We left Kampala by the Jinja road, and as always it seemed that the mess of semi-urban development had destroyed the nature of the land and almost destroyed old systems of community. Near a 'trading centre' we turned off the main road and drove for some time along a red-dirt road: old Uganda again, the green bush acting as a screen, so that it is often a surprise what lies at the end of these unremarkable roads. There was a sign for the waterfall; and then in the middle of simple bush a high iron gate barred the red road.

Some young fellows were sitting about the road cutting above the gate, apparently idle. But one was our guide; an arrangement had been made with him on the telephone. He began to work right away. He slid down the cutting and said the site was of cultural value. That was promising, but he didn't really have much English. In fact, he had pretty much shot his bolt with that sentence.

We heard the falls before we saw them: in the opening

before us, a stream or river, coming from our left, falling over a rocky cliff, which was about a hundred feet high. Unexpected, this opening in the land, this flow of water, this violence. The water split into many channels as it slid down the rock and crashed into the river pool. Around the pool, away from the violent fall of water, was a grassy basin, lush from the spray. Everything here was very green. Much diminished now, but still brisk, the river continued out of the quieter end of the pool, running from left to right, and then winding away at the foot of a low hill until it was lost to view. On a clothes line in front of us, after the sublime falls, were men's clothes hanging out to dry, perhaps the laundry of the guardians of the shrine. Above the disappearing stream, on the sunny hillside far to our right, were the conical thatched roofs of small huts, perhaps the quarters of the guardians.

The most sacred spot is at the very top of the falls. The spirit of the place dwells here, and there is a tribal story that tells you why. The water there washes away curses. You must be barefooted, though, to show respect for a holy place; and you must wash your face and hands nine times.

I had seen a greenish picket fence up there and had thought it was to prevent people getting too close to the falls.

It was easy to understand how people would have been moved by the beauty of the place. Its beauty would have always been known, and the idea of its sacredness must have come from far back, but the puzzling story was that the first person to visit the site and recognise its qualities was the Kabaka Mwanga, the successor of Mutesa I, who in 1886 ordered his Christian pages to be burnt.

Mwanga also planted a tree, which is still honoured, as did Mutesa II, who was sent into exile by Obote and died in London in 1969.

A footbridge led across the pool to a rocky slope. There was a stand of young eucalyptus trees on that slope. Our guide said they had been planted ten years before, but it was now accepted they were a mistake (perhaps because they were foreign), and there was a plan to have them replaced by purely local trees. The topmost line of eucalyptus had been hacked down with a machete, leaving small stumps. A slippery path zigzagged up the rocky slope, over the exposed roots of trees planted beyond the eucalyptus.

At the top of the zigzagging path was the first part of the formal, religious shrine. It looked modest: a low cave in the rock, not going in very deep, where there were clay bottles, spears, and a few baskets with offerings. The guide said that eggs were the standard offerings. A python lived in the little cave and came from time to time to eat the eggs. I could see no sign of the python's passage into or out of the cave.

We were on the path to the shrine hut. It was hidden by trees, but there was no diviner present that morning and no one volunteered to take us higher. When the diviner was present there would of course be fees. But we were only visitors; we had no needs that called for a diviner's attention. We didn't have questions for the oracle of the waterfall; and I felt we shouldn't intrude any more.

Later I learned that the shrine – possibly only the shrine hut – had been burnt down more than once by Christians who, extraordinarily, were claiming this ancient site for themselves. A high man of the church had come to the shrine and cleansed it of its ancient spirits. To get rid of spirits, therefore, the church had to acknowledge that they existed. And, to add to the confusion, there was a signboard (close to the footbridge across the pool) that appeared to make a legal claim to the place in the name of the Kabaka Foundation.

It was time to go. And time to pay. The guide had to be paid for attending, and for helping me up the slippery path over the exposed tree roots by the eucalyptus. And when we got to the iron gate there was a further charge, for entering. It would have been like that, too, at the oracles in the classical word. The world always had its dues.

Later there were Prince Kassim's words about the sacrifices of Mukono district and the sacrifices especially at the Sezibwa waterfall.

I had asked about the burning down of the shrine there. It seemed to me a strange thing to have happened at a place sanctified by the visit of Kabaka Mwanga in the 1880s.

Prince Kassim said, 'The shrine was burnt because it is a place where a lot of human sacrifice was going on. Three months ago they found a body of a young child very mutilated.'

As always, there were many sides to the sacred.

PRINCE KASSIM stood for an important segment of the Ugandan jigsaw. He was a prince of the royal house of

Buganda and was related to the Kabakas. At the same time, by this same royal descent, but from the Muslim side of Mutesa I, he was the Muslim leader of Uganda.

He said, 'It is true that the foreign religions took over the command of the society. They converted the leaders and the flock followed. They did it by putting up institutions of education where the young were taught that African gods were many and they required animal and human sacrifice. I am not an authority on traditional religion. I don't know where traditional religion begins and voodoo starts, but I do know that both are entwined. The Kabaka was head of traditional religion in the old days, but he abdicated in favour of the Anglican church, and is now seen as the head of the church here. My own attitude is that the power of traditional religion is myth and superstition. Because of my educational background I have been told it is a pack of lies. I grew up comfortable with the idea of one God. The Arabs came to Kabaka Sunna's court for ivory and slaves, and according to our history an Arab slaver called Ibrahim Battuta challenged Sunna's brutality to his subjects. He told the king he could not behave in this brutal way to his subjects as there was life after death and accountability. The king who was a god in his own right was surprised, and fascinated that there was life after death. Before Sunna there was a belief that death was final and one just went in to the spirit world. They broke the king's jaw, to make the king's ghost powerless, and he simply went into the void. The saying that "he has dropped his jaw" meant that the king was dead. Many things happened afterwards. The religious wars from 1888 to 1894 turned Bagandan society upside down.'

I wanted to know about the royal tradition of music-making. There was so much about it in Speke.

The prince said, 'Yes, it was always there. What else was there to do in the palace? It was all about feasting and merry-making and fooling around.'

But wasn't it sad that so much of the tradition was lost? So much that came from so far back and linked people to the earth?

The prince began to speak like a man of the Bagandan royal family. 'Well, there is so much to feel sorry for. In 1966 the Kabaka went into exile. It was, and is now, a period of moral degeneration, and a period of anarchy. In which there was no respect for anything, and even the environment was destroyed. The Kabakaship is an institution. He is the fountain of honour for the Bagandans and when he went into exile the political institution was destroyed. It was unimaginable that it could happen. That the Kabaka and the palace could be attacked. Buganda was a nation in its own right and they spoke their own language. When people tell you of that world where honour meant everything you feel the shame.'

'Within this decay, how do you live your life?'

'I have a dynastic duty and I aim to do it. We have to have honour for the sake of our fathers and forefathers.'

'Do you have any memento of your past?' I was thinking of the palace.

'It was all destroyed. Our heritage was looted and

destroyed.' Sunna's tomb was in a bad way, and there were others. 'We have to wake up to our responsibility. Rightly they belong to us. It is a unique architecture. Such amazing grass thatch where despite the heavy rainfall there are no leaks. There is a lot of skill and we have the human resources and they still hold on to their culture and are loyal to the king.'

But nearly at the end Prince Kassim let fall a sentence which seemed to reassert his pessimism. He said, 'With the new religion people became insubordinate.' And that of course would have been true for both Christianity and Islam. To belong to either was to be part of a great world faith, approved and organised, with a great literature and famous solid buildings; the temptation to look away from the much smaller thing, of grass, that was one's own was great.

7

IN THE 1840s Arab merchants from the east of the contin-ent, great travellers and explorers in their own way, came to Uganda looking for slaves and gold. In return for what they got they gave poor guns and trinkets. They gave the Kabaka Sunna a mirror, and this murderous man was enchanted to see his face for the first time. Perhaps in gratitude he allowed the Arabs to talk about their faith and especially about the afterlife in paradise that awaited believers. Now the Arabs were no longer suppliants in Uganda. Their mosques, of every denomination, were on all the hills of Kampala, and the Brother Leader of Libya, Colonel Ghaddafi, of limitless wealth, was coming to open the biggest mosque in Uganda, the Libyan, in the presence of four or five African presidents.

Habib, a Ugandan Muslim businessman now of great wealth, had fostered the Libyan connection. He came from one of the oldest Muslim families in Uganda. Habib's grandfather had converted in 1846, almost at the beginning of the Arab presence, and they had lived through the bad years of the religious wars, between Muslims and Christians, in the late 1880s. The Muslims lost that war, and were exiled by the British colonial administration to the bush in the west.

Habib's grandfather did not give up his faith. He became a preacher for Islam. He went everywhere on foot, and lived to be a hundred and four. He walked with one hand behind his back; this was how Habib remembered the tough old man. Walking and preaching, he got as far as Rwanda, which was quite a distance away, and he took three more wives there, one Hutu and two Tutsis. He had twenty-one children.

It was a poor life for Habib's father in the beginning. He was not well educated. He kept cows – the kraal was three miles away from the house – and he also had a small business mending bicycle and motorcycle tyres. There wasn't a lot of money in that, and he later went to the

Congo, which was just across the border. There – no doubt following other people – he began to mine gold, then traded in gold, and became rich.

'We lived in a collective fashion. We all ate together. Each wife had her own vegetable garden and every wife had to cook for one week of the month. It was her duty to cook for the entire household while the others helped her. We were around thirty people at each meal. About ten in the morning the other wives and their daughters would gather in the garden of the wife whose turn it was to cook, and they would peel the green bananas. Then they would call the boys or men to lift the food or peeled bananas to the kitchen. Water was brought from the well by the boys. Water and firewood and picking coffee was the boys' turf. No woman could do that.'

They were a rich family now, with a car, and the only people in the village to have a concrete house with glass windows. Other people had mud-and-thatch huts. Habib's family had outside latrines, but each wife had a room to wash and bath in.

When Idi Amin was overthrown, in 1979, the people of the village went around killing Muslims. But Habib's family was respected – they used to lend their car for village weddings, to fetch the bride – and they were not touched.

Habib did well at school, and his father took him to Buganda, so that he could learn English in addition to Arabic. In 1971, when he was eighteen, he was one of thirty-two boys chosen for scholarships.

He went to Libya, and studied Sharia and Muslim law.

He became fluent in Arabic; it was the turning point in his life. He became an interpreter for the Ugandan embassy, and did the job well. There were not many people who knew the languages and understood both African and Arab ways. He impressed Amin (still at that time the ruler of Uganda). Later, after Amin, he came to the notice of the Brother Leader, Ghaddafi. It was the beginning of his Libyan connection, which flowered in all sorts of ways.

Was he Libyan or Ugandan, African or Muslim?

'I see myself as a Muslim. My grandfather was circumcised with a reed, and my father and I were circumcised by a Gillette blade. I still remember it. When the man came to circumcise the boys they were taken to a separate place and kept behind a kind of screen. I was five years old and very curious to see what was happening. I went to see, and they saw me and grabbed me too. I am still angry about that.'

As a Muslim child he was trained to have nothing to do with African religion. 'We were brought up in the faith, and that dictates that African religion is paganism. We were trained to despise it. I will not allow my children to go near it.'

And then, speaking in the same voice, the same firm tone, Habib said, 'Now that I have grown up and had exposure, I see it was a tool to control our African mind. It is how the imperialists worked.'

I wasn't expecting this. I asked whether he meant what he appeared to say, and included Islam among the imperialists seeking to control the African mind. He said he did.

I would have liked to hear more. But at this stage he

was called away by some business friends – the hotel was full of them after the Ghaddafi visit. He said he was going to come back to us, but he never did. And the next day he was off to Dubai.

8

TO BELIEVE IN the traditional African religion was to be on the defensive. There was no doctrine to hold on to; there was only a sense of the rightness of old ways, the sacredness of the local earth. It was, in a small way, like the fourth- and fifth-century conflict between Christianity and paganism at the time of the religious changeover in the classical world. Paganism could not be a cause; the most that could be said for the old gods and temples was that they had been around for a very long time and had served people well. The doctrines of Islam and Christianity, world faiths, had a philosophical base and could be expounded. The traditional African religion had no doctrine; it expressed itself best in its practices and in things like the hundred fearful charms the witchdoctors presented to Mutesa I before the naval battle against the Wavuma in 1875.

And now people who cherish the old African religion have begun to develop – or rediscover, it may be – a cosmogony, a kind of *Paradise Lost*, for the people of Buganda: an affair of God and the angels, the first people, their disobedience, the replacement of the angels by the ancestors, the appearance of mediums who can invoke the ancestors. The powers of God, the guiding being who knows all and has been in existence forever, can reside only in a royal person, a kabaka. The Kabaka is linked to the spirit world; the mediums are linked to the ancestors. This is where the cosmogony touches earth and the Baganda.

This theology – difficult when it separates from *Paradise Lost* – was outlined in the Bambara lounge of the Serena Hotel by Madame Sehenna, a former cultural minister, who now gives cultural and religious talks on the radio and generally guides culturally troubled young Bagandans. Susan brought her to us one afternoon: an educated middle-aged woman with a close-to-English accent sometimes. We sat below a beautifully carved wood panel – the Serena is full of fine African carving – and heard about the stigmata or signs of the Kabaka.

He has a mark on his right hand and is born with two umbilical cords. Only people of the monkey clan, one of the fifty-two clans of the Baganda, can install the Kabaka. When he is holding court he hears a voice from above that speaks to him alone. A separate house has to be created for him where he sits in seclusion and no woman can enter. It is here that the angels come and guide him. Now that things have begun again to go badly for the Baganda – the government is even claiming some of the nine thousand square miles of the sacred land of Buganda – there are people who say that the installation of the Kabaka was not well done. Perhaps certain rituals were left out; now as a result the people are suffering and lost.

Madame Sehenna said, 'But you mustn't think it will end. We are doing work. Many of the angels who were protecting the Kabakaship have now come back. We have a prince of the royal blood who has the connection. He gets revelations and he tells us. The prince can be consulted. He lives in his shrine. You buy an exercise book and write the name of your first ancestor, your name, and your problem.'

The first ancestor, known to God, was not born but created, and this ancestor doesn't die; he disappears.

'The exercise book with your name and your problem is taken to the shrine, and the answer is given. You have to buy back the answer. The royal drum is tuned by someone from the lion clan, and the lion is the symbol of Buganda. You also have the fallen angels who live and are underground. If you offer them great sacrifices, like your mother or your child, something very near and dear to you, they give you great riches. Wealth beyond your dreams. In this case you go to a medium and you go to the lake and, if you are a woman, you meet a handsome man, a spirit, who takes you beneath the lake. If you are a man it is a beautiful woman who will take you and give you the wealth you want. But once you invoke the spirit world you have to obey their rules. You cannot marry a human then, as the spirit of the man or woman will live with you. You see many such people driving these big cars and living in big houses like palaces here. You cannot escape their rules. If you do, the riches vanish and you are punished.'

*

FOR A FEW DAYS Luke was my guide. He didn't have much to show me because he didn't know a great deal, and because he lived in a far-off part of Kampala where the roads were unpaved. When it rained the roads around his house became impassable, and then he would telephone to cancel whatever arrangements we had made. Later, when we tried to work out what I owed him, he would claim these blank days as working days because he had set them aside for me.

He worked in a university, one of the many new universities of Uganda. He got 170,000 shillings a month, a little under 600 pounds or 1,200 dollars a month, which I thought sufficient for his needs. But he and the other teachers and many of the students as well were on strike. This meant that he had great needs. And when he came late one morning and said he wanted to take me to a diviner or witchdoctor I became anxious. I was worried about the fees those people might charge. I said I thought we were going to look at Bassajadenzi that morning, a famous rock-shrine. He had spoken at length about it the day before. He said no, I had asked for witchdoctors. That was why he had asked a friend of his to come with us, a man in touch with witchdoctors. This man was waiting for us at a police post. This official-sounding detail made me doubt my memory. We went to pick the friend up.

The police post was in an awful part of the city, the ground scuffed down to red earth, children everywhere, the ditches unsavoury, and there was often a spread of garbage between the rough shacks.

The sloping dirt road we turned into had been diagonally trenched by rain, and the car bumped up and down in the most worrying way. A further side road, narrowing, suddenly full of green, brought us to the witchdoctor's house.

It was a proper little cottage, modern and newly painted and pretty, fenced with concrete blocks. Luke and his friend, suppliants in their demeanour, as though they didn't want to make too much of a noise, undid the two leaves of the wide side gate, and went into the yard and waited for the witchdoctor. He came out of his house wearing what were clearly his home clothes, an off-white singlet and red jogging shorts. He looked sour; it seemed he didn't like being disturbed. Many words passed between the three men, the witchdoctor firm, Luke and his friend speaking more softly, as though they didn't want me to hear.

The driver told me that the witchdoctor was saying it was Wednesday and he didn't receive on Wednesdays. That was his day for gathering herbs.

This would have been a small but valuable part of the witchdoctor's business. People in Uganda believed in the magical value of herbs; men liked to have herbs in their wallets, to protect the money they had and to attract more.

So, from having to plead with me, Luke and his friend now had to plead with the witchdoctor. They had told me, 'He is not an ordinary witchdoctor. He is modern. That is why we brought you. It will be good for you to see him.' I didn't know what they were telling the witchdoctor.; there was a torrent of words between them. I suspected they were tempting him with the promise of a good fee.

In a room like a garage at the side of the house a woman could be seen through the big open door washing down the concrete floor, soaking a rag in a bucket and dragging the rag over the floor. She was taking her time over this, washing the same piece of floor again and again; it seemed she was more interested in what was being said in the yard by the men. She was standing in the remarkable African way, bent at the waist, legs straight; a naked baby was crawling about behind her.

Luke and his friend came back to the car and said it was all settled. The witchdoctor would see us. But he had to purify himself before he went into the shrine section of his yard. This was a connected but separate fenced plot next door to the house. We should go there, taking off our shoes beforehand, and wait for him. We left the main yard, went out into the street, and then almost immediately turned into the shrine area, which had its own entrance. Ismail, our hotel car driver, was by now sufficiently interested and awed to lay aside his Muslim anxieties about the occasion. He took off his shoes with the rest of us, and said that if the witchdoctor didn't purify himself before he came to us the spirit who guided him would become very angry. The witchdoctor himself had said that.

I felt the witchdoctor's bill was growing by the minute.

There were about five small huts in different parts of the shrine yard. The huts were modern, with concrete walls; they were too small, I thought, for anyone to live in; and they were connected – as though for a game – by a raised walk in red concrete about a yard wide and six inches high.

But perhaps this red concrete walk was only another modern touch: no visitor need walk either in dry-season dust or rainy-season mud.

To one side of the entrance, where we were, there was something like a little office, with a few books, a telephone, a small steel safe. A framed green-printed certificate on the wall was the witchdoctor's official licence; it was like the certificate issued in other countries to professional people like accountants and pharmacists. Everything here was modern and correct; no believer need feel ashamed.

Below a mirror was a small wash basin with a thin wafer of used soap. A proper painted black-and-white sign pointed, with arrows, to where the toilets were. They were next door, in the yard of the main house, and they could be reached through a gate in the middle of the fence. It wouldn't have done for toilets to be in the shrine area.

While we were considering all these things, and arriving at some (not all) of the subtleties, an assistant or servant of the witchdoctor came in through another side gate, and began to open up the padlocked huts. In one hut he managed to get a wood fire going. Perhaps it was a fire of welcome, done expressly for our sake; or it might have been a more general purifying fire, a commissioning of the shrine area.

Whatever the fees, I now had to stay. After all that had been done for me I couldn't say I wanted to go back to the hotel. Even Ismail the driver, Muslim though he was, would have turned against me.

The witchdoctor himself now appeared. He had replaced

his red jogging shorts with a pair of long trousers, and was wearing a sports shirt. His purification had given him a freshness and formality which he didn't have before. He had lost his sourness and looked ready for business.

He went and sat on the floor in one of the huts at the far end of the yard. The open door framed him. It was now as though we were really clients and he was receiving us, sitting behind a spear head, the spear head being one of the Baganda emblems.

Luke's friend said that each hut had a different purpose. In one the witchdoctor would receive the client and assess his needs. Another was a kind of pharmacy; the medicines here, compounded by the witchdoctor, were in small jars; they were doled out to the client according to advice from the spirits. The witchdoctor had to hold himself ready at all times for communication from the spirits. It was how he healed. It was the great difference between him and ordinary people. It explained his success.

We went to look at the witchdoctor in the hut where he was sitting in his mystic posture below a portrait of the Kabaka. The hut, concrete and modern on the outside, was traditional and African inside, completely hung with lengths of bark-cloth, stitched together in the way bark-cloth had to be stitched, and concealing the foreign material of the roof. A spiritual or magical quality attached to bark-cloth, which was the special material of the ancestors, as was shown in the tomb of the Kabakas at Kasubi, where it hung from dome to floor and concealed the 'forest' where the spirits of the Kabaka resided after death.

Everything in that great tomb had to be made of local materials, and the witchdoctor knew that in his shrine area (and perhaps also in his house) he was going against tradition. He had a reason for that. The world had changed since Kasubi. He had now to compete with the Christian church and the Muslim mosque. He had to build in modern materials; he wanted people who came to his shrine to feel good.

The witchdoctor came out of the hut. He went to where, not far away, there was an open fireplace with much grey wood-ash and a length of partly burnt wood still in place. He said that was where he sat sometimes, in the living fire. He was moved to do so by the spirits; and when the spirits were on him he didn't feel the fire. Inspired words came to him from above or below, from the earth.

Ismail, snapping back into his Muslim faith, said to me in English, in an undertone, 'I would like to see him do that.'

Luke and his friend didn't hear. They were completely taken up with the witchdoctor, who was explaining the uses of the various huts. When this was done the witchdoctor called to his assistant, and the assistant, like a man well trained, went to the house and brought a thick square album of colour photographs. The photographs were of people who had visited the shrine here. The witchdoctor turned the thick pages of the album one by one, and Luke and his friend and even Ismail fell silent, because we were looking at photographs of famous local people who had come here as suppliants.

Then the question of money came up. Luke said in his dangerous way that it was up to me. I gave 20,000 shillings, just under seven pounds, fourteen dollars. I gave that because I had not put any questions to the witchdoctor. To my amazement the money was accepted without trouble, and I was sorry that worry about the man's fees had slightly spoilt the occasion.

The trouble came later, when I had to settle with Luke. I offered him a hundred dollars – this was on the telephone – and he appeared to agree. But later that evening he telephoned and wanted to know whether he had heard correctly: had I offered a hundred pounds? I had been thinking that a hundred dollars was really too little. So I said yes, I had offered him a hundred pounds. But when he came to get his money in the morning he made it clear that in his mind the bargaining was far from over. He went over the little we had done together and said that a fair price would be two hundred pounds. This was his way, doubling an agreed figure, not moving up in smaller increments. I began to know the exasperation and blackmail Speke had to suffer with one chief after another a hundred and fifty years before over the *hongo*, the entry tax that had to be paid a chief for being in his territory, before the 'drum of satisfaction' could be beaten, which told people not to trouble the visitor.

In the end Luke so tied me up in dollars and pounds, always mixing the currencies, that in the end I believe I gave him a *hongo* of a hundred and fifty pounds, far too much.

9

EVERY WEEK there were two or three items in the newspaper from various parts of the country about witchcraft.

In one village people were reported to believe that malaria, a great killer in Uganda, was caused by witchcraft and mangoes. They had good reason for linking mangoes to the illness. Mangoes were plentiful in the rainy season; that was also when mosquitoes bred, seeking out even small accumulations of stagnant water. To others witchcraft seemed a more natural explanation. One villager said, 'Malaria is caused by witchcraft or bad spirits. When I got malaria, I found out that my neighbour was responsible for it. And when he was sent away from the village, I got cured.' One procedure – a visit to the witchdoctor – would have been responsible for finding out about the neighbour; another, more violent, procedure, probably involving the village, would have been necessary to send him away.

When it came to witchcraft, violence was never far away. In Easter week, in a village in the south-west, four brothers strangled their forty-two-year-old aunt. They removed her jaw and her tongue, no doubt for some private magical purpose, and then dumped the body in a nearby banana field. Not long after, dogs began to gather in the banana field. The village people became suspicious. They went to look, and found the dogs feeding on the dead woman's body, which was lying in a pool of blood. The dead woman was well known. Suspicion at once fell on the four brothers, who were believed to practise witchcraft. About twenty of the village men went to look for them. When they found them they began to beat them with sticks and anything else that came to hand.

Two of the brothers got away and went to the police. The other two brothers were killed and buried in a latrine. Four goats, five hens and two pigs belonging to the brothers were slaughtered; this was what happened to animals belonging to people who were thought to be bad. The police, when they came, arrested fifteen people. They recovered the two bodies from the latrine and took them away for a post-mortem: a strange legalistic note in this story of country wildness.

Sometimes, of course, it goes the other way: witchcraft in a setting where it doesn't fit. The story begins peacefully enough, in a village, with animals looking for pasture. A cow enters a secondary schoolyard, sees a shirt put out to dry, and begins to eat it. The student, whose shirt it is, chases the cow in the hope of getting his shirt back. He hits the cow with a stick. A few days later the student's leg – not the cow's – begins to swell, and he becomes paralysed. The students at the school recognise magic and witchcraft when they see it. They deal with it in the only way they know. They attack the village in a body, burn eight houses, and they try to lynch the cow-owner, an old man of seventy, whom they accuse of bewitching the paralysed student. In their rampage through the village they kill a dog, six cows, fourteen goats, three sheep and eleven chickens; they also destroy four pit-latrines, and the banana and coffee plantations of eight villagers. Three of the villagers, armed with spears and pangas, later hide in the school, to counter-attack; there — somewhat unfairly — they are arrested by the police; and the affair fizzles out.

Witchcraft is not a joke to these people. They cannot laugh at what they fear. The students at a senior secondary school in a major town, a boarding school, become very agitated when they see one morning, in the school compound, a fresh goat's head and a whole goat's skin. They see these as witchcraft fetishes. They blame the headmaster; already, they say, the food at the school is not good; and that morning when the boarders got up they found some school windows broken and the school generally in a mess. This is a clear 'sign' of magic afoot. The students feel they are being threatened in an unpleasant diabolical way, and (speaking now in a code which they expect to be understood) they say some 'big people' are behind it all. Later they parade through the town, sturdy young men in their school uniform, dark trousers, white shirt, and they declare a strike. The police, when they come, are conciliatory; they understand their country.

To live in a world ruled by witchcraft, a world liable to irrational dissolution in its details, is to be on edge, to be on a constant lookout. Add to this the eternal anxiety about politics, the fear of a land being lost; add the great population of Uganda, the constant feeling of a crowd too great for the land available, the roads, the jobs available.

The land can look so open and unused (as it did to the early explorers), but you never can tell when you are encroaching on protected wetlands that are now known to filter and cleanse water for Lake Victoria; or when, hunting antelope for food in the Mount Elgon area, a traditional hunting ground of your people, you are trespassing on land protected by the Uganda Wildlife Authority, whose guards carry guns and shoot to kill, and where, as they say, poaching is 'like shaking death by the hand in the forest'. There are many regions where as a herdsman you never can tell when you are occupying land reserved for cultivators, or sometimes driving your cattle over the border to Tanzania, where they are not wanted. In Kayunga you cut down trees, with others, to burn charcoal; and then, because there is now no forest cover, the hailstorms destroy houses and fields and animals, and people quite suddenly have nowhere to sleep and nothing to eat. It is so easy to make matters worse.

That feeling of being on edge can easily turn to a feeling of being torn, can turn to pain. It is of this pain, of people driven to extremity, of a world now beyond control, that many of the items in the newspaper speak every day.

Man burns 10 to death in hut: this is an item from the north, from an internally displaced persons camp. The name of the camp suggests the tensions. Within that, a family quarrel: a man settling accounts with his estranged wife. It was a grass-thatched hut; after it had been sprinkled with petrol it would have burnt fiercely. Seven of the ten people killed were children; some of them belonged to other families; shortage of space had caused them to be brought to this particular hut. A photograph showed the little charred bodies in the burnt-out hut, lying together, for that little bit of last-minute comfort, and lying face down, instinctively protecting their faces.

My husband was hacked to death as I watched: this is an item from the same issue. It was a second marriage for both parties. The husband had fifteen children from his first marriage, six from his second. They were returning home from a trading centre when they were attacked by a man with a panga coming out of a banana plantation. The attacker, while he hacked and chopped, accused the husband of being a polygamist. So – in addition to possible resentment from the husband's first family – there was some Christian feeling here. After the husband was killed, the attacker turned to the woman. He chopped off one of her hands and would have done more, but he ran off when a *boda-boda* cyclist with a bright cycle light appeared. The woman was taken to hospital and there her other hand was amputated. Without hands, she has to be fed by other people. She told the newspaper, 'I do not know where I am headed with these children, and now that they are going back to school, who will feed me?'

Accused of burying her son alive: again, this is from the same issue of the newspaper. A thirty-three-year-old casual labourer, a woman, working at a flower farm (of all places), is accused of burying her eighteen-month-old son in a potato garden. The child had been wrapped in a sack and his legs had been tied. The photograph of the mother shows a woman undone and helpless. A neighbour tells the paper that people so desperate should be allowed to take their

unwanted children to any police station. And in the description of the buried baby – the sack, the tied legs – there is a
strange echo of the witchdoctor's advice to a seeker to make
an offering of something very dear to the seeker. As though
the poor woman had heard of this advice and was trying to
do it all by herself.

So much for the pain of the poor. But for better-off
people, even people of a royal clan, there is an equivalent
kind of distress.

'We had independence and we lost it. We have never
recovered from the years of destruction that followed
independence. Twenty years of it till 1984. Traditions are
fading away by default. Are you going to Mbarara? You
should go there and see the destruction with your own eyes.
See the deserted palace with weeds growing there because
of the politics. Once you remove cultural restraints you
have chaos and anarchy. People put under this will do
anything to survive.' This was like the point Prince Kassim
had made. 'They will do anything and at the same time
they want the technological advances of the world. The
race for these technological luxuries has replaced culture.
Our religion was not savage. It was based on the venera-
tion of the ancestors. If your father dies you venerate him.
You give a libation to the ancestors before you drink. The
destruction of traditions and the lack of cultural restraint,
especially for people who have been brought together by a
colonial power and told to form a nation, could only bring
disaster.'

And from someone in the middle, an educated woman,

not poor, not of a royal clan, and from quite a different part of the country, someone overtly Christian but with a love for her roots: 'Modernity wants us to sweep our culture away, and that will manifest itself in a political upheaval. A conflict between Christianity and traditional religion. In the Lango tradition when there was a drought, or it was prolonged, all the elders got together and made sacrifices, and it would rain while they were there at it. My grandmother told me this. But the missionaries called it devil worship. Culture does not die – today it is called witchcraft. My grandmother produced twins who died. They had to be buried in a special way, in hollow pots, and a shed had to be built over the grave, to protect and shade them. Every year my grandmother went there, to tend the shed, feed the grave, and sing and dance there. When she became a Pentecostal she had to stop that, as it was not allowed. She had to remove the shed, and she was so afraid that the twins would come and kill her living children. I talk to myself so as not to get confused. To me it's all about belief and what treats you well. In traditional religion it was not about money. It was a communal spirit and people came together for a common cause like the drought.'

And gradually, from the tragedies the newspapers report, and from conversations with good people, the visitor arrives at the unsettling idea of a poor country still vulnerable – in its people, living on their nerves, and even in its landscape, which might be despoiled – after forty years of civil conflict, still waiting for an upheaval which may solve nothing.

10

I HADN'T THOUGHT in 1966 of going to look for the source of the Nile. No one among the people I knew talked of that. They talked about the game parks and fishing in the western lakes; they talked about the politics of the country; they talked about their colleagues; they talked about doing long drives. I hadn't myself read Speke at that time, and so I hadn't been touched by the romance of the great river, though we crossed the river at Jinja on our way to Nairobi, a regular outing, and crossed it again when we drove back to Kampala. In Stanley I read that 'jinja' meant the stones, the falls, which occurred just after Lake Victoria poured into the Nile.

And now I was to see that this pouring into the Nile, seen from the Busoga side, was one of the majestic things in Nature: a great smooth sheet of water of immense force, not muddy like the Congo or the Mississippi, but fresh-looking, grey-green, dotted with mysterious small green islands, and between high green banks, dividing and coming to life over the stones. Speke, when he first saw it, the object of his dreams, sat on the bank on the Buganda side and 'saw the day out' considering the play of water. It has that effect still, of encouraging the visitor simply to look, sending the mind back over the centuries, perhaps even over the millennia, when what we see now already existed (though a speeded-up camera would show islands and vegetation disappearing and reappearing); and sending the mind also on an unimaginable four-thousand-mile journey north to the Mediterranean.

Speke saw thousands of 'passenger fish' flying at the stones, and many rhinoceros and crocodiles in the river. They are not there now. Speke was himself a great killer with the gun, with a jaunty Victorian sporting vocabulary to match; and many thousands of sportsmen would have followed where he led. Even at that first sight of the stones, while his master was content to sit and stare, Speke's well-trained assistant, Bombay, shot and killed a sleeping crocodile.

In the next century a dam was built at Jinja. River dams alter river life and alter the aspect of things; and what we see now at the stones wouldn't be quite what Speke saw. Another dam is planned for lower down the river; when that is done the visitor would no longer see what we see now.

ON ONE OF the islands of Lake Victoria a world wildlife or conservation body has set up a small chimpanzee sanctuary – forty-two animals, whose parents had been killed and eaten by Africans, who are great relishers of what they call 'bush meat' and, given guns and left to themselves, would easily eat their way through the continent's wildlife.

The conservation people do boat trips to the sanctuary from Entebbe. It seemed to me a trouble-free way of being on the lake where a hundred and fifty years ago Mutesa I, with some boats of his navy, liked to go picnicking with his court and harem.

The gardens or grounds of the conservation body grow lush and green almost to the water's edge. It should be idyllic, but in the early morning the lake flies, feathery and brown, swarm over the lake. After what must be a life in the air, a short life, they are looking for places to settle down, and they do so on hair and clothes. For some inches below the boat-jetty cobwebs hang down pale-brown and heavy, like decorative swags, with their load of trapped flies – Africa prolific in life and death. The boat, starting up and moving on, cuts through another cloud of lake flies, which fall twice as fast on faces and clothes, and settle where there is no wind to blow them away, especially on the floor of the boat.

Then, mercifully, the fly-cloud is no more. The water is choppy, dark green, and you soon start to see fishing dugouts. There are two men to a boat, which sit so low in the water that the fishermen (who might be showing off a little) appear to be skimming the water with their bodies, and you find it easier to believe the newspaper item that five thousand people drown every year in the lake.

The romantic lake islands begin to appear, forest and parkland, their colours softened by the haze. What seems near is farther away than you think. Much white smoke comes from behind an island, from a fishermen's settlement which is slowly but surely polluting the lake, making it a carrier of typhoid and cholera. It would have been like that in Mutesa's time, but there is no mention of it in Speke, who has trouble describing an asthmatic attack he suffered over many weeks.

It was an hour and a half to the island of chimpanzees. Immediate order: mown grass, neatly thatched huts, paths and signs, with the brilliant yellow weaver birds busy about their extraordinary nests. Twice a day the chimpanzees are fed. The launches from the mainland arrive in time for this.

A pebbly red path led up to the fence that marked off the chimpanzee and forest area from the rest of the island. A tremendous racket from somewhere in the bush told us that the feeding had begun. There was no meat for the chimpanzees, only cut fruit thrown from a platform. This was fought over with mighty blows that when they landed on a chimpanzee seemed to strike hollow ground. The cries of beaters and beaten were overlaid with a continual squealing, relish indistinguishable from pain.

The chimpanzees might have been orphans, but in the sanctuary old ideas of size and authority ruled. The leading male ran back and forth the length of the viewing platform and beyond, thumping males not as big as he was. Only the very small, close to infancy, and strangely melancholy, were allowed to eat quietly, long, jointed fingers fixed round their pieces of fruit. One or two chimpanzees were made to perform little tricks for the visitors, using sticks or twigs to drag within reach pieces of fruit that had been deliberately thrown outside the wire-mesh fence, so that we could see the trick.

Gradually the feeding was over, and there again the bigger animals led the way, being the first to lope back to the forest, moving swiftly on arms and legs.

One couldn't help remembering that in times of national

emergency, it was the zoos and the animals that were the first to suffer. Just a little weakening of the central authority here, and all the elaborate support of the chimpanzee sanctuary would wither away. The chimpanzees had skills, as we had been told; they were close to human beings; but against guns they, like all the world's animals, were helpless. Fifteen minutes or less with a gun could reduce these animals to the African bush meat their parents had become. The paths of the sanctuary, maintained now with so much trouble, would become overgrown; the neat grass roofs of the huts would slip and collapse. When Speke and Stanley had come this way the forest and forest life would have seemed eternal; but now, like everything in Uganda, it felt frail.

We returned by another route, going round an island where there was a fishermen's settlement of about a thousand. So one of our boatmen said; but the settlement, with the dun-coloured shacks tight one against the other, looked like a very full mainland slum, and I thought there might have been more people there. This was where the thick white smoke of the morning had come from. On the way out we had seen a few fishermen's settlements, and some had looked romantic, picture-book places, with dark dugouts drawn up on pale beaches. But this big settlement that mimicked a mainland slum would have had no electricity and no water except what came from the lake.

Soon in one part of the sky there appeared the thin brown tornado-like whirls of the lake flies that had troubled us in the morning. Before we could get back to Entebbe

five or more of these light-coloured whirls defined themselves against the pale lower sky, thin, rising high, wavering, constantly changing shape: like emanations of lake
water.

11

THE BAGANDA people had great skills as builders of
Roman-straight roads and majestic grass-roofed huts that
didn't leak even in the rainy season. They had a detailed
social organisation; every clan was like a guild, with its
special duties. Worshipping their Kabaka, they were ruled
by the idea of loyalty and obedience. These qualities, taken
together, made them a great fighting force, and gave the
Baganda their empire, which lasted some centuries.

Their history, however, has no dates and no records,
because the Baganda people had no script and no writing.
They have only a limited oral literature, which is a poor
substitute for a written text that can be consulted down the
centuries. Strangely, the absence of a script doesn't seem to
trouble academic or nationalist people; it isn't a subject that
is talked about.

I found only one man who had thought about this
deficiency of the Ugandan or central African kingdoms. He
was a middle-aged melancholic and he was from a neighbouring kingdom (or kingdom area). He was passionate
about the kingdoms, believing in the power of the imprisoned and irreplaceable royal drum of his area, with its

particular heartbeat. He grieved for the recent past. The terrible Milton Obote had imprisoned the royal drum and sixty-two items of its regalia in 1967; and though the kingdoms had been technically restored, nothing had been the same again; and the drum had still not been recovered. The drum still had power, but it suffered in its imprisonment. Like a wounded patriot, the melancholy man exaggerated the pain to come: he lived with the vision of all this part of Africa being swept away by some new political force. He pointed to the demure woman, a relative, who was with him. He said, 'In a few years you wouldn't see her here.' He wasn't saying that the woman would migrate; he meant only that in a short while people of the royal clan, to which his relative belonged, people known for their fine and distinctive features, would be squeezed out.

I took him back to the question of the absence of a script and writing.

He said, 'Script? They didn't know the wheel.'

This was news to me. But then, reviewing everything I had read about old Uganda, I felt that what I had heard was right; though it was hard to imagine everything being manhandled or loaded on to donkeys on those straight Baganda roads.

He thought that the geographical isolation of Uganda in central Africa, beside lakes the outside world didn't know, would have gone some way to explaining why there was no script. And I felt he was right. The Baganda had their own language; it would have been reasonably easy, given the stimulus of literate neighbours, for a script to be devised to match the sounds of the language. In the neighbouring kingdom of Bunyoro Speke found people writing Arabic: some people felt the need for a script and writing.

To be without writing, as the Baganda were, was to have no effective way of recording the extraordinary things they achieved. Much of the past, the thirty-seven kings of which they boast, is effectively lost, and can be talked of only as myth. The loss continues. In a literate age, of newspapers and television and radio, the value of oral history steadily shrinks.

The Baganda built roads like the Romans, very straight, up hill and down dale, filling the awkward depressions with the stalks of tall papyrus, which grow on this water-logged land in profusion, as they did in ancient Egypt. But the Baganda have lived for so long with the sight of their old roads that they take them for granted; there are some who even say that the roads were built by the British. And what must have been refined tools or systems for aligning and grading those roads have been forgotten.

In about 1870 Mutesa I was fighting a war against one of his neighbours. For this war he built or caused to be built a road along part of the lake. Stanley saw this military road two years later. It still existed as a road. Very little grass had grown over it, which was quite remarkable in a fertile area, which had heavy rains in the rainy season.

PATRICK EDWARDS was the Trinidad ambassador. He was an African expert, having served in Nigeria for some years. He was interested in my travel and did what he could to help. He thought I should move out of Kampala and have a look at some of the other kingdoms beside Buganda. He wrote an official letter to the kingdom of Busoga (which Kabaka Sunna had spectacularly punished in the 1850s). After some time there was a reply. The officials were concerned to an extraordinary degree about their expenses when I came to see them, and specified what these might be: meals, travel, hotel charges. I felt that in one bound, because of Patrick's letter, we had gone back a hundred and fifty years to the arbitrary world of the tribal *hongo*, which could at any time be doubled for the traveller and then doubled again, before the drum of satisfaction could be beaten, to free the traveller. I decided to stay away from Busoga.

PATRICK THOUGHT we should persevere, and try with the more famous and beautiful kingdom of Toro in the west. In the Serena Hotel, where we were staying, there was as it happened a man who, in addition to his hotel duties in the human resources department, was head of protocol for the kingdom of Toro. Patrick made his usual correct approaches to this man, whose name was James, and in due course we heard from James that the Queen Mother of Toro was going to be in the hotel in a couple of days.

On the afternoon of the appointed day we sat in the Bambara lounge on the first floor of the hotel, waiting for the Queen Mother. In a far corner of the lounge were three big women, of brown complexion. They were there when we arrived. They made a distinguished group. One of the three was noticeably handsome and vivacious. She was wearing a shade of powder red that suited her complexion. I suspected that she was the Queen Mother, but we couldn't presume without an introduction. That was made only when James, the protocol man of the court, came.

The Queen Mother and her companions then left their corner and came to where we were sitting. The women with the Queen Mother were her sisters, and I imagine they were her official chaperones.

The Queen Mother said of one sister, when she introduced her, that she was a born-again Christian. That meant she was part of the Pentecostal crop of Uganda, where there were hundreds of Pentecostal churches, extravagantly named, and matched in their number only by the private junior and secondary schools, whose signboards ('Day and Boarding') appeared in unlikely places, like the boards of the churches, a kind of private enterprise gone mad: an unlikely, twisted fulfilment of Mutesa's wish in 1875 for British missionaries.

'Do you want to be saved?' the Queen Mother asked ironically.

But the irony had no effect on her born-again sister who, in an undertone, immediately began to talk to us about the need for Jesus.

With equal irony the Queen Mother said that the other sister was married to an old man, leaving us to work out what that meant.

The Queen Mother told her own story easily. She had clearly done it many times before. Her husband had been in

the foreign service of Uganda. He had served in Latin
America; and she, in her jolly way, spoke some Spanish
phrases she still remembered. *'Cómo está? Todo va bien?'*
('How are you? Everything all right?') They were a happy
couple, although he was older than she. They had three
children, two girls and a boy. One of the girls became very
ill with leukaemia. They took this girl to the Royal Marsden
Hospital in London. For three years, while the girl was in
hospital, the family stayed in London. At some stage her
father, the diplomat, had to go back to Uganda to deal with
various matters. While he was there he died of a heart
attack; shortly after, the girl with leukaemia also died.
So, at the age of twenty-seven, the Queen Mother became a
widow and regent.

Her son was now sixteen. In two weeks or so he was
going to open the parliament at Toro. It was going to be a
splendid three-day occasion. Prince Kassim had spoken of
this as part of the culture and discipline of the old ways;
it was moving in Toro, he said, to see distinguished old
men reverencing the boy king. And the Queen Mother now
told us a little more about her son. He loved animals. He
allowed no one to kick a dog or kill a cat. She was hoping
to send him to England to be educated. She invited us all
to come to Toro for the opening of the parliament. And
Patrick, returning courtesy for courtesy, invited the Queen
Mother to come to Trinidad for the carnival in the coming
year.

James, the protocol man, seemed delighted that the
meeting in the Bambara lounge had gone so well. He was

as squashed in appearance, and dry and formal, as the
Queen Mother was full of bounce. He said later, in his
delight, 'The royal family of Toro are big and handsome
and light-skinned.'

It was strange hearing this from him. He himself was
very dark.

I HAD BEGUN to feel that I had done what I could do in
Uganda, and I was planning to move on. But now, after the
Queen Mother's invitation, I thought I should hang around
until the opening of the Toro parliament.

I had a few memories of the kingdom from 1966. The
main town was Fort Portal, named after an early British
surveyor of the protectorate. In 1966 it had a kind of
expatriate life. There were tea planters. Unwillingly one
day I went fishing with one of them in Lake Albert, to
the west, and quickly made a mess of things, fouling up
line and fly on an underwater snag and amusing no one.
The best known bar was The Gum Pot. The ruler was the
Omukama, and his palace was at the top of a hill. There
were stories about him (or, possibly, his father). When he
had drunk too much his major domo would keep visitors
away, saying, 'The Omukama is tired.' One year, in a
decorating mood, he laid a coat of green paint on the stones
beside the hill road to the palace.

The days passed. No word came from James about the
arrangements that had been made for us. Patrick, with his
ideas of diplomatic etiquette, didn't press. On the Saturday
when the boy-king was to open the parliament Patrick

telephoned James in the morning, and we were told that
there were many guests and we couldn't be fitted in. The
ceremonial weekend passed. James said, 'You know these
royal people. They don't care.'

On the days that followed – perhaps Patrick had deliv-
ered a diplomatic rebuke – James became more and more
agitated. We had been let down; he felt responsible and
very much wanted to make it up to us. He wanted us to go
to Toro. He even wanted us to spend the night there. He
became quite frantic. He said he had planned everything,
and he was so full of remorse for his royals we thought it
would be churlish, for his sake, not to go to Toro.

At the last minute, however, some good fairy made us
decide not to spend the night there, but to drive back to
Kampala. Patrick, always correct, put on a formal grey suit
for what could be thought of as his visit to royalty; and
we went in his ambassador's car, with his Trinidad standard
unfurled.

It was a four-hour drive to Fort Portal. At least half of
that was on the straight royal roads of Buganda which,
went they went up a hill, seemed to disappear into the sky
at the top of the hill. But these Buganda roads were in a
poor way, in spite of the editorial in the paper that morning
which said that the people of Uganda were 'hoodwinked'
into believing that the roads were not good; and speed-
breakers across the road in every peopled area shook up the
bones.

We came in time to the British-built roads of Toro: not
straight, always curving, laid down in cuttings in the red

soil which often shut out the view. But for some reason –
perhaps the population was sparser and there was less heavy
traffic – these roads were in much better shape than the
Buganda ones; and we were able to travel at speed. The
stone markers on the roadside were engraved every four
kilometres with the distance to Fort Portal. That distance
seemed to melt away, and the landscape all around was
wonderful: parkland between mountain ranges.

James, on the telephone from Kampala, guided us
through the small town. We came to the hill with the
palace. As we climbed I looked for the roadside stones that
might have been painted green by an eccentric omukama
before 1966. I couldn't see them. The stones might have
been removed as being too disfigured, or the story might
have been false. On every side the view was grand: we
looked down to wide parkland, pale grass, darker trees, and
the roofs of the small colonial town of Fort Portal.

The hill was isolated; every view was grand. It occurred
to me that this hill would always have been the seat of a
king or chief; it would have had a history. If Africans
hadn't built with the perishable products of the forest, it
would have been worth excavating.

We came to a gravel area between the palace and a
small, featureless modern building. When we got out of the
car we were welcomed by a small team of smiling, busy
men who darted about and took photographs of us and
managed to make a lot of noise. They must have been the
palace officials James had talked about. So, reassuringly,
James had kept his word.

We were led to a small room in the palace where there were copies of family photographs on two big boards. Immediately, then, not giving us time to rest after our long drive, a red-eyed official in a long gown and with a heavy-handled stick, began to harangue us about Toro and the royal family. He didn't simply point at the photographs; he used the heavy handle of the stick to knock hard at various photographs on the boards. He generated a lot of noise and he had a strong accent. I couldn't follow what he was saying, but I felt he had already begun to repeat himself.

There was a photograph at the top of one board of the old palace: a large rectangular thatched building. When the British came to Uganda Africans became ashamed of their round huts; as soon as they could they began building rectangular concrete houses. So what had happened here on the royal hill in Toro was a curious reversal of what had become standard practice in Uganda. The old palace was rectangular; the new palace was circular. It had been built like that for the sake of the all-round view; but it was also like a rejection of the old colonial idea of modernity. The new palace, with its various political messages, had in fact been built by Brother Leader Ghaddafi as part of the Libyan expansion in Africa. The new round palace had concrete uprights and its drains were exposed. This exposing of the drains was the Libyan style; the grand new mosque in Kampala had a similar feature.

I would have liked to see more of the palace, but we were not able to do so. When I asked where we might rest we were led to the smaller, rectangular building on the other side of the gravelled area. In the drawing-room area there was an old leopard skin, mark of kingship — (poor leopard, doomed to extinction) — thrown over an upholstered chair. I imagined the young king sat there and discussed affairs of state with various people. There was another small room with two plain divan beds set against two walls, their heads at an angle one to the other. This was where we were supposed to rest. The lavatory had no seat; through a big hole in the ceiling we could see the beams and rafters of the roof. This was where James's arrangements petered out; it was clear now that no amount of telephoning could improve matters.

We dragged some chairs out to the wide verandah, and the warm air from the gravelled yard and from the road below came at us. Patrick telephoned James and said without complaint that Toro was beautiful, so beautiful he was hoping to be allowed to buy a piece of land. James, missing the irony, told us that if we wanted lunch we should go to the Mountains of the Moon Hotel in the town. We decided to forget the palace officials — we had some idea that they might have laid on lunch for us — and make a run for this hotel. We heard later that the officials were hoping to come with us.

In the Mountains of the Moon, new to me, we sat in the spacious back verandah, at the edge of the bright green lawn. A pretty little kitten, three or four months old, wailed piteously for food. I wished I could have taken him away with me. I went and talked to a waitress. She told me that the kitten was the last of a litter; they had got rid of the others. The kitten lived in a drain pipe in a concrete gutter; when it was there it was perfectly hidden. It was alone in the world; it kept alive — perhaps for not much longer — by its instinct. Hunger alone had made it come up to the back verandah. The waitress brought a saucer of milk. This little bit of nourishment comforted it; it stopped crying, and a little later I saw it in the hotel garden, not far from its drain-pipe home, licking its paws.

It was not far from here, in the kingdom of Unyoro, to the west of Buganda, that Speke, near the end of his journey, bought a little kitten from an Unyoro man. He doesn't say why he bought it, but it could only have been to keep the creature alive for a few more days. The Unyoro man wanted to eat the kitten; it was good eating, he said. He begged Speke to give the kitten back to him if it looked likely to die. It is a strange episode in his book, just four lines long; and he doesn't say how it ended.

There had been some talk from James of the palace officials taking us to see places and people connected with the traditional African religion. But since our arrival my interest in this part of the programme had gone down and down. And it was just as well, because when we went back from the Mountains of the Moon to the palace the red-eyed official, talking of the religious things we wanted to see, said they had sent away all their cars; and since we couldn't all fit in Patrick's ambassador's car, they would have to go ahead of us on a *boda-boda* motorbike. That would cost three thousand shillings. It was only a pound, but in Ugandan shillings it sounded a fearful amount; and I dreaded to think, if we showed ourselves indifferent to money at this stage, how much we would have to pay later to have an audience with a local diviner.

I said we were leaving out that part of the programme. They didn't seem to mind. But they wanted us to sign the visitors' book. They especially wanted Patrick to sign it, since he was the important man among us. And, since he was important, they wanted him to sign by himself on a whole page.

They then took Patrick off to the small room in the palace where there were the two boards of photographs. He came out after a while with what looked like a framed souvenir photograph: it had been taken of him in the morning with a lot of noise and busyness. Patrick thanked them. They said there was a charge. Seven thousand shillings. A little over two pounds. Patrick gave them 20,000 shillings. He was expecting change, but they said he had misunderstood. The charge wasn't 7,000 shillings; it was 74,000 shillings. Twenty-four pounds and fifty pence sterling; or thirty-seven US dollars. Patrick, too stunned to argue, or to think about pounds and dollars, paid. He awakened to outrage only after we had left, and for a long time he could think only of what was in effect the *hongo* he had been made to pay.

All the way back to Kampala, along the curving roads of Toro and the straight roads of Buganda, there were schoolchildren in uniform coming out at the end of a school day, walking home to simple dwellings in the fierce sun. It was just after three, the deadest time of the tropical day: the heat at its worst in all the green, the freshness of the morning long burnt away, together with whatever optimism the new day might have brought. The light and the heat cast a gloomy clarity on what we were driving through: small houses, small fields, small people, and it seemed that nothing more uplifting was being offered to the children we could see on the road. Uganda was Uganda. Education and school uniforms, giving an illusion of possibility, was easy; much harder was the creation of a proper economy. There would be no jobs for most of the children we could see — some dawdling on the way home now, killing time in spite of the heat.

The latest employment news, presented in the newspapers as good news, was that, even with all the suicide bombers and mayhem, there were six thousand Ugandans working as security guards in Iraq. There was also a report of a call for Ugandan English teachers from North Korea.

TWO

Sacred Places

I HAD BEEN TOLD — by someone who said he wanted to
warn me about Lagos airport — that that Nigerians liked
to travel with lots of luggage. I took this to mean that there
would be trouble collecting luggage in Lagos. But we had
luggage trouble even before we left London. Someone had
checked in with his luggage and had then disappeared. We
waited a while and then the pilot said that the absent
passenger had checked in nineteen pieces of luggage. I
thought I had misheard. But the Nigerian passengers didn't
turn a hair; and later, in Nigeria, I understood why. Why
fret about nineteen pieces when at that moment there was
a Nigerian bigwig travelling the world with thirty-seven
suitcases, and doing so on a diplomatic passport to which
he was not entitled?

Nigerians have their own idea of status. They make
sport with things that other people might take seriously;
and a diplomatic passport, with its many immunities, was
one of the toys that had come to them with independence

and statehood. To possess a toy like that, almost a fetish, sorted the men from the boys, and important people jostled with one another for the ennoblement. A man with thirty-seven suitcases would make enough of a show, you might think. But in Nigerian eyes such a man would make much more of a show, would put the seal on his grandeur, if at Immigration, in full view of the waiting crowd, he could saunter through the diplomatic channel.

We were waiting that morning or afternoon in London in the parked plane, and the man who had abandoned his nineteen pieces didn't show up. At length the pilot said that those nineteen pieces would have to be taken off the plane. This would take time; we were a full flight; many more than those nineteen pieces would have to be taken off before we could come upon the unclaimed suitcases. At the end they were found and taken off. We were now two and a half hours past our scheduled departure. For all this time we had been idle in the aeroplane, looking at the airport buildings and the busy life of the tarmac.

It was horrible when we got to Lagos. Beyond the immigration and customs hall, deceptively brisk and soon quite clear, there was chaos. Three flights had come in, close to one another; and there was only one unloading facility. Down the aluminium chute, from time to time, came the swollen black suitcases of Nigeria, like fragments of cooling lava. Unexpectedly conservative in style, those suitcases, done in a kind of fabric, and oddly similar.

In the dim light people lined the carousel and some stood against the wall. Others stood as near as they could get to the debouching point, almost amid the dangerous tumble of fat suitcases, like people who believed in magic, and thought that to be near the source was to be halfway to success. More important people walked up and down with the assistants (in suits or fine Nigerian clothes) who had come to the airport to welcome them, and were now, instead, like everybody else, only looking for luggage. After the style of business class and first class, all were equal here. The unloading and reloading of our own plane had made a mess of the original order in which things had been stowed.

I was standing against a wall behind a Nigerian family who had boarded the plane in London and were still full of beans. They had a couple of trolleys, but so far no suitcases. From time to time, for no reason I could see, the teen-age daughter, setting her face, gave her much smaller younger brother a good hard kick or lashed out at him with a vicious cuff. The blows would have hurt, but the boy made no attempt to hit back; instead, like a puppy or kitten with a short memory, he went to the girl again and was again kicked and cuffed.

While I was watching this piece of Nigerian family life I was accosted by a man in a dark suit and a coloured tie. He seemed to suggest that he was a driver and was waiting for me. He seemed so good and correct and logical in all the noise and hopelessness around me that I forgot all that I had been tutored about Lagos airport. After that introduction I looked, while I waited, for the man with the suit and the jaunty tie; he became my anchor in the rocking, jumping crowd. Sometimes (no doubt for some pressing private reason) he melted into the scrum around the carousel, and then I was frantic until I had a glimpse of the red tie again.

When in the fullness of time he guided me to a car (my two little pieces of luggage now found) I was happy to go.

The airport building had been chaotic inside. Outside was full of menace: raw concrete beams overhead, raw concrete pillars in front, and a kind of canopy that offered no protection. It was raining. The road, though shiny in the rain, was not well lighted. After the fug of the luggage hall every drop of rain, slanting in below the teasing canopy, felt cold and seemed to sting. There were beggars coming out of the dark now, around a corner, from nowhere that one could see: spectral at first, these figures, and then very real and sturdy. They all offered to help, and every one seemed a threat. The women beggars, at this time of night, were especially disturbing.

Here, without understanding how it had happened, I lost the man in the suit. Here, left alone with a man who said he was my driver, I heard that the man in the suit was not himself a driver; he organised drivers at the airport for people like me.

This man at least knew where I was going, and I allowed myself to go with him.

It was a slow, long journey to the other end of the sleeping town. The driver appeared uncertain about the route.

All kinds of doubt came to me, but then, miraculously, there was the hotel tower.

The man who took me up to the room drew the curtains

dramatically and said, like an impresario, 'The Atlantic Ocean!' I had to take it on trust. It was too dark to see clearly and I was too tired to concentrate. I had an impression of rollers coming in, heard some of the ocean noise (as I thought) muffled by glass and concrete; and that was all. The man then spoke about the television, took his tip, and was gone, leaving me alone with the deficiencies of the small, bare room: the broken safe, the empty refrigerator.

I telephoned the desk. They said they would send someone to look at the safe. He came up promptly, a sour-looking fellow in blue dungarees with *Locksmith* in big white letters on the back. He did a few things to the safe and said he had fixed it. He gave a little demonstration, but a short while later the safe went back to its bad ways, and the desk, not at all put out, said they would send the locksmith again. He did come up, too, as promptly as before; but by this time I thought the room was beyond redemption and I should look at another room.

That too was unsuitable. And then the people at the desk began to send me zipping up and down, from floor to floor and room to unsuitable room. It began to seem that a gratuity was called for, if I was to be shown a good room. And almost at the same time the idea came to me – thinking of what I had seen downstairs – that I had been booked into the wrong section of the hotel (it had various sections, and separate actual buildings) and that this error had led me to something like a Nigerian *maison de passe*.

I remembered that a warning of some sort had been

given me by a friend, but he had done so in too coded a way and I had not understood. This friend was now in Dubai, on the Persian Gulf. He had a friend whom he trusted in Kano, five hundred miles away in northern Nigeria. I telephoned them both, and though it would have been early Sunday morning for them, they were marvellous.

The man in Kano must have been a man of some authority, and perhaps also with a gift of correct language. The hotel's attitude changed at once. I was given a room in another, more suitable building. The man in Kano said I was to go there right away and not wait for morning. Like the hotel itself, I was happy to obey. The hotel sent its shuttle van to ferry me over. Everyone was civil. New world, new day. It was now about half-past two.

Later, when I was settled in my room, the telephone rang. The caller was impatient, on the brink of rage. He was a car-driver. He said he had been sent to the airport to pick me up but hadn't been able to find me. He had been hanging around for hours.

I understood then that I had fallen too easily for a suit and a tie and had allowed myself to be kidnapped at the airport. There was a card on the table in my room, warning clients about this sort of thing, urging every kind of precaution before stepping into a taxi. I felt, then, that I had had the luck of the innocent — it does exist: it has looked after me for all of my travelling life — and that, whatever was to come later, this luck had brought me to the hotel.

This was my first day in Nigeria.

In the open lobby of the first building I had noticed —

there are many levels of consciousness at any given moment, and perhaps it will be like that at the moment of death itself, even if it is painful – I had noticed, in spite of the anxiety, which was uppermost, and in spite of the fatigue after fourteen or fifteen hours of travel, an attractive and mysterious sculpture: African, but realistic, and not apparently magical: a life-size figure of a veiled man in a high hat, and in a long coat, holding a thick stick. The hat, like a top hat, and the coat, like a Victorian frock-coat, gave an odd touch of Europe to the figure. The veil was reticulated, and kept in place on the forehead by the hat, so that it was a little away from the face. There was a smaller version of the sculpture in the office area of the new building, and there was a version, in pale-blue shadow, on some of the hotel stationery.

The motif was clearly well known, but no one I asked could tell me with confidence what the mysterious figure stood for. Or perhaps they didn't want to tell me. I was told it was emblematic of Lagos; I was also told it was a figure of masquerade. This didn't help me.

Help came later, in *Travels in the Interior of Africa*, by Mungo Park (1771–1806). He had travelled, by horse and on foot, in this part of Africa more than two hundred years before, in the late 1790s (strangely, at the time of the Napoleonic wars: war did not then close everything else down). I had read Park's book nearly forty years before, and had liked it, but (as with so many books that are part of one's education) had forgotten much of the detail, preserving from that reading only an idea of dust and cruelty and deprivation, the writer's deprivation and the deprivation of his companions, mostly African slave merchants driving their chained-up slaves from the interior, taking them in sickness and half health and on half diet, all of five hundred miles to the coast, to be sold into the holds of Atlantic ships.

The figure with the hat and the veil and the stick occurs early on in Park's book. Park called it Mumbo Jumbo. The name changed its meaning later, became the pejorative which we all know; and yet, of the English dictionaries I consulted, neither the Oxford dictionary nor Chambers credits Park with the first, pure use of the word.

On the 8th, about noon, I arrived at Kolor, a considerable town, near the entrance into which I observed, hanging upon a tree, a sort of masquerade habit, made of the bark of trees, which I was told on inquiry belonged to Mumbo Jumbo. This is a strange bugbear, common to all the Mandingo towns, and much employed by the Pagan natives in keeping their women in subjection.

Africa was polygamous. The women often quarrelled, and a husband was at times hard put to it to keep order in his household. That was when he called upon Mumbo Jumbo. He might act the part of Mumbo Jumbo himself, or he might call upon someone he could trust. Just before dark one day Mumbo Jumbo would begin to scream in the forest outside the village in a most fearful way. This terrible screaming would tell people in the village that Mumbo Jumbo was coming; and when it is dark Mumbo

Jumbo does come with his strange disguise, his stick and high hat, his veiled face and his long coat.

Mumbo walks through the village to the village meeting-place, the equivalent of the village square. The villagers gather there; no married woman can stay away, even if she feels that Mumbo Jumbo has come especially for her. There is singing and dancing; it continues till midnight; and then Mumbo Jumbo declares who the offending woman is. She is seized, stripped naked, tied to a post, and flogged until dawn by Mumbo Jumbo with his stick. The villagers shout with pleasure; they mock the woman and show her no mercy.

Africa is no longer polygamous; only the Muslims among them have many wives. Africa, away from its Muslim segment, thinks of itself as Christian, even if ancient currents of thought and belief and custom flow below. And it is easy enough to understand that the figure of Mumbo Jumbo might create an embarrassment for a modern African, and that people who know very well what the figure stands for – the playacting, the comedy of the old bush culture – might not know what to say to a stranger about it.

Mungo Park didn't get down to the Nigeria region, but he wasn't too far away. The difference between his West Africa and what we see today is incalculable. This may be obvious, but its very obviousness makes it easy to forget. Yet it is the necessary background to any assessment of Nigeria. Nigeria is rich now, with its oil. But modern

Nigeria is new; it is only about eight or ten generations old; and some of the most gifted Nigerians carry this burden of newness.

I had been given an introduction to Edun. He was a handsome, athletic man of fifty, and an investment banker. I felt it was still a source of wonder to him how he had become what he was. The world was new for him. In this new world he saw everything as possible for him, and his patriotism, of an entirely new sort, took the form of wishing people to understand their new possibilities.

He had been born in Manchester in England. So he was an immigrant, with the immigrant's drive. It wasn't something one associated with Africa. It was new. It wouldn't have happened one hundred years before; the Africa of that period would have been close to the Africa of Mungo Park.

When Edun was three he, with an older brother, had been taken back to Africa by his parents. The brother died, and Edun had been taken back to England; this was how it happened that all his education had been in that country. His parents were passionate about education; it was something they had brought with them from Africa. Edun, as a child, felt that concern. 'My mother said that if I had a good education I would not look back.' When Nigerian visitors came to the house they always asked the little boy what class he was in, and what his position was in the class. So Edun, growing up, found himself different from his West Indian friends, who gave up school without thought. Now these friends (descendants of the people Mungo Park saw being walked down to the coast) look at Edun and say, 'Well, we dropped out, but you carried on.'

This, about West Indians, was strange to me. In Trinidad we had overcome some of the effects of history. We had a distinguished group of black professionals; their children reflected the confidence of their parents. We were able, without trouble, to distinguish these people from the general black population. Black and ordinary, black and distinguished: we carried the two ideas in our head, and it could even be said that their blackness added to the distinction of the distinguished. Perhaps this group had required time to grow; my feeling is that they began to come up fifty or sixty years after the abolition of slavery. The West Indian children in England (some of them descendants of the people Mungo Park saw being walked to the coast) didn't have this professional background, this idea of what was possible; they stayed with old ways of thinking and behaving.

Early in his banking career, when he was working in an international bank in Washington, Edun had an illumination. It was very simple. A Nigerian friend said to him during a general conversation, 'I want to own my own bank one day.'

Edun at that stage could imagine a cook wanting to own a catering firm, or an artisan wanting his own workshop, or a driver wanting to have a car-hire business. But a bank! In fact, it was already possible for a Nigerian to own a bank; the formalities were not insuperable. Very quickly, as

I heard from someone else, there were 126 private banks in Nigeria. Most were simple deposit-takers, but many of them went on to develop proper banking skills; today, after regulation, there are twenty-five Nigerian banks. Edun's friend now owns a bank. Edun himself started his own bank, with a friend; that bank was later merged with an important South African bank; its branches can be seen in many African countries.

Edun said, 'This is the mindset here. I did not have it as I was brought up and educated outside the country, but I soon picked it up. People often say to each other, "You can be anything here. You can reach any height." And this mindset is our great strength.'

But Edun, growing up in England, was spared the other side of the Nigerian mindset, the side that fell down a deep well into ancient beliefs and magic, the side that resisted rationality.

2

THE CONTRACTOR said, 'You know Edun? Tell him to give me another contract.'

I said I would do what I could for him.

He was a portly but muscular man of fifty, quite tall. When he was asked to describe himself and his community, he said, 'I am a Christian contractor who is a Yoruba.'

So he knew a lot about Yoruba culture?

He said, in a series of apparent non-sequiturs, which yet

had meaning, 'I am well read. I come from a staunch Catholic background. My mother was a papal medallist in the days when you really had to work for it. I was with the Celestial Church of Christ. And then I attended the White Garment church – an orthodox form of Christian Cherubim and Seraphim Church Movement.'

Why did he call it orthodox?

'In the books I have read it is more African than Western. There is more uniformity in it. They use the Bible. The service usually lasts for four hours. It starts at 10 a.m. world-wide.'

There was a lot of singing and dancing during the service. It excited him. He liked the burning of incense. The order of the service was also more interesting.

Did it change him spiritually?

'I shouldn't say that it opened another vista in my life.' But then he said something different. 'One day I saw a little girl who was possessed by the Holy Spirit, and she was being cleansed. I was taken aback by the things she was confessing to – the things she had done in the spirit realm of darkness. The experience made me more spiritual. I now believe there is an Alpha and Omega who watches over you. One hundred and twenty million Nigerians or average Nigerians can contend with the vicissitudes of life only by turning to the Alpha and Omega. Other people call it something else. I guess I am an optimist. I have lived here and I have also seen other African countries, and I thank God for Nigeria. I have seen Liberia after the war, and Sierra Leone, and I have seen Angola before and after the war. Your average Nigerian is more educated than the other African. By the time a man is really educated he can rationalise better. In Nigeria you have educational processes where you can carry on improving yourself.'

I asked what he knew about traditional African belief.

'We have traditional deities that are well known internationally. Then there are sacred sites or shrines and festivals. There is a grove here. It is a recognised UNESCO site and here they have the festival of Osun Osogbo. Followers of the goddess gather here in hordes and they pray for what they want with the priests and priestesses. The sheer scale of human traffic at this festival is awesome. People come from Brazil, Cuba, the USA and Haiti, and it goes on for a week. On the final day a virgin with a big calabash on her head walks to the river followed by legions of people, and she pours the contents of the calabash into the river, giving it a libation. I was crushed by the people. I could not see the virgin.'

The Yoruba gods and goddesses are many, their stories involved. Did the contractor learn about them when he was a child? He said no. His knowledge came from talking to other Nigerians when he was grown up, and it opened his eyes. He didn't think of it as juju. He didn't like the word. It had a negative connotation.

He said, 'The priests and priestesses hate that word. They call it tradi-religion or tradi-medicine. 'Juju' is debasing. There *is* magic. Look at that girl. The girl I told you about. Look at the things she said – how they went under trees to create havoc and accidents, and how they afflicted people with misery and poverty. She was in a trance, and she was open about it during her cleansing. I believe in this dark side. I am very careful. I don't upset people who threaten me. I don't know what dark abyss they are coming from, and what powers they will use to hurt me.'

I had a romantic idea of the earth religions. I felt they took us back to the beginning, a philosophical Big Bang, and I cherished them for that reason. I thought they had a kind of beauty. But the past here still lived. People like the contractor were closer to it, and his words (with their Shakespearean echo) gave a new idea: the dark abyss of paganism. Others spoke of that as well, in their own way; and it seemed to me that people near the bottom, who responded more instinctively to things, had the greater fear. The fear was real, not affected, and I felt it was this, rather than ideas of beauty and history and culture (as some people said), that was keeping the past and all the old gods close.

A Lagos city councillor said to me, 'Even the pastor of the church will go very quietly, if he can, to the traditional priest and the shrine. Let me tell you: the average African is very afraid of the pagan, and the pagan is there. Muslims and Christians practise forgiveness and cannot harm you. In the pagan religion there is no forgiveness. It is a tit-for-that religion. There are rules you have to follow very strictly, and if you go against them you either die or go mad. They punish swiftly and they stick to it. They adhere to what the priests in the shrines or the gods demand. So you see it has a strong hold.'

3

THERE WAS a king of Lagos. He was called the Oba. There are obas or chiefs all over Nigeria, some hereditary, some appointed (and paid) by the central government. The Oba of Lagos had nothing of the antiquity and mystery of the Kabaka of Uganda; he didn't have subjects, properly speaking; he didn't call up the religious awe. This Oba was a businessman and a policeman. His Oba-ship had been challenged by someone, as I had heard; and the case was still before the courts. In the meantime the Oba ruled and was generally accepted. He had had a long and distinguished career in the police service; he had retired at the very top, as DIG (Deputy Inspector-General).

The Oba knew Edun, and Edun thought I should see him. When I said the meeting was a good idea, Edun right away took out his mobile and telephoned the Oba. That was like Edun. He didn't like to waste time; it was one reason for his business success. I could hear, from what was taking place on the telephone, that the Oba had his doubts, perhaps about writers generally, or perhaps just about me. Edun talked him round: there would be no interview, no direct quotations. So a meeting was fixed, and Edun promised to come with me. I was glad about that; it made the business of the royal audience more manageable.

He was a king of the people here in Lagos, and he lived in a popular part of the town, off a very long street of traders and their small shops. The Nigerians love to trade;

there are traders in the unlikeliest places. The visitor, seeing a crowd in constant movement, can often find himself wondering who the buyers are and who the sellers, and (since the quantities dealt in can be so small) what accidents have led them to choose their respective roles. A buyer, it seems, can easily be a vendor, and a vendor the other thing.

All at once, in the long street of traders, and after a house with a roughly painted notice on its upper storey which said that the house belonged to a royal family (not our Oba), after this in a side road there was a concrete arch of two interlocking V's, one inverted. This arch framed the royal purlieus. On the right-hand side were more small shops, some selling plastic trinkets; in front of them were food vendors with trays. On the left-hand side was the royal street, properly speaking. A big black iron gate barred the way. There was a sentry in a sentry-box. Edun rolled down the glass window and the sentry waved us on. We passed a small concrete house, unremarkable in every way; this was the old palace of the Oba, before Nigerian oil and money. The new palace was just ahead. It was like a middle-class residential house.

The crowd outside seemed ordinary at first, but very soon the eye began to take in more. The people, men and women, were attendants on the Oba. They were bright-eyed and expectant and smiling. Some of them were drummers; others made a lesser kind of noise with bits of old metal. This took me back to Trinidad and the nineteen-forties, when the steel band was being perfected. A sweet metallic noise was called up from the discarded wheels of motor-cars. Men held the old wheels aloft in their left hand, to keep the sound pure, and struck with smaller pieces of metal. But now, outside the palace of the Oba of Lagos, it was women, smiling at the visitors, who were making this metallic noise.

Edun brought out crisp new banknotes from the pocket of his formal Nigerian tunic and gave them to the musicians, stilling them. I hadn't known about this aspect of the ritual, and hadn't prepared for it. I had no banknotes or other money on me.

We went up the steps of the new palace to a marble hall. On the left was a small reception room with a white throne between two red chairs. This room was empty. The main audience hall was ahead of us. We were ushered into it by a tall man in a cream-coloured silk gown. Yorubas are big men. The audience hall was empty. It was big, about forty feet long, with sofas pushed against the side walls, and with two blue-and-cream Chinese rugs placed end to end down the middle of the room. Through a half-open door at the far end, beyond the throne and the formal chairs, you could see a dining room.

The Oba's chair was high and with a royal canopy. On either side of it was a lesser chair, equally well upholstered. We sat on a sofa on the right. The chiefs who had been waiting outside began to drift in for the audience. They sat on sofas facing us on the other side of the room. So, even before he appeared, the Oba had been given this aura of majesty. It was hard not to yield to it. And when at length he did appear, coming in from the dining room at the back, I instinctively got up, with everybody else.

He was wearing a light-blue long tunic. He had big red coral beads around his neck and wrists. Again, he was very tall; this added to his impressiveness. He didn't look at all absurd sitting beneath the canopy of his throne.

He sat down. In the silence that followed, Edun, my sponsor, stood up beside his sofa and – to my amazement – threw himself flat down on the Chinese rug and made his African obeisance.

Three of the chiefs in silk gowns then half-fell on the floor and made their own obeisance, resting on elbows and knees, a little like sprinters in their starting blocks. In that posture of respect they clicked their fingers rhythmically, slapped their palms and chanted. The Oba took it all in graciously.

I found it extraordinary. The display was very much like the ritual of respect Speke had witnessed in 1861 in Mutesa's Ugandan court (still an affair of grand huts and elephant-grass enclosures); and Uganda was very far away from Nigeria. Speke described the ritual as the 'nyanzig'; he thought that was what the Kabaka's subjects were saying when they were flat on the ground. Thirteen or fourteen years later Stanley said that Speke had been wrong. The people greeting the Kabaka in this way were only expressing their thanks to him.

When the other chiefs had done their obeisance to the Oba, Edun stood up again and addressed the Oba in

English. He told him who we were and what we were trying to do. The Oba made a gesture of welcome with his left hand and pointed to the chair at his left. I went and sat on that chair.

A woman appeared at the back of the audience room. She knelt on her haunches and smiled at the Oba. He gestured to her – it was like a little private drama – to come up to where he was, and she came and sat on the chair on his right.

I spoke a few words about my interest in old cultures and religions of the earth. The Oba, when he replied, felt around for a suitable subject. He settled on the history of Lagos and his position as Oba. He said that as Oba he was trustee of the local people, trustee for the dead, the living, and those to come. It was moving. I had heard great landowners in another country talk in this way, and I had felt it was something they had been trained in. They had a particular way of referring to what they owned. They never said they owned it. They said, 'When I inherited this' or, 'When this came to me'; as though with great wealth had come philosophy and the idea of trusteeship, a way for the transient human being of dealing with transient wealth. I felt there was something of this in what the Oba was saying. It might have been his way of putting the dispute about his Oba-ship to one side. And, indeed, in this audience room, with the majesty of the Oba, his undoubted style, the dispute seemed not to matter.

He spoke of the history of Lagos. It had been Portuguese before it was British. (Portugal: how often it comes up in these far-away places! To see some of the outposts of the Portuguese empire in Africa and Asia, to feel the heat of the desolate shore and the unfriendliness of the grey ocean, to get some idea of the awful distances, eating up many months of a human life, already austere, is to admire anew the spirit of the people, who were just a million strong at the time of their greatness.) The Oba spoke about an early nineteenth-century skirmish – this was hard for me to follow – that was important in the history of Lagos. He said there were guns from that war in front of the old palace, which we had passed on the way. He hoped we would want to go and see them.

Edun stood up and with a few words brought our audience to an end. I stood up and bowed to the Oba, and as I moved through the long audience hall, making for the door, I bowed to each chief and received a bow from each of them. There was some private business or courtesy Edun had to deal with. He stayed behind. I went out alone down the palace front steps. I saw again the guinea fowls and the turkeys, regal creatures, but standing here in their own mess. The musicians were still hanging around, with drum and metal. They were friendly. They might have been less friendly if Edun hadn't given out his banknotes.

Some of the chiefs came out and led me to the earlier palace. It was a smaller affair, more a pavilion than a palace, built around an open courtyard, with wire netting spread below the openness of the roof. Here in the old days the Oba and the chiefs would have sat on mats and talked to one another across the open courtyard. This small room and its simple appointments gave a scale to the new palace; it showed how far Nigeria had travelled, and how much more money there now was.

In front of the small palace were the three small, even stubby, Portuguese guns the Oba had talked about. They were stamped 1813. They might have been mortars, designed to spit out hot shot over a short distance. They looked as though they would have been at least as dangerous to the users as to the people shot against.

It was strange to think that this simple technology might at one time have helped to create a colonial empire. It was a little bit like wealth in a time of inflation. To have money first was to be rich; it didn't matter what money came to other people afterwards.

I saw now that on the gable of the new palace was a mosaic, elegantly done, of a Mumbo Jumbo scene. In this version Mumbo Jumbo wasn't alone; he was chasing women. The scene was repeated in a large free-standing sculpture at one end of the compound. It was an attractive, humorous piece. The frightened woman, bursting away from Mumbo Jumbo, her mouth open and her arms raised in alarm, was very thin and painted black and white: very effective.

There was a certain amount of street rubbish at the foot of this sculpture. This didn't imply rejection or neglect; it was just the African way, as I had grown to recognise.

One of the chiefs who had been showing me around had his own interpretation of the sculpture. It was of funeral figures, he said. These figures were celebrated at a time of death. In this interpretation, then, Mumbo Jumbo with his high hat and veil and coat was nothing less than death. It was strange, if this interpretation was right, to find the figures lovingly rendered in elegant mosaic on the Oba's palace.

Edun came out at last and we went back the way we had come. We passed again the wide central reservation on the street where the traders had placed many small bowls and fragments of pottery with offerings. The traders did this to get good luck. These offerings were made every day, and they were not as public as they appeared: most people knew that it was dangerous to be the first to look on these things, which had been prepared by soothsayers and were intended for higher spirits.

4

ON THE BEACH (or marina, as some said) of Victoria Island, one of the islands of Lagos, far inland from the coast – the Portuguese chose amazingly well – there appeared sometimes on Thursday, and more often on Friday and the weekend, fine chestnut horses. One or two were tethered in patches of fresh grass beside the road, near building sites, but most stood saddled and bridled and still in the great heat with their keepers and waited for custom: the children of the Lagos well-to-do whose parents might want them to learn to ride. The keepers then sat far back, and the children sat between their arms.

These horses were rejects from the local polo club. At first, I was told (and had no means of checking), the rejected horses were simply turned loose and left to forage for themselves; they became scavengers. The wife of a European diplomat, too distressed by the sight, began to shoot the animals. My friend from the polo-playing north (he had got the hotel to give me a proper room on the night of my arrival) thought it was the most humane way of dealing with the rejected horses; it saved them from degradation and suffering. But the diplomat's wife was no longer in Nigeria, and I heard from someone else that the marina horses now had proper owners and were being worked for money. Some of them still looked good, still had the gift of clean movement, but they were all on the way down.

(Two or three years before, I had heard that this kind of cruelty had begun to be practised in Trinidad, where abandoned horses had been seen on a popular beach, looking for food. I don't think this had happened when I was there as a child. It was shocking to me that such a big animal, which needed constant attention, could be subject to such bad treatment. The unpleasant fact stayed with me, and soon I saw that in most countries horses had always been ungratefully treated: tormented during their life, and killed and cut up into meat after their racing days were over. Cruelty, it seemed, was inseparable from animal racing. Poor greyhounds were constantly run to the limit of their strength until, at three, they were killed or turned loose.)

Whenever in Lagos I saw the horses on the beach I consoled myself with the idea that in the feudal north of the country there was a horse culture and that horses might be better looked after there.

My friend from the north said, 'They might have a horse culture. But Nigerians are not animal-lovers.'

A moment's thought told me that he knew what he was talking about. There were no common dogs and cats about. Christian prejudice and African ideas about spirits and familiars combined to make life hard for cats especially, and even Muslims were affected, though in other Muslim countries people liked to tell a story about the Prophet: he was unwilling to disturb a cat that had fallen asleep on his gown.

Adesina, a self-made man, now an important business executive, was the only Nigerian I met who was an animal-lover. He was a man of sixty. His mother had been fierce with him as a child, beating him often. But it was from her that he had got his love of animals. There were always cats and other animals in his family house; he woke up to them every day; and it was his mother's rule that no animal or bird that had been reared in the house was to be killed. He was now close to retirement, and it was his wish when he retired to do something for animals in Nigeria.

All the children before Adesina had died in infancy. When Adesina was born his parents thought he was the same child, always coming back to torment them, and so they made small cuts on his face, to frighten him into staying. The cuts were still there; Adesina liked to show them; but they were not as prominent as Adesina thought they were.

Adesina's father was born in 1904. To understand a little of his history was to understand the important history of conversion (to Islam or Christianity) in Nigeria. He did not go to school. He converted first to Catholicism, but he was unhappy with it. He didn't understand the church service, which was in Latin. Later he met Arabs who had come to northern Nigeria with the trans-Sahara trade. These Arabs were teachers and missionaries. They translated the Koran into Yoruba, and they also preached in Yoruba. This was much easier for Adesina's father and he converted to Islam. He always wished after that to be a good Muslim; he didn't think Adesina was a good Muslim, and so he didn't eat in Adesina's house. But he was open-minded. He let people in the family read the Bible and he liked to debate with friends who were Jehovah's witnesses.

It seems from this that religion had become a kind of intellectual activity, perhaps the only one, in the newly educated house. Adesina's father's younger brother stayed a Christian, while the third brother remained firm in the traditional African religion. Adesina, growing up, had the full range of available Nigerian belief to choose from. He was technically a Muslim, following his father, but he liked the uncle who practised the traditional religion because this uncle was a great one for sacrifices and in that house Adesina was always given meat from the sacrifices to eat. His parents disapproved and beat him, but still he went to the unconverted uncle's house. He would go and watch the sacrifices, eat his meat, and come home to a beating.

It was a hard childhood. He had to get up at a half-past five, wash and go to the mosque. Then he went to school; when he came back in the afternoon he had to go to the market to sell the *foo-foo* his mother had made. *Foo-foo* was a local food made in the main from pounded yam; people thought it was easy to make, but it wasn't. His mother made it well, in her own way, and Adesina had no trouble selling what she had made; but he had to stay in the market all afternoon. He was back home in the early evening, and by eight-thirty they were all in bed.

When Adesina was ten – this would have been in 1958 – his father lost all his property. The reasons were political and very Nigerian: the family tribe was accused of using charms to kill a powerful man from another tribe. Adesina's father called the young boy and made him sit down and talked to him like an adult. It was the Yoruba tradition. The family houses are all built around the main house, and whenever there is something to discuss the extended family gather in the compound and talk. Everybody, from the youngest to the oldest, has a say. Adesina's father told him that they were now poor, but there was hope for the family if Adesina worked hard enough and said his prayers. Adesina understood; because of these family discussions he knew the history of his family.

During the week he worked on the family farm. At weekends he went to construction sites and worked as a labourer, carrying bricks, mixing cement. He learned a few things; he got to know, for instance, that a bricklayer with two helpers could set one hundred bricks or blocks a day. He saved the labouring money he got; he liked going to Christmas and New Year parties and he needed to buy clothes for himself. His parents didn't like that. When he came home from the New Year party he was beaten. But when he was fourteen he was able to give his mother five pounds. She needed the money for an operation; and after this they got on much better.

He didn't go to a secondary school. He took private lessons. He bought books and read them at night by the light of a lantern. He was helped by his old teachers. They taught him English and Calculations (Arithmetic) and he studied history to improve his English. He was attracted to accountancy, and especially to the sound of the IAA, the International Accountants Association. He did three parts of the accountancy course they offered, but his English boss at the firm where he was working said the course was not recognised in all countries. Adesina gave it up and began to study to be a chartered accountant. He was encouraged by his boss, who told him that if he studied diligently for three or four hours every day he could achieve whatever he wanted.

He was thirty-five when he became an accountant. For all the years of his study he worked at other jobs. Some were menial; he never minded. His father had told him that he was now the head of the family and had responsibilities;

he took that seriously. He got a job in the Swiss firm of Nestlé by chance. He used to go every Thursday to the race course to gamble. One Thursday, at the race course, he met a cousin who was going for an interview with Nestlé. He went with his cousin for the interview, and when he got there it occurred to him to tell the Swiss man in charge that he had sent in his own application form. There was an argument. Through the intervention of a Yoruba officer Adesina was given an interview and was selected. He impressed people with his talent for calculation. He didn't use conversion tables; he arrived at answers quickly; and he made no mistakes.

He began to rise in the firm, doing all sorts of clerical jobs. His ambition at that stage was to be a shipping clerk. He thought that in that job he would become familiar with the port and would get to know sailors, and this would help him to be a stowaway. He thought that everything would become possible for him if he could stow away to a friendly country. But he didn't become a shipping clerk. He stayed in the office as an accounts budget clerk. He was trained by an Englishman and then by a Nigerian, one of the first professional accountants in the country. What had been a disappointment (for the would-be stowaway) had in fact set him on the business path which took him to where he was now.

Twenty-five years of work and ambition (and what was implied: the overcoming of many disappointments) had made him a modern man, but he would have been supported in those years by old ideas of family and tribe, and old habits of belief that reached back beyond the conversion of his parents and his uncle.

Adesina said, 'Look, all rich people and warriors in our tribe consulted their soothsayers before they went anywhere or did any transaction. If they had any problem they went to their soothsayer. My grandfather had his own soothsayer or *babalawo*. They were part of the extended family, and that was their profession. Even the Yoruba obas have their own soothsayers. They are the highest level of soothsayers and are called "Arabas" in Yoruba-land. Someone might say, "I feel there is going to be this problem in the town. What shall I do to avoid it?" The soothsayer will say they will have to consult the Ife. Then they may do rituals to ease it or make it go away. The Ife will tell us. There are two types of Ife. One is the chain type, and the other is the sixteen kernels. The soothsayer will throw the chain or kernels in a certain way and read the message of the oracle or Ife.'

Adesina knew a soothsayer who was very good, but was now dead. He used to work in the multinational firm of Lever's. After he retired from Lever's he had a traditional African church in his house. He ran it like a church and had services.

Adesina said, 'He was educated and knew the Koran and the Bible. This man told me there were three astral high languages – Hebrew, Arabic, and Yoruba. If you go deep in the Koran you will find that Ife originated in Mecca. The Yorubas are Arabs from the Yahuba tribe, according to Koranic records, and those sixteen kernels were given to a man called Setiyu. It is in the Koran. Because he was an invalid and had to be carried from place to place he was given the Ife. He was killed during the Hijra when the Prophet had to flee. He was the first Ife.'

I knew that Adesina was complicated. I understood now that he was more complicated than I thought.

When I had first met him, at a restaurant dinner with someone else, he was wearing a suit and a tie, essential businessman's clothes in Nigeria, but on him like protective gear. He was not a handsome man; his face, with the now shallow scars on his cheeks, was small and tight. He didn't talk much at first; he might have been self-conscious about his appearance. It was only when he began talking of his mother's animals that he engaged me.

Later, when he opened up and I got to know his story, I saw – or began dimly to see – how far he had travelled. He had started with nothing, in a far-removed world. He was now the managing director of a great corporation; he worked for one of the richest men in the country. One day, driving in the centre of the city, he showed me the house of this rich man: it was of glass and marble, like a bank.

Adesina's business language was half modern. His speciality was 'numbers and calculations', logistics and stratagems. He had pride in what he did, and I was half expecting him to say at some stage that the success that had come to him was a tribute to the country and its movement forward. But he said nothing like that. He was, in fact, gloomy in every way about Nigeria; and he didn't talk of himself as part of the elite. He talked more of the poor, drinking 'erosion water' in some districts and sleeping nine to a room. Perhaps he had waited too long, and the wait had been too punishing, more full of indignity than he knew at the time. Perhaps it was only the encouragement of the Ife, the pull towards the past, that had kept him going in the dark days.

He felt that Nigeria was now paying the price for its colonial history, which had begun not long before his father was born. 'The French wanted to break this region into smaller divisions for their own reasons. The British dealt with us in a regional way. There was no Nigerian in the centre. So when we came into the centre we had no idea how to run it. Missionaries were never allowed to go to the north. So the north is very Muslim and we were all ruled by tribalism. Every political party that came up was really a regional party. Then a parliamentary British form of democracy added to the confusion at independence. So we had the Biafran war and then the coups. All our presidents and prime ministers came up by accident. No one was actually trained or prepared.'

He didn't believe in the Nigerian boom.

'There is no boom. It is only a small stock-market boom where the elite thrived, and for a short time too. I know because I made money in it too. Booms are judged by the GNP and by the income of the lowest-grade worker – what will his income buy in the open market? Most Nigerians like to be self-employed, but on the farms it is subsistence-level agriculture. Eighty per cent of our land is not cultivated. The farming people will have a few goats and a few plots of yams. It is not mechanised farming, and they have no meat except the rabbits they trap. I was recently in a state where they are good farmers. But the oranges they grow rot, and the tomatoes. You need infrastructure to create a processing industry, but that kind of support is not there. What are Nigerians abroad coming back to invest in?'

As for politicians, there was no point in looking to them to do anything. They were in politics for the money. Even the old religion got dragged in and chewed up by their politics. Shango was the god of thunder; to swear by Shango was the most terrible kind of vow; because if you broke your vow Shango was certain to take his revenge. And that was why at election time the politicians didn't simply want you to promise to vote for them. They wanted you to swear by one or other of the old gods, who were all as implacable as Shango.

5

FROM THE WAY Adesina talked, I imagined his favourite soothsayer or *babalawo* had been the man who worked at the international firm of Lever's and after his retirement ran a traditional African church (with services) in his house. It was said that this man could even foretell the coming of visitors. Adesina, I suppose, had regularly consulted this wise man and since the man's death would have been a little bit at sea. But he was on the look-out for wise men. There was one he wanted me to meet; this could be combined with a deeper look at Nigeria.

I had already had something of a deeper look; it had happened by accident. On a day of rain, a couple of days after I had arrived, when I had the sketchiest idea of the layout of the city, I had had a sight of the slums of Lagos. I wasn't looking for the slums; I was paying a business call. The driver was late; the shortcut he was taking led us to streets so flooded that cars had had to stop.

The road where we were was hardly a road. The drains were over-full; the flood had scoured the gutters into an unspeakable dark mess, added plastic bottles and other vegetable rubbish, and this all bounced and raged down in one direction on this side and in another direction on the other side. In this water rage every obstruction showed: miniature rapids, water always finding a way. Stall-holders, mainly food-sellers, were pulling back from the edge, and pulling back again. In front of a closed stall a jaunty little black-and-white sign in small italics, professionally done, said *Pepper soup is now ready*; though the idea of food didn't go too well with the garbage rocking past.

Apartment buildings, at a lower level than the flood, looked drenched and rotting; it was easy to imagine them collapsing; and at the same time they looked smoky, as though from fires within. So they looked at once cold and warm. It would have been dreadful to live there, to wake up there, to go to sleep there. Around these blocks were lower, flatter living areas, seemingly covered from end to end with bumpy old corrugated iron, with no apparent room below for lanes and alleys.

In the distance, hugging the shore of the creek, was the great fishermen's settlement, a degraded Venice, shacks on stilts, just above the dark water which fed the shacks and which they in turn soiled.

I talked later about what I had seen to some local councillors I met. I said I thought the area couldn't be improved; it had grown too big; it could only be rebuilt. The councillors were politicians, hardened people, used to going among the poor of Lagos, but they felt that nothing could be done in that area around the creek. The people in the fishermen's settlement and in the neighbouring slums were migrants, constantly on the move, and as constantly replaced by new arrivals. These people didn't like sending their children to school; they preferred sending them out to the roads to hawk and trade, to add to the family income. They were not settled people, a fixed community. You couldn't build them new houses with proper sanitation. You couldn't talk to them about poverty alleviation. You couldn't do anything for them; and they bred and bred.

One councillor said, 'Islam permits four wives and Catholics don't practise birth-control and you know Nigerians are very religious people.'

Another councillor said, 'With the population explosion comes social apathy. They fill the open drains with rubbish. During the rains this rubbish floats everywhere. They encroach on the drains and put up their shacks over the drains. We were equipped for two thousand people and we cater for twenty thousand. So something gives.'

This was what I had in my head. I thought that Adesina had more to show me. But in spite of the passion with which he had spoken at our earlier meeting, he didn't seem particularly interested now in that side of things, and my feeling was that his thoughts that morning were more of the *babalawo* we were going to see.

Adesina's new *babalawo* (if indeed he was that) lived on the mainland. A ten-kilometre bridge and highway connected Victoria Island to the mainland, and it seemed on this wet Saturday morning that a fair sample of the life of the island and the mainland was laid out as if for inspection on this highway.

There were the usual crowds at bus stops or taxi stops, people becalmed and resigned in the rain. Almost no traffic on one side of the road, and a lot of traffic on our side. Boys or young men, hawkers, swarmed down the middle of the road, and sprang into action when the traffic came to a halt. They sold quite a range of goods. They sold colour pictures. They dangled various foods in clear plastic bags (boiled guinea-fowl eggs, potatoes of a curious squashed shape); they dangled miniature open accordions of telephone cards; fake designer dark glasses, fake designer watches, wallets, even clothing. It was an industry; behind these boys there would have been active suppliers, getting the goods out every evening and every morning.

The houses near the road were solid, of concrete and

with glass windows; the slums were behind them. Between the houses were places of education, especially for computer training. The Ilupeju industrial area – food processing, textile manufacturing – was gated. Just beyond this area was a big bus and wagon station, with much rubbish on the wet ground.

This was like the jumbled semi-cityscapes of Lagos that I had already got to know. They were like places that seemed waiting to be knocked down or completed, but they always spoke of energy. They did not especially depress me. I saw the jumble as superficial, and felt that with the resources of Nigeria, and when the people were ready, the jumble could one day be undone.

Was it only this that Adesina wished to show me? He was some years younger than I was, and it was possible that I had travelled more than he had, and seen more hopeless places – in Jamaica, Bombay, Calcutta, and many rural localities in India.

We pass a church, 'Mountain of Fire'. Always churches with grand names on the Nigerian highways. These names trying not to repeat one another. (Other names on this run: The Redeemed Church of God, Christ Apostle Church.) Then the bleached concrete quarters of the Nigerian Air Force, tarnished as if by smoke A while later we have the modern splendours of the domestic airport, which go some way to balancing the air picture. A big complex for the Concord Press ('Truth is constant') is deserted; the business is in liquidation. Settlement after settlement of unpaved roads, wet and red and gritty, full of children standing about: children of the Nigerian boom preserved by a new kind of health care, to add very soon to the slums of the towns. In one settlement a number of the newish houses are roughly daubed with signs saying that they have been repossessed: boom turning to bust at this level, with the roughly daubed signs about repossession like an additional insult.

The town we get to is big and rich, in spite of the garbage. You can tell from the number of banks: Zenith Bank, Skye Bank, Ocean Bank. We are now near the *babalawo*'s territory. We need a guide, and we twist and turn back onto a parallel road to pick up Adesina's brother. He is friendly, in a flowered shirt, and seems much simpler than Adesina. He would have been waiting for some time, but he doesn't seem to mind. He sits next to the driver and guides us to a small and bumpy side road with open gutters. Many herbalists here in small wooden shops, offering to cure syphilis, gonorrhoea and breast cancer. Clearly this shop has been set up here to benefit from the nearness of the true medicine man, our *babalawo*, and to give him a little competition. So we are on the right track. Our quarry can't be far away. But we can't find him. We go up and down some muddy lanes, asking. Still nothing.

At this stage Adesina's brother wanted us to stop and take on another guide. It turned out now that Adesina's brother didn't really know, hadn't known, and he had commissioned a proper guide. This new guide was waiting for us in another place. He too would have been waiting for some time; and he too didn't mind. But it turned out again — after he had taken us up and down a few small streets, indistinguishable one from the other, asking people all the time — that the new guide was himself at sea, and wasn't too sure where the *babalawo* lived. It was the new man's idea then that, just to make sure, we should ask one of the commercial motorcyclists, the *okadas*, who for a fee gave pillion rides to a particular destination, to go ahead of us and guide us. And the *okada* man knew. His fee was modest, one hundred naira, about eighty cents.

I suppose we had been using the wrong word. In Lagos I had been told that if for some reason I needed a witchdoctor in a village I was never to ask for the witchdoctor or the juju man. It was better to ask for the medicine man. Juju was too demeaning a word; people resisted it.

And the *okada* man led us immediately to the side street where the unprepossessing house of the *babalawo*, the soothsayer or magician, was. It was a low house of unpainted concrete, flat to the ground, below a corrugated-iron roof, and with an entrance in the middle.

From the car this middle entrance gaped black, and when we picked our way to it over the wet road and yard we saw that the corridor in front of us was dark, even at this bright time of day. On the threshold there were slippers, doubtless of people inside. Adesina and his brother and the new guide were ready for this; they were wearing slippers. But I hesitated. In 1962 I had got ringworm in Delhi after padding about barefoot, a little too freely, in temples and gurdwaras. Adesina noticed my hesitation and said I wasn't to bother. This was African or Nigerian courtesy: of course it mattered, tramping about a house with muddy shoes.

The floor of the central corridor was of concrete, and plastered grey and smooth. It was broken in patches. The woman of the house, appearing in the corridor, greeted us civilly; and from that small corridor space we were led to a smaller, darker space, and then another dark little corridor, really a space-divider, with a view on one side of a bedroom with an unmade grey bed. On the other side was the sanctum of the soothsayer, the herbalist, the magician, the *babalawo*.

The sanctum was really very small. Our little party – five of us – covered the floor. There was a bench and a stool, but our two guides had to remain standing. I sat on one end of the bench.

The *babalawo* sat on a low stool. He was very thin, in a white gown that now came out grey from the wash in local water; and he wore a white cotton cap embroidered with a simple wavy pattern in blue and yellow.

The little sanctum was full of unassorted things. A rusted electric fan on the floor, near the *babalawo*'s feet, looked abandoned. Near the ceiling was another fan in better condition. It was fixed into the wall and set horizontally. It wasn't working now, but soon it was going to be put on for us. An unlikely looking plug was going to be fitted into an unlikely looking socket, and the fan was going to play over us, a nice breath of air in the muggy room. They had modern conveniences here! A mysterious object took up much room: it was part of an electric work table, a slice of a table, in new satinwood, and with an electric motor in a grey casing. This was clearly a found object of some importance, and the *babalawo* didn't intend to let it go; he sat next to it.

Directly, with no beating about the bush, he asked our business.

I didn't know what to say. I couldn't say I had come only to have a look.

Adesina, though, knew how to deal with diviners. He said he first wanted to know whether our visit was going to do him, the *babalawo*, any good.

It was the kind of question the *babalawo* liked. He replied right away that we were going to be of immense value to him. I felt there was an element of ritual in the question and the answer, and both parties were satisfied.

On the little table in front of the *babalawo* were some of his magical things. A school exercise book resting on its front cover was sensationally dirty. It was furred with dirt, as though handled and handled by unwashed thumbs and fingers, and the mathematical tables on the back cover of the exercise book had suffered: the dirt and the fur had lifted some of the printed numerals off the paper. Not far away was a matchbox, in the same condition as the exercise book; a give-away bottle-opener, recognisable only because I had seen the little tool many times before; and a little green bottle loosely stopped with things I didn't wish to look at too closely.

Adesina and the *babalawo* were now settling the fee for

the consultation. The *babalawo* wanted a lot: five hundred pounds, a thousand dollars. Adesina, used to this kind of outrage, remained calm, and began to beat him down. He settled in the end for something much smaller.

I now had to ask my question.

I had it ready. I asked, 'Will my daughter get married?'

The *babalawo* was thrown by the question. He said, 'I thought only black people had such problems.'

But he was willing to give an opinion. He lifted the dirty exercise book and showed what it covered. Sixteen cowry shells (I assumed that was the number: Adesina had spoken of sixteen kernels as one way of divination); two tiny gourds tied together with a piece of string, the gourds not much bigger than marbles; and a small metal figure, like the top of an apostle spoon. The cowry shells had been much handled. I had known cowry shells to be grey, brown in the interstices in the middle, and dirty-looking; but these shells, from the handling they had received, were very smooth and wonderfully white.

He passed the shells to me, saying, 'Blow on them, give your name, and throw them on the table.'

I did as he asked. He took up the tiny gourds and muttered some incantation. After a while the gourds began to swing from side to side. That meant no. If the gourds had swung out and then back, it would have meant yes.

The *babalawo* said, 'The girl is not going to get married. You have many enemies. To break their spells we will have to do many rituals. They will cost money, but the girl will get married.'

Everyone in the room was quite excited. Adesina, his brother, the guide: the *babalawo* had them all in the palm of his hand.

I said, 'But what he's told me is good. I don't want the girl to get married.'

The *babalawo* looked appalled. He must have felt I was trifling with him. I believe that only the reverence of Adesina and the others saved the day.

I pointed to the apostle-spoon figure and said, 'What's this?'

He held the little figure and said, 'He travels at night. He goes to the shrines where I send him and he brings back news.'

And Adesina's brother and the guide, correct in their Nigerian floral clothes, added a little to my credit by looking horribly awed.

Adesina said, 'He wants to know about creation and the gods.'

Once again Adesina's obvious fervour helped to calm the *babalawo*. One of the seer's friends, like a man who knew his way about the place, came and plugged in the fan on the wall. To my surprise it began to work, whirring horizontally above us.

The *babalawo* began to talk about the gods. He took his time. He acted out the dramas he was describing, and he spent so long over the first bit of creation that I feared we would be in that airless little cell all afternoon. Already something in the air was pricking my nostrils, a sign of trouble to come. Casually the *babalawo* poured some stuff from a bottle against the wall next to him, adding to the general mess of the place; but in fact, as he soon said, he was 'feeding' one of the oracles which were against the wall. He said one of those oracles was asleep and had been fed. To take the name of another god at this stage he would first have to make a libation to the unfed oracle. He would need spirit for this libation, and he meant spirit in the normal way: hard liquor.

Adesina sent the guide out, to get the spirit. And the *babalawo* went on with his stories about gods, stopping every few words to allow Adesina to translate and amplify.

My heart sank more and more. The *babalawo*'s cell became like the ship's cabin in *Room Service* with the Marx Brothers, endlessly receiving new people. At one point a young man in a polo shirt came into the cell. He wanted to see the *babalawo* privately. The *babalawo*, like a man with no time for village idlers, shooed him away roughly. The young man in the polo shirt withdrew with bad grace, and the *babalawo*, using his bony fingers a lot, went on with his weighty stories about the gods, more important to him at that stage than any petty business the young man in the polo shirt might have brought.

The *babalawo* broke off and said, 'I believe I told you I cannot mention this god unless we have poured a libation to him.' He pointed once more to the dingy splash on the wall.

At this opportune moment the guide returned with a square bottle of Nigerian gin. The *babalawo* had already had a tot from his own bottle, and now they all drank to the god.

The *babalawo*'s mobile rang. The *babalawo* put it on speaker mode. The young man who had just been with us was heard remonstrating with the *babalawo*. 'The people you have with you are going to make a lot of money from what you tell them. Don't tell them everything.'

The *babalawo* was perfectly calm. The gin had had a soothing effect on everybody. The *babalawo* offered to show us the oracles in his yard. The very small space in his cell gave way to something even smaller as we followed him outside. We followed him to a passage barely wide enough for two people. We were now near the boundary wall: the small house was on a very small plot. And in a corner, looking like something lavatorial and disagreeable, were the three shrines with the oracles the *babalawo* had made with his own hands. For the believer it would have been a high moment, being permitted to see these sacred things; but for me the moment came with a noticeable tickle in my nostrils: a touch of asthma on the way.

I thought we should be looking for a way out. That soon came, because Adesina, though he might have wanted a serious personal reading from the *babalawo*, now understood that because of my frivolity there was going to be no further seriousness; the moment had passed.

There was no rebuke from him; and soon back to the gritty red lane we went, and into the car. A thin dog with swollen dugs came out of the *babalawo*'s yard; some children had been tormenting it. Adesina shouted at them. He had the right words and the right tone. The children held off at once. The dog came up to the street and trotted about its business undaunted, its tail up, its dignity intact.

And then once again we went past the little shops and dwellings of the settlement, the advertisements for extraordinary medical cures, the other advertisements for musical shows, and always the children; and then the houses with the big, humiliating, daubed sign on the walls: *This house has been repossessed.*

In Lagos the next day I told a man at the hotel where I had been and what I had done. He was genuinely frightened for me. He said, 'They are bad people. Even if you want nothing from them they will damage you. You go with one problem and you come back with ten.'

And, indeed, the tickle in my nose had by this time developed into something that called for antibiotics, threatening me with the loss of precious days.

6

THE ONI OF IFE: it was a memorable title. Once you heard it, it could play in your head as sound alone (especially if you didn't know what it meant), and with its easily interchangeable vowels could take fantastic shapes. Even Dickens, master of made-up names, had sought to parody it somewhere in his writings (perhaps in his journalism, but I was no longer sure). I discovered now that the

Oni was the religious head of the Yorubas of Nigeria, and Ife an actual place somewhere in the interior and within reach: half a day's journey from Lagos.

The necessary arrangements were made, and I went. The Oni wasn't going to be in residence that day, but there would be people to receive me. The Oni was in England. Like many Nigerians of means, the Oni usually went to England for his summer holidays; he was said to have a house in London. This was unexpected. It modified my idea of the Oni.

We left Lagos by an easy, uncluttered road. On the other side of the same road thousands and thousands of cars were taking their time to get to the capital: the Nigerian weekday paralysis. In the late afternoon and evening matters were reversed: it was easy to get to the capital, not so easy to get out of it. So we, morning travellers, heading out, were fortunate. Outside the city were business sites, luxuriating in space, and long walls that spoke of big churches to come. At last, then, we were in open country. The land was green: not the dark green of primeval forest, but the fresh green of land that had grown things many times over and was still fertile, requiring only rain and sun to burst into new vegetation. Adesina had said that eighty per cent of Nigeria was uncultivated, but I wasn't seeing that. I was under the spell of the empty green landscape, which I hadn't seen before, not in Trinidad, not in India: wide and green and empty.

The road to Ife was part of a projected trans-African highway. Near Lagos it had two wide lanes; and just as, in

India, it lightened a journey to study the wrecks of over-loaded small trucks on either side of the road, some on their backs, some on their sides, some wheel-less, front axle broken, rear axle broken; so here, in Nigeria, it drama-tised the long highway and the unchanging green through which the highway ran, to look for the big articulated lorries that had slipped or skidded or been driven off the asphalt and had been abandoned, left to rust and rot, since that was the cheaper and easier thing to do.

Ibadan was a great city on the way. It had a university, founded in colonial times, and branches of many British educational publishers. Yet it was a surprise when it came, because nothing in the land before the city had suggested there was a big city to come. It was simply there, at the end of the green, just as in Argentina Buenos Aires was at the end of the Pampa. Ibadan, a city of low houses on rolling hills, spread far in the distance, up to the horizon. It showed no city amenities, no public gardens or squares.

There was some such mystery about Ife, too. It too simply appeared, and was raucous. We followed road signs and went to the Oni's royal compound. We were some minutes before the appointed time, and there was at first no one to greet us or guide us. It was a big compound and seemed to have grown organically. It was a series of small buildings, government-style, undistinguished, some one storey, some two. There was a crowd outside one build-ing in a corner, with people crowding the steps, and they appeared to be following a debate that was going on inside. I was told it was a divorce case. I thought that if all the buildings in the compound were in the traditional African style, with the fine grass roofs of Kampala, say, the compound might have been as impressive as Grant's drawing of Kampala's royal hill in 1861–2.

My visit had been arranged by an educational publishing firm – it was always necessary here to be sponsored – and some people from the firm, together with a tall man in Nigerian costume, came to greet us. The tall man was from the tourist board, very important here; he gave our group some kind of official standing. The tall man and the publishing-house group led us – with our driver: Nigerian courtesy – to a big air-conditioned audience hall, like a theatre hall, and we sat down on plush seats.

The tall man from the tourist board told us that the Oni was away, but the Oni's deputy and some other chiefs were going to welcome us. He said that we were not to misunderstand the background and nature of the chiefs who were coming. They were highly educated people. And a little while later – though no one had challenged him – he said it again. It was as though, as a man from the tourist board (and perhaps after some misunderstanding with a recent tourist), it was his duty to put the record straight: local chiefs were not mere villagers.

Soon the chiefs began to come in. They arranged themselves in some order of precedence beside the Oni's throne. They were in wonderful embroidered silk gowns, and so much grander in appearance than we were, that I feared that at any moment they might decide to call our bluff and dismiss us.

There were speeches. The tall man told the chiefs that I was from Trinidad. This had an amazing effect on the chief who was the Oni's deputy. He said, in the tall man's translation, 'You who have left your ancestral land have now returned to your father's land. *Wali, wali, wali.* Enter, enter, enter.'

It was moving. My anxiety about my own style seemed base. I returned the deputy's kind and poetical words as best as I could. Patrick Edwards, the Trinidad ambassador in Uganda, who had served some years before in Nigeria, had told me about his ceremony of welcome in Ife. He had cried, and now I understood why.

Our party (now rather large) was taken on a tour of part of the palace. The tall man from the tourist board told me that this ground of Ife, where we where, was the source of civilisation. It was sacred for all Yorubas and the black race generally. He said this more than once, and I felt that this was how in many cultures national traditions would have been inculcated.

At the back of the audience hall there was a gate decorated with cowry shells. This gate opened on to a small garden. The garden was formal and neat, with grey concrete borders and flat hard beds of reddish earth, and quite bare apart from an old and suffering tree.

A sign said, 'The Source of Life.' This referred to a concrete well in the centre. The well held a sacred and undying memory of the wife of the very first Oni of Ife. She was very beautiful and her marriage to the Oni was a success. It would have been a perfect marriage if she could have had a child. It was important for the Oni to have a child. But there was no child. So the good woman sacrificed herself. She had the Oni married to another woman, and she became a water sprite, an eternal protectress of the Oni and his family. This was the origin of the well. It was said to be bottomless. It had a brackish smell, and when I looked down I saw something like a very pale nettle growing in the mouth of the well.

The tradition was that at the time of his enthronement the Oni's feet had first to be washed with water from this well. And because the well looked after him and his children, the Oni had to tell the well when he was leaving Ife.

In a quadrangle at the back people were being fed; this feeding was connected with our visit. Women helpers had done the cooking in big stainless-steel pots and were still there, handling long spoons. Some of the people in our party, overcome by the idea of food, settled down to eat. On the wall, at the back of the tables, were many colour photographs of important people who had come here on other occasions; one photograph was of a previous Archbishop of Canterbury.

We went back with our guides to the air-conditioned audience hall, with all the fine chairs, and went out the way we had come. Outside the main door we saw the bust of a woman, rather squat on her stand, her features not absolutely clear. I had seen her as I was going in, but I had not been told much about her.

I was told now. She was the great Yoruba heroine. The

story about her was something like this. At some time in the remote past the Yoruba were fighting a traditional enemy and were on the verge of defeat. This woman went to the oracle and said, 'Please give me the secret of our enemy's power.' The oracle said, 'No trouble about that. I will give you the secret of your enemy's power. But first you must give me what is most precious to you.' What was most precious to the woman was her only son. She had him sacrificed. The secret of the enemy was then revealed to her, and the enemy was defeated. Up to this day the woman and her son are venerated by the Yoruba. In fact, the son has taken on the lineaments of Christ, because of this story of sacrifice, and in this form has been received into the Yoruba pantheon.

It was a perfect story for a place that was the cradle of civilisation and the black race. If I had been introduced to the story cold, so to speak, just as I had arrived, it wouldn't have meant much. But now, after a meeting with the grave chiefs, and after a sight of the garden that was the source of life, I understood a little more. For myths to take on life, they have to be supported by other myths; and there was enough support of this kind in Ife.

There was more to see. There was another garden some distance away, but still in the town, where the central object was the staff of an ancient Yoruba warrior, who was a giant. The wood of the staff, which was, of course, very big, had turned to stone. The staff stood upright in a garden as formal and clean as the Source of Life garden. The white-robed priest who looked after the staff said he had been trying for some time to get the government to put a canopy over the staff, to protect it from the weather and to prevent it from being worn away.

The story of the staff was like this. At the very beginning of things the giant ruled the Yoruba. He protected them and made them prosperous. In due course the giant was called to the world of spirits. He left behind his staff and a trumpet, and his instructions were that whenever the Yoruba needed him the trumpet was to be sounded. One day an idle young fellow, having no regard for the story, blew on the trumpet. A giant figure began then to stride over the earth, laying people low left and right with his sword. A woman ran out to the giant and said, 'Madman, can't you see what you are doing? These people are your own.' The giant picked up a severed head by the hair and saw that the head did indeed belong to a Yoruba. He was mortified. He laid down his weapons and vowed never to come back to earth. But he wished before he left them for good to give his Yoruba people a final boon. The boon was this: the Yoruba people would always be successful in war. Then he went away.

His weapons stayed where he had thrown them down. Over the years, perhaps millennia, the staff became petrified, and it is now one of the holy relics of Ile-Ife. There was a proper shrine connected with the staff. It was in the tangled green at the back of the garden. But time was pressing; we had made arrangements to see other things in other places, and we told the priest in white that we had to leave his shrine for later.

7

Osun State has the reputation of being very religious, full of shrines and sacred places. The old world was like this in many countries. (Even England, though not thought of now as a religious country, is full of sacred sites at many levels of its history.)

We were going to a sacred grove of great beauty, but we had first to get the permission of the Oba of Osun. The wide highway from Ife to Osun, built for festival crowds – like those from the black diaspora and elsewhere who came for the climax of the river festival, when the virgin walked to the river with a big calabash on her head and poured the sacrificial contents of the calabash into the river – was empty now. We made good time. We were not going to be as late as I feared.

The Oba's palace was in the centre of the town. A number of carefully dressed officials were there to greet us.

(When I considered their clothes, and their happiness in the occasion, I thought how awful it would have been if, as I had half wanted, we had telephoned and cancelled this part of the trip. I had thought of doing so because it was exceedingly hot, the heat of early afternoon, and also because I thought that we were going to do a long drive only to be shown another version of what we had already seen that morning, another piece of Yoruba myth.)

A fine woman in pink came out of the Oba's palace. She was from the Osun tourism department. She said that the Oba had gone to change his clothes, after the earlier receptions, and she led us to a durbar hall, where we were to wait. We waited there for some time.

Two servants came and sat on the low steps in front of the Oba's throne and they held us in their gaze. They were stylishly dressed, in different costumes, and I thought, because of their direct gaze, they were chiefs of some sort, with special duties. I didn't know they were servants.

Someone in our party asked when the Oba was going to come out. We were told what we already knew, that the Oba was changing his clothes. So we waited.

Eventually he appeared, coming out through a door at the back. Two policemen in black uniform came out before him; and some chiefs, coming out through another door, stood on the Oba's left. The Oba was a tall man with a wide, kindly face. He carried a whitish whisk made from a horse's tail. He handled this whisk in an impressive way. He used it to thank, to acknowledge, and to suggest in the most delicate way to a speaker that enough was enough.

The Oba's wife, who had come out with him, and was sitting demurely on his left, was young, with a lively questioning face that made her appear separate from the court formality. She considered us, one by one, and I felt she liked us.

The fine woman in pink, who had greeted us, and was now sitting with us, as though she was part of our group, said in an undertone, speaking of the friendly young woman on the Oba's left, 'She is the real power behind the throne.'

There followed the speeches and the formalities. The

Oba, with his soft voice, cut in with a little piece of business. He asked the people from the tourism department how they were getting on with the pavilion for traditional religion. The men among the officials stood up, made the royal obeisance, doing their half crouch, touching the floor with the tips of their fingers, so that (like the courtiers before the Oba of Lagos, but those courtiers were wearing gowns, and these officials were wearing suits) they looked like sprinters waiting for the starter's pistol. Then they stood up and correctly, holding one hand over the other, they told the Oba that many things had been done and, in fact, they were hoping that one day when he had the time he would come and have a look. He said he would, one of these days.

Then the officials, speaking on our behalf, asked for permission to visit the sacred grove. The Oba gave it graciously, making an encouraging gesture with his white horse-hair whisk. We were dismissed. He went out by the door through which he had entered, and the policemen and the rest of his suite followed. We had a few words then with the Oba's wife. She was as friendly and interested as she appeared.

We left the durbar hall, with the officials from the tourist office. As soon as we went out of the main gate the ragged court musicians started up: drums, metal on metal, and pebbles shaken in calabashes. The man who was our sponsor – he was from the publishing house – made as if to give money to the musicians. But another man rounded on him, saying, 'I've already given them money. Don't give any more to the scoundrels.'

THE SACRED GROVE took my breath away. After the Oni's palace, the garden of the Source of Life, the Yoruba heroine of long ago, the petrified staff of the Yoruba giant, I had expected only more myth-making, something calling once more for a suspension of disbelief.

But the grove was real and it was beautiful: a piece of tropical woodland which had been left untouched for some time, and where no animal or creature was to be killed. That was what we had been told; and that was what we found. At the limit of the grove families of monkeys took their time to cross the public road. Smaller, sad-faced monkeys, tormented elsewhere, looked without fear at our party and the cars that had brought us.

The grove was walled off or fenced with a fascinating wall of masonry or terracotta, the work of an artist whose melting forms recalled the playful designs of the Barcelona architect Gaudí. The textured wall was touched with moss; it was in keeping with the design. Through the wilderness of tree-trunks and hanging lianas inside we had glimpses of the river that ran through the sanctuary. It was a muddy tropical river, and no attempt had been made to beautify or soften the turbid water; the scalloped melting forms on the wall were intended to match the bounce of the fast-moving river, narrow at this point. As in the design of the Kabakas' tombs in Uganda, where the design had been religiously laid down, everything had to be local, had to be of the place as it was.

It was all very moving to me, especially the idea of the grove as an animal sanctuary. It was said to be a hundred and sixty acres in all, a quarter of a square mile. I wished it was ten times the size.

A big gate opened into a short lane – this was for the procession at the time of the river festival. The lane led down, past a number of small home-made shrines at the foot of trees, to what was said to be a pavilion, just where the yellow river curved. It was an open pavilion, thatched, with timber uprights. To one side of the pavilion was the big shrine. The shrine was also thatched, and had mud walls decorated with figures in white, chocolate, rust and black. The priests and the soothsayers lived within those walls. The legend was that the pavilion stood on the site of the palace of the first Oba of Osun. At the time of the river festival, as people said, thousands of people of the black diaspora, came here. There were morality plays in every corner of the wood.

Perhaps it was artificial, as some people said; perhaps it was all made up. The site was too beautiful, the symbolism of the ritual too easy; perhaps it had been all put together by someone whose business it was to stage events. But it was also possible that all rituals began like this, in artifice.

The event had now taken hold; and the people of the diaspora who came for it would understand that though they had taken many of the Yoruba gods across the water, and though the whole apparatus of the supernatural had also travelled with them, reminding men of the precariousness of their hold on life, and though they had taken much of this Yoruba magic to the New World, making that difficult world safe, they could never take the sacred grove with them. That remained in Africa.

ON THE WAY back to Lagos our driver stopped a few times. He was looking for palm wine. The palm wine here, in the country, was the real thing; in Lagos the palm wine was diluted. He eventually got his palm wine, but he didn't offer the rest of us a taste. He was saving it up for the evening. He would call his friends over – they didn't live very far: it was almost the driver's definition of a friend in Lagos: someone who didn't live far away – and they would 'kill' the bottle.

We should have had a clear run to the city. But just inside the city the traffic caught us, or we caught up with it, and it wore us down. It even began to look as if the driver might have to postpone his palm-wine evening.

8

THE NORTH OF Nigeria was Muslim. I had heard from Adesina that in the colonial time missionaries – he meant Christian missionaries – had not been allowed in the north. All the intellectual life of the country had been in the pagan or Christian south; but it was the more populous north that with independence had come by the greater power.

My friend from the north – he had helped with the hotel on the night or morning of my arrival – said one evening at dinner that the south was 'degenerate'. He might have been speaking lightly; or he might only have been making a standard provincial joke; but jokes are always more than jokes, and this one spoke of the cultural fracture between north and south.

It is better to go to the north by air.

Somewhere before Kano, the great city of the north, you start to look down at what might be parkland: isolated big trees, dark green, on pale grassland. It is the kind of soft landscape that is created after forbidding forest has been cut down, all but the isolated big trees, which have been left for shade or beauty.

Outside the small airport building there is an immediate feeling of strangeness. Men in blue or white Muslim gowns, working garb for them, standing in a semi-circle well away from the passengers. Some of them are selling prayer beads and white Muslim prayer caps. You quickly get to the town outside, since there are no immigration or customs formalities for people from Lagos. The town is seen to be a town of dust and dirt. The road is a wavering path between dirt and garbage, which people here seem reluctant to get rid of; and Christian churches. The churches are surprising in this Muslim area, but I am not to get the wrong idea. I am told, 'Only foreigners live here.' And this is the only place where churches are allowed, on the periphery of things.

There were two dogs on a mound of garbage, and the poor creatures were the colour of garbage.

Beyond this is the town proper: many goats eating garbage, plastic and paper. The goat is the perfect animal for this area, living on air until it is slaughtered. And children: innumerable, thin-limbed, in dusty little gowns, the unfailing product of multiple marriages and many concubines. Horses, in this place which is supposed to have a cult of the horse and horsemanship: but the horses thin, like the boys. Garbage here, gathered up in little mounds. Innumerable *okada* motorcyclists, doing their routes, picking up pillion passengers.

Only one active building site, with seven people working on it, one man mixing mortar, which is then passed from man to man, and finally to the mason on the brick wall. In the centre of the town there is a big abandoned multi-storey building: this is a relic of the time when Kano was a boom area, but now, with the absence of power, that boom is far away. The children that are now unceasingly produced by wives and concubines, boom or no boom, have no future, except buying or hiring or leasing motorcycles, to add to the city's *okada* force.

We were told later that one of the great sights of the city, well worth coming for, took place every Friday, the holy day, when after prayers the garbage-strewn streets erupted with hundreds and hundreds of thin little Muslim boys with their begging bowls, waiting patiently for alms from the pious who had said their prayers.

The good Muslims of Kano see their situation as 'dynamic'. For these people, once the state is Muslim, and the culture Islamic, there can never be a crisis; the world is whole. This sets them apart from the rest of Nigeria, which lives in a perpetual state of crisis.

THE HOTEL had an unusual number of black-and-white signs, perhaps done on a computer, asking guests not to take away the hotel fittings.

Some friendly local intellectuals in white gowns came to see me after dinner, and we talked by electric light in the sandy garden, away from the parked cars, between the hotel proper and the hotel's Calypso restaurant. We fought off mosquitoes and sand-flies while we talked.

One man, a former Fulbright scholar, taught literature at the university. A man in a red fez did media, and worked for the government. A third man, modest and attractive, said he was 'a tiny writer' in English.

They were all proud men of the north, and they had done much thinking about their identity in the mish-mash of Nigeria. They didn't appear at first to see the Kano the visitor saw. They saw growth and dynamism. Kano, they said, was an ancient trading centre and it still held its place, although the trans-Sahara trade had gone down.

Later, not understanding that they were saying something different, they said that Kano was conservative, and the challenge to it came now from education. There were two kinds of education. One was Western; the literature-teacher said he was part of that. And there was the traditional Koranic system. This made people literate in Arabic, and sent them out into the 'informal' network. That was a formal academic way of saying that the Koranic system sent them out to shine shoes, to drive *okada* motor-cycles, to hawk things in the street, and generally to do 'low' work which kept them at a subsistence level. The Koranic way, in fact, made the streets of Kano what they were.

This couldn't have been an easy thing for these proud Islamic men to live with, but their heads were full of the problem of identity as reflected in language, and they let it pass.

The literature-teacher said they were inward-looking people. They wrote in Hausa, a language of the north; they had very few English writers. He said, 'We want to look out, but all these writers write in Hausa.'

The man in the fez, the media man, said 'We need new ideas.'

The man who said he was a 'tiny writer in English' said, 'Kano is a strange place. I look at people who are happy one minute and very unhappy the next. All right and then angry by turns. I look at them because they are my characters, and I want to understand them.' He couldn't say why they are angry. 'They are not vocal. I don't know why they are so alienated. I feel their anger even though we are an urbane and commercial centre.'

The academic, the literature-teacher, didn't feel the anger the tiny writer felt. 'It is not so palpable to me. It could be an identity issue. What pigeon-hole they fit in.'

They then talked about what was closest to them, the question of Hausa identity.

When did that identity crisis begin?

They said it was started by European anthropologists. And, indeed, there was an American academic in the hotel at that moment, who had come to write about the Hausa and was now at the end of his 'field-work'.

The tiny writer in English said, 'The inwardness of people in Kano is part of our identity, and maybe this is why the social and political advancement is limited.'

We had gone far beyond the brave attitudes they had adopted at the beginning.

I wanted to know how they were reacting to the dilapidation of Kano. In the beginning they had appeared not to notice it.

The media man in the red fez said it was growing, both the city and the dilapidation. 'They are all like ants milling around. We do not have much new development.' Again, very different from what they had said in the beginning. 'There is a great influx of people, but no jobs, and so many people just do the *okada* thing.'

The literature-teacher said, 'It is a lament these days, but there is no magic wand to solve it. People will have to solve it on an individual level. Just as I solved my power problem with a generator.'

I wanted to know about the position of the Amir. Was he like the Oni of Ife, or was he more?

They all said that people respected the institution. There was no coercion.

The writer said, 'The Amir does not control production. He is identified with Islam and he stands for the inspiration of the people, and he is revered.' The people of Kano did not think of themselves as Arabs. In this they were different from the people of Sudan. 'They are black as night but pretend to be Arab because they speak Arabic. We will never want to be Arabs.'

IN THE geography books I read at school, Kano was a great mud-walled city. Photographs showed smooth-plastered walls, pierced with narrow drainage pipes. I had wished then to see Kano, but now I had to be content with that faint memory, of an old photograph seen long ago. I couldn't find anything like that, and I found in the end that some cultural arm of the Germans was looking after the little stretch of mud wall that had survived. Its surface was dug up, and very far from being plastered and smooth.

The first palace I saw was the Amirs' weekend palace. With a name like that it should have been many miles away from the city, but it wasn't, leaving one to worry about its purpose.

The walls were high and ochre-coloured. Their only decoration was a series of abstract designs in raised concrete, which might have been created by moulds. Here too children ran after visitors and waited patiently for the gratuities that were doled out at the end of the visit. The doorway or gateway was set in the middle of the wall, which was apparently many feet thick, but when you looked up you saw that the thickness was an illusion, that above the ceiling (of corrugated iron) was a vacancy that reached to the very top.

The ceiling was broken in many places and open to the

sky, and there were birds nesting in the corners. The wall was hollow. Inside there were courtyards around small low buildings that were shut. Against one wall was a very old tree, with a thick trunk. At the very back there was an orchard, walled again, where the concubines of the Amir of two generations ago might have relaxed, if they weren't too old or if they hadn't been discarded.

The main palace, to which we came in due course, was more challenging on this day of heat. It was in a big open dusty semi-arid *maidan*, sun-struck and bare except for the neem trees in the driveway, with great distances between the cool of the three gateways. The walls were high and brown.

In the second gateway a small white kitten with a patch of colour on its back was crying. It was like the kitten I had seen in Uganda in the Mountains of the Moon Hotel. It was possibly the last of the litter, surviving heaven knows how. It would have taken very little to comfort it, but I was with people to whom cats were spirits and familiars; and I had to leave the dainty little creature opening its mouth and crying, still remarkably whole, still nourished by the milk of its mother, now perhaps persecuted and killed.

This little tragedy, and my own helplessness, cast a shadow over the rest of my visit to the palace, to the various durbar rooms, including the England room, where framed photographs on the wall showed Queen Elizabeth being received many years ago by the Amir of Kano.

These inner rooms were being repaired or redecorated, especially the ceilings with their raised decorations and earth

colours, the colours of sand and gold in one room, and
grey, black and white in another. There was a harem area
in the palace, unlikely as it seemed, with wives and concubines and slaves and eunuchs, Islam living out its good old
ways at its African limits.

The harem was, of course, off limits to me. I sat on a
dusty chair in a durbar room and waited for the rest of the
party to come back.

9

DELACROIX'S PICTURE of the ladies of the harem in
Algiers shows idle women in colourful clothes. The vacancy
of their minds shows in their faces. I suppose some such
picture – the clothes, the idleness – had worked on the
imagination of the Indian woman I met in Delhi some years
ago who said she would have liked nothing more than to
be one of the harem of the Emperor Akbar. This woman
was not a Muslim, had no idea of a harem, and even with
her folly would have been dismayed to find that the harem
of an African ruler (no doubt in this woman's mind some
notches down from the real thing) was in the main a place
of homeless derelicts – slaves and concubines (many of
them gifts from other African rulers), discarded older wives,
eunuchs (bought from Egypt) – people who had outlived
their usefulness, had no talent, no family, no outside life.

Old age and idleness gave them the freedom to go
outside (the eunuchs always in their uniform), and they

used this limited freedom to do little errands in the town for people in the harem. Apart from this there was nothing for them to do. They were waiting now only for death, were fed like dogs, and slept on the floor of the harem in such corners as they could find.

This was the picture that was given me later, by a woman whose mother had spent some unhappy years in the harem of a small northern Nigerian chief.

Polygamy, the way of life of the harem, had its own rules. The most important of these was the separation of women from their children. This happened when the children were born. The children were given out to other women and were brought to the natural mother only to be fed or suckled. While this was happening the natural mother covered her face with a cloth; the child was not to get to know her or think of her as a source of special affection. When a child was six or seven it could be told who its natural mother was. That caused no disturbance; the child did not lose its affection for its foster mother.

These complicated rules – like a little religion within the larger religion – were intended to break down any idea of the 'nuclear' family and to inculcate the idea of a broader family unit within the walled harem. Polygamy as the sound Islamic way had its champions and theoreticians, and they could be well educated. For these people the nuclear-family idea was the origin of the selfishness and breakdown of other societies.

Laila was the romantic name of this woman's mother. And perhaps it was one of the things that had helped to give her some idea of the life she wanted for herself. She had grown up with television; she read the Mills and Boon novels, and believed in love. Her family were big landowners, rich enough and secure enough to have some idea of the modern world. They had sent Laila to a convent school in the cool plateau of Jos for a couple of years. There she caught the eye of the ruler or caught the eye of one of his matchmakers. Her family were delighted, and so was Laila. She knew, of course, that Muslim men could have four wives, and a ruler any number of concubines. But her education, her secure family background, and her imagination had made her believe that when she married she would enter the realm of love and somehow be exempt from the common destiny of women around her.

She became pregnant. She had a daughter. She called the little girl Mona. They, the ruler's court, wanted to take the child away and give it to a foster mother. She refused, and her passion was so great that the court, fearing that she might do something to her child, let the matter drop. One of her servants brought back the story that some people were calling her the white woman. She thought this funny, and it seemed to her that she had won. But what she next heard wasn't funny at all. She heard that her husband was paying betrothal visits to the parents of the young girl whom he wanted to make his second wife — visits just like those he had made to Laila's parents.

Laila felt herself sinking. Her husband tried to calm her; he told her that nothing would change the love he felt for her. This other marriage was something he had to do as an

Islamic ruler; it was expected of him. His father had about thirty children. He couldn't be more precise about the number of children because it was unlucky for a man to count his children. His grandfather had about fifty, but things were different in those days.

Nobody in the court could understand why Laila refused to be comforted, and continued to make a fuss, threatening the harmony of the harem; many of the women said that the white woman had been unhinged by the English books she had read and the convent education she had received. And Laila was cast into the very pit of despair when her parents made it clear that they couldn't support her; she had expected them at least to understand.

The second marriage went ahead, without reference, it seemed, to Laila. She felt shut out of her own marriage. She felt that her humiliation was complete. She felt mocked by the past. She began to think of withdrawing from the ruler, having no intimate contact with him. It was hard for her to decide; there was a part of her that thought everything could still be made all right. When that idea faded, she discovered that she was pregnant again.

Now began a strange time for her, living alone with the mess of harem life, the rivalries and quarrels, the hatreds, the constant tension. She was protected to some extent by her solitude, her ambition for something beyond the harem, which the others couldn't even begin to suspect. Within that solitude she discovered a cause: she became determined to spare her daughter what she had gone through.

Her second child was a son. They wanted to take him

away. She let them. She covered her face when she nursed the boy. The boy grew up. Thereafter she let the years pass.

The idea that she might do something to save Mona never left her. It gave her a kind of solace, though – living within the walls of the harem, a kind of prisoner – she had no idea what she might do for her daughter. But she felt that because she wished it so much, she would one day be shown a way.

For a year or two a relation of the ruler had been appearing in the harem. He was a doctor from Dubai in the Persian Gulf, a man of mixed Arab and African family. He had become one of the physicians of the ruler. (In the old days the ruler would go to London for his check-up, to Harley Street or the Cromwell Hospital; but prices in London were going up and up, and this London jaunt was now too expensive, especially as the ruler was required by his style to travel with an entourage.)

The doctor enchanted the women of the harem with stories of the wonders of Dubai, of grass and gardens being made to grow in the desert, of aeroplanes constantly flying in and out from all points of the globe, of hotels being built next to the ocean.

Laila loved his stories. She liked his clothes. They brought back her old dreams of a world outside. When he discovered that she could read, he brought her English-language newspapers from Dubai and other places. He, for his part, appeared to be more interested in Laila than was correct. People noticed and talked. She was disturbed. She didn't feel she could at this stage of her life handle more enmity. And if someone in the harem hadn't said one day, 'This doctor is more interested in Mona than in anybody else,' Laila might never have noticed. She studied the doctor when he next came. She saw that he was, indeed, interested in Mona. She wondered that she had missed it. And then she saw the hand of God in the arrival of the stranger from Dubai. She pushed Mona towards the doctor. In time he asked for the girl's hand.

Perhaps it wasn't the best arrangement in the world. Laila had no idea what life in Dubai would be like for Mona, but she saw the hand of God in it.

Mona had heard her mother's stories many times. Laila's suffering, and the harem life she had known, had hardened Mona, prepared her for whatever might come her way. She was better able to withstand the shock of the doctor's second wife, and it did come; and the further shock of the third. She never told her mother.

THREE

Men Possessed

A LARGE PART OF the contemporary West African state of Ghana belonged to the kingdom of the Ashanti. The Ashanti kingdom was huge. An old English map shows the area of 'Ashanti authority' as about four hundred miles wide and two hundred miles high. On this old map you have to look hard for Accra, the modern capital of Ghana, among the many sea 'castles and forts' set down since the fifteenth century – by Portuguese, Danes, Swedes, Prussians from Brandenburg, Dutch and English, all dreaming of gold and slaves – on this long east–west stretch of African coast.

Kojo was an Ashanti, and his wife was the daughter of the previous king of the Ashanti. The king, Kojo said, had asked him to marry his daughter. It is one of the more straightforward things about Kojo. But when he tells it in his own words it acquires a strange tone: 'My wife's father was the previous king. He very tactfully suggested that I marry his daughter. She was studying medicine in school and I was a dentist. She was Ashanti, and I agreed.'

I saw a lot of Kojo when I was in Ghana. At one time we had dinner together every day. He was always ready to answer questions, always helpful and civil. Yet at the end he remained mysterious, almost as mysterious as he had been when he talked in his deadpan way of his marriage to the king's daughter. At first it seemed to me that in spite of his readiness to talk, there was a reticence about him, an aristocratic African reticence that made him underplay everything. And then I thought that his life had been too varied, full of unconnected or disparate parts, and he hadn't worked out a way to present himself. I suppose that meant he hadn't been able to make a whole of his experience.

Here are pieces of the jigsaw as they came to me. Kojo's father went to Achimota, the famous secondary school set up by the British to train the children of chiefs and local dignitaries for 'public duty' (Kojo's words). The Achimota student became a schoolmaster and served in different parts of Ghana. The schoolmaster's father (Kojo's grandfather) was a palace chief, a senior adviser to the king on cultural matters. Kojo said he received a 'special' African education.

Kojo (in his reticent style) did not say what this African education was. He only said, 'It taught him to fulfil his inherited designation. He was not a top chief or a very powerful one. His fiefdom was limited. He had less land. Land here means status and power. He did not have that kind of power although he was a wealthy man. He was wealthy because he had cocoa farms outside Kumasi. His tenants grew the crops, harvested them and dried them, and then bagged them in sisal bags and sold them to the agency. He had to spend time in Kumasi because of his court duties.'

Kojo said, 'My clan produces the kings of Ashanti. There are five other prominent chiefs who can also produce chiefs. But we, of the Oyoko clan, give the leadership on my maternal side.'

The famous Ashanti wars that gave Gold Coast and then Ghana its final shape took place in the 1890s. This would have provided Kojo's grandfather with enough drama. But the big disturbance in Kojo's life came with independence and especially with the dictatorship of Nkrumah, the first president of independent Ghana. Nkrumah wished to re-draw the Ashanti borders. He wished to make the Ashanti people less dominant. He brought in mining acts that took away the mining rights of the Ashanti. The Ashanti lands were famous for the gold they produced; in colonial times Ghana was known as the Gold Coast. Nkrumah's mining acts decreed that below a certain depth in the ground all the mines belonged to the government.

Kojo said: 'I could see myself in trouble. I was used to living in a country where there was the rule of law and where there were human rights and everything was regulated.'

From this period come his London stories, where his addresses are in Belgravia; this is when his three sons ('three of my boys') go to Eton.

I met one of the boys at the very end of my time in Ghana, the evening of my last day, at the airport. He was charming and resourceful, full of manners, a great help in the airport mess and crowd; and I felt that it might be possible for this boy (though lacking his father's experience) to have a steady way of looking and acting that his father (whose memories went back too far) wouldn't begin to have.

Kojo was brought up as a Christian. In this part of West Africa this usually means a background, or indeed a foreground, of traditional African belief. But Kojo said this was not so in his case. He loved the 'Ashanti spirit', but Christianity had made it mellower and less warlike. Paganism did not pervade Ashanti; Kojo was not exposed to it. The Ashanti have ancestral gods, but they are figures of healing. Certain cultural rites have to be performed at times of death, birth, and puberty. Every family has an elder who can do the rites; the knowledge is passed from generation to generation.

2

THIS ASHANTI religion, if what Kojo said was true, was not too intrusive. The same couldn't be said of the religion of the coastal Gaa people, at one time enemies of the Ashanti. This religion is so encompassing, so full of signs and portents that the true believer (rather like the devout ancient Roman) might live in a constant fever of anxiety about the messages of the gods. This Gaa religion is rooted in the spirits of the departed and is at the same time so much part and parcel of the living world that it surrounds us, this world of prophecy and divine messages, even when we are not aware of it.

If we are walking on a road and we stub our toe on a stone, that has meaning. If we sneeze, that has meaning. To sneeze on the right side is good; to sneeze on the left is bad. Nature itself has been programmed; we have to learn to read it. Even the velocity of the wind is a sign. The high priest will interpret it; so will the elders who guard the properties of the stool, which stands for the ruler, and women seers.

It was Pa-boh who took me into this understanding of his complex faith, where so much has to be explained. He never spelt his name out for me or wrote it down; so I write it according to my phonetic memory. It may be that I have written it wrongly.

The son of an important chief took me to see Pa-boh. I thought that the house we were going to was Pa-boh's house. The house, when we came to it, was in a populous but uncluttered part of Accra, without garbage. I was told later that the garbage here, as elsewhere in Accra, was collected by a private garbage-collecting firm. There was also a system of drainage, and that made all the difference to the appearance of the place.

The houses were small but not hemmed in by garbage or fences; so there seemed to be a lot of openness. Children ran in and out of every free space and the street sounded like a schoolyard at recess.

At one end of the street there was a small white concrete structure, like a sentry-box; at the top of this strange box two crosses leaned away from each other. I thought it might have been a very small local chapel, with the leaning crosses showing how the imported religion of Christianity had been made to fit into the older African framework. I learned later that the sentry-box was, in fact, the oracle house, important to local belief, and open only to the religiously qualified.

We walked a little way down from the oracle house, past a few parked cars. We turned into a narrow passageway between two proper houses. The floor here was of concrete, broken in places. We were joined here by Pa-boh. He was wearing a local shirt-jacket, with a wide flare. I didn't know who he was at this stage. I noticed the stylishness of his dress, and I thought he might only have been an idler, one of those who stare and push themselves forward when strangers come to their place.

At the end of the passageway between the two houses we came upon a little area of openness which enabled us to turn and start on a narrow staircase to the upper floor. So space was cramped again. The narrow staircase was made of roughly sawn timber, not planed or painted, showing diagonal saw-marks. The woodwork upstairs had a similar rough-and-ready quality. Our party edged its way into a small room that overlooked the street. The cries and shouts of the playing children came up to us.

The left side of the room was dominated by a big man who was sitting at a Hewlett-Packard laptop, completely given over to what he was doing. He was of polished appearance, and was sitting, big and chief-like, dressed in white, on a brown-and-white goatskin that was thrown over his chair and came down to the floor. He was told by the chief's son, who had come with us, who we were. He was civil, but no more, not interested enough in us to look away for long from his laptop; and I was puzzled, since at this stage I thought he was the man we had come to see.

We sat down on the cream-coloured leather chairs set against the outer wall. The street was just outside and below, and the children's cries came up sharp through the open window at our back.

Pa-boh began to talk.

He stood beside a high stool, and sometimes he sat on the stool. His shirt-jacket, flaring out from the waist, was in a varied but mainly striped black-and-white pattern. He faced the big man in white working at the laptop, but he, Pa-boh, was talking to us, and the big man continued to look at the screen of his laptop, adding a few words from time to time to those he had written.

It was not easy for me in the beginning to concentrate on what he was saying. It was too simple, about God and the spirits; I had heard it before. But then he became more personal and direct. I understood at the same time that the man in white had offered his room as a meeting-place, and had done so as a courtesy, both to me and to the chief's son, and that Pa-boh was the man we had come to see.

I had to look afresh at Pa-boh. I began to be held. There was a shininess to his face which made him hypnotic whenever, to confirm a point, he smiled and pressed his chin down. He was then like an academic lecturer.

One of the early things he had said was that by the time

he was twenty-six he had mastered six jobs or disciplines. At the moment he was administrator-secretary to seven chiefs.

The chief's son had told me the day before that whenever we went to see important people about religious matters it was common courtesy to offer them a bottle of schnapps. No beer, no whisky, no wine; only schnapps. I suppose this was because it was a colourless liquid.

I had been told, but I didn't have the schnapps with me. I wasn't expecting a serious religious moment that morning; I was expecting only a preliminary discussion, a discussion about a discussion; and I feared now that we would have to pay a fine to Pa-boh. In everything he had told me about the high priests of his faith this power of theirs to levy fines was important. It seemed to be one of the sources of their livelihood, just as the schnapps was part of a traditional tribute (the *babalawo* in Nigeria had required a bottle of gin to pour a libation to the gods or spirits in his room).

And then I noticed, on the floor to the right of the big man in white, a half-used bottle of a clear-coloured liquid. Clearly everywhere one went here one should be armed with a bottle of schnapps.

3

I ASKED PA-BOH about the oracle house on the street outside. He said that the area at one time was all forest and neem trees. The government recognises these sacred spots, and they should be left alone. The community takes it amiss if these spots are interfered with or in some way desecrated. Pa-boh guessed that inside the oracle house there would be offerings of palm oil or eggs in an earthen pot. But he didn't know for sure. He hadn't been inside. To go inside you had to be invited or chosen by the high priest; and Pa-boh, learned and reverential as he was, didn't have that privilege.

This led Pa-boh to give an outline of the traditional religion. He had the academic manner, and he spoke so much like a book that I wondered how much of what he was saying was scholarship, from a university course, say, and how much came from personal experience. Perhaps the two were mixed; or it might have been that Pa-boh had a special gift of language.

The spirits, the lesser deities, and the gods (Pa-boh said) bridge the great distance between us and the supreme being, who is like Jehovah. The biblical comparison or link is often made when Africans seek to explain their faith; it is done to clarify what would otherwise be hard to describe. This supreme being is very powerful and is not to be used in daily rituals. The others, spirits and gods and so on, are invoked daily. They have physical representations: they can be trees, stumps, stools, carved idols, rivers and pools. Every community has its own set of deities of this sort, who protect and heal; these deities also settle difficult matters that can arise in communities. These deities have their own spokesmen, who are high priests and prophetesses. They have to be initiated into the cults. Both the high priests and the prophetesses are possessed.

When a difficult issue arises the people seek the prophetesses. If the prophetesses take up an issue they go into frenzy; they tear their upper clothes off and bare their breasts, and start talking in unknown languages. These women normally speak Twi, the language of the Akan people. But when they are in frenzy they can talk other languages.

Religious beliefs and cultural practices go hand in hand. Religious beliefs dictate the culture. When a child is born water and palm wine are poured into its mouth. This links the baby to the earth. At puberty the child is covered in ash or a greenish-coloured clay and presented to the village. The villagers sing and dance then. The songs are important. They spell out the history and moral expectations of the community, and the child gets to know what its responsibilities are towards the family and the community. An ancestor is a point of reference for the young. Anyone who behaves well can become an ancestor when he is old or when he dies.

At death traditional religion comes into play. There are different rituals for different deaths. If someone dies in childbirth there is one kind of ritual. When both the mother and the child die, all the pregnant women in the village go to the sea and bathe, to wash away the bad omen. (The Gaa are a coastal people. The sea is always present for them.) So from birth to death the supreme being, through his appointed deities and spirits, protects the people.

Chiefs are embalmed. In some cases, depending on the status of the dead chief, the rituals can go on for a year and longer. The elders and the high priests know what they have to do. At this time of death, a time of horrible taint, so to speak, a special kind of language has to be used, to protect people. It wouldn't do to say that the chief is dead. It is better to use the language of life and say that the chief has travelled, or he has turned round against life, or he has gone to pluck a leaf, or he has gone to his forefathers' village. The coffin is to be called 'a dead house'.

Since life (and death) are so full of snares, there are many ablutions to be done and many taboos to be observed. It is better to be barefoot. For the high priests especially it is taboo to have the soles of their feet covered; these important people must always have a link to the earth. If they are caught wearing shoes they can be fined. Full shoes are allowed in some shrines, but not slippers. Wherever the high priest walks becomes holy, because he is the physical representation of the spirits, and is possessed by the spirits. The high priest wears white and carries a broom in his hand. The broom stands for his cleansing function.

THE GAA (Pa-boh said) migrated from the east with their high priest. In those days they did not have a king. Rather like in the days of Jesus, the high priest was both king and priest. (Again, this need to refer an African story to a biblical or Christian model.) When the Gaa reached the coast, they found the Portuguese. Later the Dutch and the British came. All these people saw African religion and its high priests as demonic. They preferred to deal with the war lord. So the war lord became the king or chief.

This downgrading of the high priest can create difficulties. Some chiefs nowadays are Christian; they don't like offering libations to the shrines or oracles. And modern laws can affect traditional practices. Slavery, for instance, is now outlawed, and parents can no longer sell or give their children to a shrine, to pay off a debt.

Chiefs get money from the government for administering government land. They fine people for breaking taboos, and that money belongs to them. They can also act as arbitrators, and then they are paid by both sides. So the function of the chief changes.

Pa-boh said, 'Traditional religion in Ghana is dying slowly. It started to die when the Europeans and Muslims came and saw us as pagans. Their superior technology killed us. We have witches who fly in the air. But when we saw aircraft we came to abhor what was our culture. I think the modern African is in a very difficult situation. He should look at it and modify it. He should not condemn it.'

4

IT WAS HARD to believe that Pa-boh, who spoke with such passion about the traditional religion, was formally a Christian, with a Christian grandfather who ran a church in a village. Sixty years before, this grandfather had had his house and church burned down by the villagers whom he wished to serve (he wanted them to repent, to leave their African gods and lesser spirits and come to Christ), and he had been pushed with his family into the bush. His sister had been assaulted, her head split open.

Strangely, Pa-boh spoke of this with passion too. Probably he was a man of passion; perhaps he needed to live at a certain pitch.

He said, 'I cried when I saw how my grandfather and my father had suffered.'

And then, to complete the cycle of passion, he said, 'But this cannot happen today even if people feel angry or outraged because there is a law, and they cannot go beyond a certain level.' Moving now with almost equal fervour from religion to something quite apart: the virtues of civil society.

When he was a child Pa-boh lost his parents (he didn't say how), and he had to shift for himself. He did odd jobs; and, in order to work in the school office, he learned to type. He also became an electrician, picking up the skill from older men who in the beginning saw their eager boy helper only as a joke. He joined a musical band and by the time he was sixteen he was a vocalist for them. He was rowdy and wild, a big fighter.

On a day in May 1970 his life changed. He became possessed by the Holy Spirit. It happened like this. He was singing with his band that day, and at midnight they had a break. He went to the midnight service and his behaviour was strange. He became noisy and disruptive. When the minister asked the congregation to pray for the betterment of their lives, Pa-boh insulted him. After the service Pa-boh went to see the minister. He wasn't at all sorry for what he had done, but he began to cry, and his crying didn't stop. He went to his dormitory but he felt very guilty and he couldn't sleep.

He felt a hand on his wrist. The hand led him to the dining room. There he saw a flashing signboard in the air, lit up with episodes from his life. A voice told him to go outside to the school ground. He said he couldn't do that because he was afraid of snakes. The voice then told him to go to the dormitory. He did so, and found some seniors who said he was late and wanted to punish him. They asked him to kneel to receive his punishment. Normally he would have knocked these boys down and given them a good thrashing, but now he fell on his knees and waited for his punishment. The boys were bewildered. They thought Pa-boh must have been affected by something the minister had said.

A little while later a senior monitor came running with a Bible to Pa-boh's bunk. The monitor said a voice had told him to do that. Pa-boh opened the Bible and then, he said, he saw the light, just like Saint Paul.

After that day many things began to happen to him. By chance one day he met a paramount chief and for some reason began telling this chief the whole story of the Gaa people since the sixteenth century. At the end the paramount chief put his hand on Pa-boh's shoulder and blessed him for a full fifteen minutes. He said to Pa-boh, 'You carry the peace of your people in you.'

After this Pa-boh was guided to do many wonderful things. For one chief he solved in days a dispute that had dragged on for seventeen years. At first this chief had no faith in Pa-boh as arbitrator, but Pa-boh pleaded with him, and the chief gave Pa-boh money for the arbitration (this money being the arbitrator's fee), and Pa-boh went to the main Ashanti town of Kumasi and spoke to the assembled chiefs, and won. In this way Pa-boh became a witness and spokesman for his Gaa people, and a lecturer on their cultural practices. In time he set up his own church, conducting a service there every Sunday.

He was bringing up his five children as Christians. He kept them away from traditional religion because traditional religion had no book and was not codified or written, and this could lead to trouble.

5

KOJO THOUGHT I should go to Kumasi, the Ashanti 'citadel', which was his birthplace. He had a house there and he offered it for the night. Accra was on the coast. Kumasi was in the interior, to the north-west. When Kojo went to Kumasi, on business, he took the aeroplane. I thought a car would be better for me, for the sake of the long drive and for the landscape. Richmond, Kojo's assistant, came along as a guide.

We went through the hills of the eastern region, and past the botanical gardens of Abrui, small but beautiful, wonderfully mature now. Some of the trees had very thick trunks, with buttresses that were like mighty tendons. The British had laid these gardens out a hundred years before. Here in Ghana, as in other places of the empire, these British botanical gardens, their founders often unknown, had become a gift for later generations.

The villages seemed to lie just outside forested areas. The land was always choked with vegetation; when you put your head out of the air-conditioned car you felt yourself driving through waves of humid heat that caused things to grow. This suggested that the forest ruled. But Richmond, Kojo's assistant, who had a nice line in cynicism, said that the impenetrable forest was an illusion. One or two chain saws could in a short time open up big clearings.

And the landscape, for all its luxuriance, was a disappointment: endlessly small and jumbled, like a tropical cottage garden, no attempt at a plantation, never anything ordered or big: small patches of banana or plantain growing absolutely between stands of teak, big-leaved and apparently always in flower. There were no paths or tracks in the bush, or there appeared to be none; so it would have been hard to cultivate these small patches commercially.

The idea of smallness continued when at dusk we reached the outskirts of Kumasi. Weak electric lights

showed outside the small houses – it might have been a
municipal requirement: to prevent the big trucks smashing
into them – and sometimes only oil lamps flickered, bright
yellow, a real flame, a real colour, more pleasing than the
dim, eye-straining fluorescent tubes in the little shops. It
went on like that, for mile after mile, Kumasi delaying and
delaying its promise.

And there was trouble when we arrived at the town.
Neither Richmond nor the car-driver could work out
where Kojo's house was. That was not too surprising to me.
Kojo gave instructions in a strange way; he could telescope
distances. When he first sent me to the Abrui botanical
gardens his directions abolished many miles. It seemed that
now something like that had happened again. But it was
important for us to know where the house was, because
Kojo had arranged for an Ashanti chief to be there, to help
us with the visit to the palace in the morning. Richmond
telephoned Kojo. Kojo appeared to repeat his instructions.
There was a big hotel on a main road not far away. When
Richmond said it would save a lot of trouble if we all
put up at the hotel, Kojo lost his temper. He said it was
nonsense to talk about a hotel when we were almost at the
gate of the house.

There were quite a few houses near by. We knocked at
the gate of one. The house was asleep. A ragged watchman
came and spoke very softly to Richmond. He was speaking
softly because he didn't want to disturb the woman who
was his employer and was sleeping. Richmond, without
being too loud, knocked at the door. The woman whose

house it was, not showing herself, merely told Richmond that the chief who had been waiting for us had got tired and gone away. And that was that. So we at least had this tender of Kojo's good faith.

Many minutes later, and a longish distance away, down a curving road, we found the house. Richmond's idea then was that I should have dinner at the hotel, while he and the driver prepared the house for me. When, after a good long time, they came for me, Richmond said that, apart from the bed mattress, which sank a little low, the bedroom they had got ready for me would have been of five-star quality.

There was some trouble about the lights – some bulbs had gone, and for some time after I had gone to bed, sinking low on my mattress, quite close to the floor, I could hear Richmond knocking against things in the corridor. But he was devoted to his master; he had done wonders in the uncommissioned house; and then in the morning he got up early and went with the driver to buy milk and coffee and bread.

Kojo didn't want me to stay in a hotel. He wanted me to see his house, which was in an Ashanti royal enclave, and though it was only the guest pavilion, as he described it, it was indeed spacious and fine.

Next door to it the morning light showed the beginnings of a palace. It was Kojo's; but the money had run out. All his instincts were princely.

At breakfast facing the garden (Kojo liked flowers wherever he lived) I saw a pretty little near-black hummingbird feeding off the red-and-yellow flowers of the *flam-boyant.*

IN DAYLIGHT the lady we had disturbed during the night, a large lady in a splendid grey and white dress, was as firm as she had been in darkness. Kojo's chief had got tired of waiting for us. So there would be no privileged viewing of the palace for us. We decided we had to live with that. It was, besides, a cleaning day at the palace; so there would be no visitors, and for us no burden of a palace visit.

The first impression of Kumasi, a royal town, was that of a British colonial settlement at the time of the conquest. The colours of official buildings were ochre and red, the architecture in the sturdy manner of the Public Works Department. The palace rails reminded me of the made-in-England rails of my own school in Trinidad (built in 1904); and the open green areas were like police grounds of the period. The treasures of the museum were small-scale, the little pieces of furniture unpolished. Ashanti was not a literate kingdom, in spite of its gold and glory. To see it as more it was necessary to be Ashanti oneself and (with the absence of spectacular remains) to consult the stirrings of one's heart.

It was a hilly, up-and-down town, in the great heat fatiguing to explore, but with oddities that were all its own: a street of coffin-makers in the bazaar area, with the painted coffins – grey, white, lilac, silver and gold – pushed out on to the pavements and creating a festive effect (abolishing the idea of grief, introducing the idea of shopping, and suggesting at the same time one kind of plot possibility for a thriller writer). Begging women had their own area in the market, and that too was cheerful. Below bright parasols the women (packed a little too tightly) sat on little stools with their begging cups, avoiding eye-contact with the alms-givers, who moved among them in a matter-of-fact way; so the business of giving and receiving involved no strain.

Richmond said (though I couldn't understand why he brought in Islam here) that Islam encouraged people to give alms, and so there had to be alms-receivers.

Away from the palace area the town had a repetitive smallness. Its crowded little streets never developed into something more interesting, an older section of the town, a fort, a famous temple. It hurried us away, and then, past the outskirts of Kumasi, yesterday's country smallness began to tire us afresh on the way back: teak amid the plantains and bamboo in the trackless bush. Though there was something else in the bush this time, which for some reason we had missed on the way out: the grey and often frail-looking concrete of unfinished buildings. There were any number of them: so many that a couple of days later, when I was driving along the Atlantic Cape Coast, I thought that some of the ancient white castles and forts were repeating the unfinished motif of the interior.

Richmond said that what looked like unfinished buildings would soon be finished. If I came back in two or three years I would see what he meant. I didn't believe him.

We talked after this of the wildlife of Ghana. There wasn't much of it left. The people of Ghana had eaten much of it out. From this talk of wildlife we turned to the cats and dogs that people were now eating with a will. In the north they ate and loved dog; they called it 'red goat'. In the south they ate cats and had almost eaten them out. Richmond knew someone who bred cats in order to eat them.

The trouble with cats was that they were tricky to kill. Cats knew when they were going to be killed and eaten; they fought for their lives and they could be dangerous for a few minutes. The best way of killing a cat, assuming you had invited someone to dinner and didn't want to create a scene, was to stretch the animal's neck, the way people in England killed a rabbit. But when you did that you could be badly scratched. The surest way – if you or your guests didn't mind the racket – was to put a cat in a sack and beat it with a stick until it was dead. Another good way was to drown it. You used a sardine as bait to attract the cat to a container with water, and then you poured and poured water. The cat swallowed a lot of water and the virtue of this method was that it was much easier afterwards to tear the bloated cat's skin off.

With this talk of local food – breaking off from time to time to look at unfinished concrete pieces in the bush – we beguiled many miles. And then, as if this talk of food had called them up, there appeared at the roadside local men holding up smoked animals, offering them for sale, the surrounding bush combed and combed for these survivors

— the agouti, together with a big rat known here as the grass-cutter, baby armadillos, long-snouted baby ant-eaters, and a few other creatures that just weren't fast enough to get away from these idle fellows.

The smoked creatures were usually split down the middle, to make for easier smoking, and they looked as though they had been run over by a motorcar. They were a strange shiny pale-brown colour — the colour looked as though it had been applied in a semi-liquid state with a brush — and were not at all like the thick black crusts of fish, monkey and crocodile that were being offered for sale on the Congo River thirty years before. Those black crusts had to be cracked open.

The bush was almost barren of wildlife, but these people were managing to squeeze out the last remnants, while their fertile land remained largely unused.

6

RICHMOND'S grandfather on his father's side had been in the police, and high up. He was given a police funeral when he died, with a one-gun salute. Beyond that was a Danish ancestor, whose surname Richmond still carried.

It sounds strange. What were the Danes doing so far from home? But that is only a modern prejudice. In fact, the Danes, though their numbers were small, were active gold-buyers and slave-traders in their time, and were known to the chiefs of Ghana. The big fort near Accra was built by the Danes in the 1660s. (At the same time they also had territory in India, in Tranquebar, south of Pondicherry, half a world and many weeks' sailing away). The abolition of the slave trade at the beginning of the nineteenth century more or less put an end to the Danish slave business, but it wasn't until 1850 that they left Ghana, after selling out whatever they still had to the British.

Richmond knew the name of his Danish ancestor, but had done no research on him. I don't think it was prejudice that kept him back; it was more likely that he didn't have the time and wouldn't have known how to go about researching the matter. 'Just out of curiosity' he would have liked to know more.

He wasn't too agitated about the slave-trading past of Ghana. But this might have been only bravado. It was said that visitors to Elmina Castle from the United States and the West Indies often broke down and wept when they saw, below the official quarters, the stone dungeons, smelling of damp (easy to imagine them crowded and airless), where slaves (already captive for many weeks) were kept before they were taken out in rowing boats to the slave ships for the Atlantic crossing. But Richmond would have seen the ocean rollers beating on those white slave forts and castles all his life; they would have been stripped of emotion for him; and so when we went to Elmina he strode about like a guide, no more.

He said: 'The colonial masters came here for business. Slave trade was a business. Maybe bad, but it was purely business. They took, but they gave us the church. That was a death knell to traditional religion. In the traditional religion, every king had his chief priest and elders to consult. It was a democratic system. It promoted sanity. People did not cross boundaries. The church came and overturned this. They brought in Jesus.'

There were so many clashing ideas there it was hard to disentangle them and to know what Richmond really felt. But perhaps the fault was mine, looking for my own purposes for a clear reply to what, for Richmond, was a complicated and messy matter: a past dying, a new way coming.

Richmond said, 'In my area in the Volta River [to the east of Accra] we all have a shrine. My father told me that in the old days we owned things, but we needed someone to own us, and so we had the gods. We were good herbalists. We had new herbs and drugs, and we used them to talk to the entity. You created the entity to rule over you, and you can misuse that entity too.'

Richmond had a story about the misuse of an 'entity'.

'My mother told me this story. Her mother – that is my grandmother – was Nkrumah's cook. Apart from Nkrumah's house in the mountains, he had a bungalow at Half Asini in the western region. Whenever Nkrumah came to visit this bungalow my grandmother and her cousin Aunty Afua would look after him and cook for him.'

That was the first part of the story: the presentation and verification of the witness.

'My grandmother told my mother that the Ivory Coast

president and king, Houphouët-Boigny, went to the high priest and asked for eternal power.' Ivory Coast was next door to Ghana, and similar in many ways. 'You should know that the Ivoirians believe that leaders are subject all the time to psychic attacks and have constantly to be purified and strengthened spiritually. So Houphouët was not behaving unusually. The high priest said to Houphouët, 'All right, you want eternal power. You will have eternal power.' He gave certain instructions. So in the shrine they chopped Houphouët into small pieces and placed him in a pot of herbs and potions and boiled it. The condition of that chopping and boiling was that Houphouët's sister had to stand guard by the pot, until the pieces of Houphouët in the pot turned to a snake. Houphouët's sister did as she was asked, and stayed by the fire until a big snake emerged from the pot. She grabbed the snake with both hands and they struggled so hard, snake and woman, they both fell to the ground, and Houphouët became a man again.'

This was Richmond's comment on the story: 'The strange thing is that it worked. No one ever challenged him. He owned the whole country. So you see how he misused the power. Now with civilisation catching up with us we are not keen to pay homage to the gods.'

The comment was puzzling to me because Richmond appeared to be saying two or three different things at the same time: misusing the power, civilisation, paying homage to the gods.

I wanted to know whether he had relatives who had

grown up in a time without education. He gave me much more than I had asked for, and what he said now was not mysterious at all.

He said, 'I have such relatives still. They are myopic in their thoughts. Reasoning and delivery is limited. They are guided only by their own experiences. Their line of reasoning is always guided by what others say or do. Everything is laid out for them, what they see or have been told, or what is traditionally done. Knowing how to read and write is not enough. It is only a tool to get out there. If in our setting we are limited we can never be smart. When I was in the USA I saw how limited the average small-town American was. He was as 'smart' as his Ghanaian counterpart. Reasoning is limited by your setting. I am sure of that.'

In a few words he appeared to define the dead end of the instinctive life. So he had, after all, a gift of analytical thought; and though it might not have been fair to say so, this had perhaps come down to him from the Danish ancestor, who might have been an engineer or a military man or an administrator, a man living by logic, full of internal resources, creating a life for himself in a hard setting far from home.

Richmond explained why the Christian church had caught on. 'It was new. It had a policy of assimilation, like the French in the Ivory Coast, but the English did it in an indirect way. They offered a faith that also brought education. It weakened the traditional religion; in that way it was like Islam. The only thing that has remained intact is the chieftaincy.'

A day or two after coming back from Kumasi he had been sent by Kojo to look for a hotel site on the east—west Cape Coast, where all the ancient forts and castles were.

Richmond said, 'I went to the office of the traditional chief and saw the homage the people were giving him by bowing. I only offered my hand because I am not from his clan and I am educated. But indigenous people will bow low to him. The land of the ancestors is held by the chiefs as custodians. You have to give gifts of schnapps to tell them that you recognise their authority. If we buy the land the paramount chief will give the money to the clan chiefs and they will distribute to the families that make up the clan.'

I said, 'The other day you told me your brother said it was a curse to be born in Africa.'

'It is a passionate statement. Being born in Africa is like being born in ignorance. We are indolent. Yesterday I encountered a very embarrassing situation. The chief I went to see lives in a finished building, but it faces a public toilet. The chief saw nothing wrong. I did not want to offend him by telling him that he was living by the cesspit. If I had sat there two more hours I would have gone to hospital, but he was comfortable. That is why I say the white man, bad as he was, brought enlightenment. We have a proverb that the man who has gone nowhere thinks his mother's soup is the best.'

7

I HAD TOLD Pa-boh that I wanted to see his Gaa high priest. Later I had thought that I didn't really need to, but it was too late to withdraw. And then Pa-boh said he was coming to see me on Sunday at midday to take me to see the high priest. He couldn't do it earlier on Sunday because in the morning he would be conducting a service at his church.

He came as he said. I was in the hotel dining room. His appearance there was startling. He wore a white gown with wide strips of purple. (White, as he had told me, was what the high priests of his traditional religion wore. The purple, which he didn't tell me about, was more complicated. It went back to classical days in the Mediterranean, when purple, an expensive colour, indicated high rank for both Romans and Carthaginians, and then was taken over by the church. It had a history, Pa-boh's purple.) He had a silver necklace which was engraved with something about Jesus.

He was aware of the impression he was making in the busy hotel dining room. He had a little smile on his lips, like a star who wished to play down his fame. I asked him who designed his white gown. He was pleased to be asked. He said the gown had been designed by an elder of his church. So, as I suspected, it had been designed – especially the broad purple band on the left of his heart.

He didn't want to eat anything, although he had been preaching for much of the morning; and I thought (since the traditional side of his religion was so full of taboos and portents) it might have been a religious prohibition against eating before a certain time of day.

What I couldn't tell Pa-boh was that I had developed nerves about making this trip with him. My friend Patrick Edwards, the Trinidad ambassador in Uganda, had told me that I should be careful of religious people in this part of the world. Patrick, the ambassador, had told me that it wasn't only the poor who had to be careful. He had a story from Nigeria. A professional person had been abducted and couldn't be found. The family of the abducted man had gone to no less a person than the Oni of Ife, and after some time they had heard from the Oni that the abducted person, now dead, was 'lying' in a shrine somewhere.

This gave another idea of what a shrine was. It was one of those words I thought I knew and had not, as it were, researched. I remember, in the early days of preparing for this book, asking a university lecturer in Uganda to come with me to a shrine. She had given a little cry of horror and said no. Other memories had come to me: a shrine was, someone else had told me, a place where body parts might be found scattered about.

It was because of this anxiety I had asked Richmond to come with me to Pa-boh's base. I needed his company and his local knowledge. Richmond knew the language of the Gaa, and had some idea of the religion.

In the beginning this precaution had seemed excessive, especially when I thought of Pa-boh's face. He was driving ahead of us in a yellowish old Mercedes to show the way.

His ecclesiastical dress showed; his face, when I caught sight of it, seemed set in a smile, above the spin of his wheels. I was trying to memorise the journey, in case we had to come back on our own. Our drive, when we left the hotel and were on the highway, was in the full sunlight of midday. No worry there; and no worry a little later when we were passing the cheerful red roofs of a new development where Nigerians, richer than Ghanaians, had been buying property, to secure their wealth, in a country less hectic than their own, and with more municipal regulation.

But then we turned off the highway, entered a gated area, left it, and turned and turned again. The roads became narrow and crowded and began to twist. Ghanaians are people of municipal order; but now this order began to break down. The shops were little more than boxes, every owner painting his box in a strong flat colour. Memorising the route became impossible; I gave up.

The people on the streets made me think of something Pa-boh had said at our first meeting. I had asked whether Accra, the name of the capital, had a meaning. (For black people in Trinidad a word that sounded like it meant a kind of food.) Pa-boh said, 'The real word is *nkrah*, or soldier ants. The Ashanti said they were going to push us into the sea, but they could never conquer us. They attacked us on 7 May 1826, but we just kept coming and coming. So the Ashanti called us *nkrah*, soldier ants.'

The people here did indeed create something of that impression. They were Gaa, Richmond said, Pa-boh's people. You couldn't do much with them. Whatever you did for them, they went back to their old ways. He said, 'They are comfortable.' It was one of Richmond's words: it meant that the people we were seeing needed little, and it was foolish to give them more. The chief on the Cape Coast Richmond had talked to a few days before – the man who had built his house in front of a cesspit and had no idea what he had done – this man, as Richmond had said, was comfortable.

At a big, right-angled turn in the road or lane, in front of a whitewashed wall that was extraordinary in its pretensions after what we had been seeing, Pa-boh's Mercedes stopped. It stopped in the shade of a tree and next to three or four big water butts in black plastic. The water was for sale, in small quantities; the buyers would have been local people, comfortable (to use Richmond's word) with this arrangement. We parked next to Pa-boh's Mercedes, and Pa-boh, in his designer Christian costume, and with the little smile on his lips, told us we had come to the 'palace' of the high priest of the Gaa cult.

He wished us to be impressed, and the palace and the wall did make an impression of size and style. But as soon as you began to look at the detail you saw that it was tawdry, in keeping with the area, and, though unfinished, already somewhat run down.

We followed Pa-boh through the iron gateway into the bare palace yard. From here I could see more clearly that there was an area of vegetation, a strip of trees, a narrow piece of woodland at the side of the yard, beyond the palace wall. This would have been where the shrine was; and though the green would have been welcome a little while before in the mess and crowd of the neighbourhood, now, thinking of it as a place that might be used for special rites, I saw it as menacing.

A side gate in the wall led to the grove. Women were not allowed to enter here.

The front door of the white palace was ajar. Various people were waiting for us inside. And since this was a palace, and in palaces in this part of the world there were usually big colour photographs of the ruler and his visitors, there were painted portraits here, such as sign-painters might have done, of three generations of the Gaa high priest. They were strong, heavy-featured men, bearded, in white gowns, and they all held the little brooms that marked them as religious cleansers. They were all barefooted; this was another sign of their religious importance.

The high priest was not in the palace. He had been called out, but he had sent a message on his mobile that he was coming, and bringing some people to see me.

There was a dignified old chief who had been waiting for some time. I don't know what story Pa-boh had told him; but it was enough to keep him quiet. He had dressed with care, in a lilac or purple silk gown, and he had white bangles. Below the bangles there were tattoos or markings on his skin; and he also had flat earrings of thin gold. His hair was done with some style. He could certainly have been expecting some schnapps, and perhaps a gift of money.

I was irritated with myself for being where I was. Pa-boh in his conversation had given all that I needed. I didn't need more. Twenty years before, in the Ivory Coast, in my dealings with magicians, I had understood that beyond a certain stage there was no place for simple inquirers; local magicians didn't understand. And it wasn't fair to them. Their faith mattered to them. They didn't like to think it might be mocked.

Pa-boh looked irritated too. He was irked by the presence of Richmond, who understood everything. But neither my irritation with myself, nor Pa-boh's with me, matched the irritation that the old chief in the lilac or purple gown (who understood that I was not a true believer) was exhibiting towards Pa-boh, who might have misled him about the visitor, might have appeared to promise some reward, and involved him in this waste of time, without even the likelihood of a bottle of schnapps at the end.

A curving wooden staircase led up from the ground floor. It led nowhere. There was no upper floor, only glimpses of rough brickwork and electric wires. I thought the staircase might have been inspired by something in a film and had been done to give an extra touch of grandeur to the palace, but Pa-boh said that they were going to create a space up there for 'archives'.

The men in the room began to look grumpy. They had good reason. They had expected me to come alone. The presence of Richmond upset them. Richmond had already begun to tell me what they were talking about. I felt all of this was adding to my get-away bill.

Pa-boh sensed that the situation was deteriorating. He decided to hurry things up. His demeanour changed. He gave a bow of great depth to the people in the room and addressed them. He explained who we were and what we wanted.

At every courtesy I felt myself sinking deeper and deeper.

There now appeared a tall man with light eyes and a strange paunch, high and round and stiff-looking. This man was the oracle-priest, the deputy to the high priest. He said nothing when he came in. He only drew up his legs on to his chair – he too, to my alarm, was barefooted – and looked at me in an assessing way.

I felt undermined. I thought we should leave. Our bill here – our *hongo*, so to speak (to use the nineteenth-century Ugandan word for a tax on travellers) – appeared to be going up and up. And Richmond, with all his cynicism, agreed.

When they tried to close the door of the palace, I said, 'No.'

I went to the door. It hadn't been locked. I made my way out; Richmond followed me. The iron gate at the front of the yard hadn't been closed. That was a bit of luck. Once we were out on the squalling street next to Pa-boh's car and the black water butts I felt free. We drove away, but not back to where we had come from. We followed the curve of the road in the other direction; and after a while we saw the other end of the green strip, the big shrine area, that had begun at the white palace.

We left Pa-boh to pick up the pieces. It wasn't fair, but it was something he could do, and do well. He thought of himself as a man possessed; important spiritual forces guided him.

Twice in the next week he left messages for me at the hotel.

8

AT THE END OF the year there was going to be a presidential election. Kojo took me to meet Nana, the man most likely to win. He was intelligent, full of charm and urbanity. His colour posters were everywhere in Accra.

There was another man, though, who couldn't be a candidate, because he had been president twice before and constitutionally couldn't run again. This man was Flight Lieutenant Jerry Rawlings. He had led two coups in two and a half years, nearly thirty years before, and had twice in that time returned the country to civilian rule. Later he had ruled Ghana for eighteen years. As revolutionary and ruler he would be a ghost-like presence at whatever new presidential feast was coming up.

There wasn't much about him in the newspapers, but he was there. Richmond's friends, when they spoke of this man, attributed extraordinary qualities to him; they said he was what the country needed; if he hadn't done all that he might have done during his eighteen years in power it was because 'bad' people surrounded him.

In this way Jerry Rawlings, even while he lived, with a pleasant house in Accra and another house in the country, was becoming mythical in Ghana, more mythical and more mysterious than Nkrumah could ever be; just as in Bengal in India in the late 1940s the nationalist Subhas Chandra Bose became mythical after his death: with many sightings reported, the man who could solve all the problems of Bengal and India, if only by some trick, some great act of faith, or prayer, or national penance, he could truly be returned to the living. It happens like this in some religions too: a great leader dies, and the grief generated by his loss turns to a widespread conviction that the great leader is not dead but only in 'occlusion', still watching from his new position on high, his vision greater than before.

The Rawlings story lent itself to myth. He was born in 1947, his mother Ghanaian, his father Scottish. He was a big and handsome man, and was the first man of mixed origin to become a political leader in Ghana. He had gone to good schools. Later he had joined the Ghana air force. He loved flying; he became a flight lieutenant. He came to power in a way that was full of romance and drama. As an air force officer he, greatly daring, had thrown in his luck with an anti-government coup. The coup had failed, and he was charged with treason. During his trial he made a remarkable speech about the corruption of the government. It was a brave thing to do; anything might have happened to him; institutions in Ghana, especially after Nkrumah, were still shaky. But in his speech he had spoken for much of the country; and his bravery on that day in court was his making as a politician. He was jailed on the treason charge, but he didn't stay long in jail. In the very next month some junior officers successfully brought about a coup. They freed Rawlings, and he declared himself head of state.

For four months after that he sought to cleanse the country of its bad elements among officials, army people, business people. He then returned the country to civilian rule. It was his romantic idea: if you cleaned a country up, it looked after itself. But people and countries were more complicated than he thought; and a year later he led another coup against the people he had placed in power. This time he stayed in charge. Nine years later he gave Ghana a new constitution. He served for two terms as a constitutional president, and then was voted out.

He had been out of office for eight years, but his myth still held. He was the man who had risked his career and perhaps life to serve the people. He had handed back power twice. If he had failed it was only because he had been surrounded by bad people.

I BEGAN TO think I should try to see him. I asked Kojo, who appeared to be able to do everything. But Kojo said he couldn't help in this matter; and I remembered that politically Kojo was on the other side. Other people were unwilling as well, and my time was getting short. I asked John Mitchell, the Trinidad consul; he said he could help, but he had to go away for a few days. I mentioned my difficulty to Richmond, the man with the unlikely Danish ancestor; and he (of course) at once said, 'My father and Rawlings are cousins. His mother is my father's auntie. This is why my father has dreams of being a politician.'

I think both requests – from John Mitchell and Richmond – got to Rawlings's office; but it was John Mitchell who, the day before I left, drove me to the Rawlings house for lunch.

The house was in an area of Accra known as the Ridge. It was well away from the centre. It had a big iron gate, and the shady compound had two big neem trees. There were a few other parked cars. A black poodle considered John Mitchell and me, but it didn't bark. Away from us, near the stairs to the raised house, a tall and powerfully built man in a loose white shirt was talking to a little group. He had his back to us. This, of course, was Rawlings, fitting every description of him that I had read.

I had a moment's hesitation, not knowing whether we should advance or wait. It was a brief moment, because almost at once a slender woman detached herself from the group and came towards us, waving and smiling. She would have been Mrs Rawlings: dark, fine-featured, striking in black slacks and a floral blouse. The earlier group began to leave, making for one of the cars parked below the neem trees. Rawlings came towards us. He was built like a boxer and he had reading glasses on the edge of his nose. We began to go up the steps to the raised house. Remarkably, at the side of the steps, among the plant pots, was a grey and white kitten, self-possessed, of great beauty. It was the first happy kitten I had seen in Ghana. Mrs Rawlings said it was a pet; they also had many dogs. I began to be prejudiced in favour of the house.

The sitting room was spacious and cool and comfortable.

There was an empty aquarium with plastic flowers on it, and there were family photographs on a wall: in one of them I recognised Rawlings as a young man. We sat down on leather sofas. He sat on the sofa next to mine, but within reach of me. He called me 'chief'. I thought it was his style; and it might have done away with the need to remember names.

He said – and it was like a puzzle, like a continuation of some of the things he had been talking about with the people before – 'Eight generals are executed just to prevent the country from sliding into chaos, but you do not take a man's life to do the same. I tried to rejuvenate this nation. This nation was ready to fly. Ghana was ready to fly. All we did was to empower the people. I say: give the people the right leadership, and they will deliver.'

He stood up and began walking up and down the room. He came back to me and tapped me on the knee and said, 'Chief, I want to tell you about language, how important it is. There is a spiritual quality to language, to words. If you use language as a tool to suppress the people it will lose all its spirituality. There is a special quality to the language of our ancestors, and we have lost that by having another language imposed on us. Our mother tongue has historical elements, and words were important.'

He was in an excited state and, like some intellectuals seeking to make an impression, he was laying down the subjects he wanted to talk about.

I said, to keep things going, 'But some people can have two languages.'

He said, 'Yes. But we are not going anywhere by having two or more languages. If we speak English we must learn to use it with its words. Once the language is spoken correctly it comes with its own spirituality. Language always evolves, but African is under threat. You attack their culture and tradition.'

He took off his glasses and looked hard at me. He said, 'Chief, let me tell you. In 1979, when I came to power, there were cases that had been in the courts for five to ten years. They were robed in the Latin language. I solved them in five to six days. Justice was given to the people.' He had begun to talk loudly. He stopped, as though he had lost his way among the many memories he had released.

(I was reminded of Pa-boh. He too had been taken up from obscurity and quite suddenly then had discovered his gifts of arbitration: in a few days he had solved for an important chief a dispute that had dragged on for seventeen years.)

Rawlings asked his wife, 'Where was I?'

She said, 'You were talking about justice.'

He slapped his knees. 'Ah. I remember. On one occasion, in the earlier part of the PNDC, angry people emerged as leaders. But as things calmed down respectable people found a place in it, and it became the NDC, the National Democratic Congress.' He was talking about old political wars. 'One of our areas was health and hygiene. I used to lead the people in cleaning campaigns. I went to a big open gutter in one village. It was full of filth and disease. I and my party wanted to give a social sense of responsibility by cleaning the gutter. It became clean and modern.'

He had begun again to talk loudly, booming across the room. And again he stopped. When he started up again he began to jump from topic to topic, as though looking for the right one. His wife looked at him (aware as she did so that we were looking at her), and so did two of his old political colleagues, a former minister and a lawyer, who had also been invited to the lunch and had come to the house before us. Rawlings stood up and told one of these men to tell us about language and its spiritual element. He then left the room, and his wife followed him.

His voice, and his undeniable presence, had filled the room, and now that he was out of it the room felt quiet and incomplete, although the former minister was trying to talk about language.

The house was well run. No word had been said but, to bridge the gap left by Rawlings and his wife, a well-dressed waiter appeared with coffee and fruit juice. I went to the lavatory. I saw the family dogs in two big paved cages at the back of the yard. One cage had small dogs. The other cage had big dogs, a Dalmatian and various hounds, all fine and well exercised and happy. While I watched I saw them fed by a servant who entered the cages with their food. I could have looked at the feeding scene for a long time.

I went back to the sitting room. After a few minutes Rawlings reappeared. He sat down energetically in his chair and, as though to get started again, called me chief. He gave me a flick on the knee and said, 'As a pilot I flew around the country, and I used to notice a green patch near every village. I never thought about it, but when I came into government I realised it was the compound of the village school. It was very clean. They were dirty in their homes, but clean in their schools. I go to a factory. It looks so clean. I beg them, I tell them, "Take this cleanliness to your homes. Why do you leave it here when you go home?" What can I do to revive this sense of responsibility?'

He leaned back, took a long breath, and said, 'Chief, let me give you one last example. In my last term in office the chaps in my castle' – some of the old castles and forts on the Atlantic coast had been turned into government offices – 'the chaps in my castle had proved troublesome in headquarters. I was very anxious. I thought: "What can I do to lower the temperature?" The culture of logic given us by the outside power was in the negative. The English word "sorry" would not have done. It was not good enough. I said, "Use the traditional way." Down here when people want to apologise sincerely they wake you very early in the morning. I made my chaps go early in the morning, and it worked.'

Someone in France had asked him whether it wasn't the uniform that kept him in power. He had said it wasn't the uniform; it was the quality of integrity.

He was talking about the rights of the people when Mrs Rawlings came in and in a nice clear voice said, 'Lunch.'

We looked at her, but Rawlings went on talking about the difference between power and moral authority. Mrs

Rawlings said with some firmness that we should move, and we did, moving first into a corridor, and then into the splendid dining room where the table could seat fourteen. It was laid with fine bone china. The food was Chinese and Ghanaian: yams and meat and goat stew, with some fish. It was an absolute feast. There were no place settings. Mrs Rawlings made me sit next to her. Everybody else had to fend for himself. John Mitchell, the Trinidad consul, silent all the while, came at last into his own. He couldn't conceal his pleasure at seeing the meat stew and the steaming yams. But Rawlings outdid him in pleasure and zest.

We talked about names. Mrs Rawlings said she had been given an Ashanti name by her father – she was, in fact, an Ashanti princess – and that had caused a certain amount of trouble when, in the fifth class, she had to be confirmed as a Christian. She was asked by her Sunday school teacher about her Christian name. She had no idea what the teacher meant. The teacher persevered: was she Esther, Veronica, Mary, Ruth? She said she had only the name she had. The teacher said she was to stay out of the class until she could show her baptism certificate; she could not be confirmed otherwise.

She telephoned her father. He was enraged. The very next day he came from Kumasi and took her to the headmaster of Achimota. He had the baptism certificate but refused to show it. He said his daughter was baptised with an African name and was going to be confirmed with that name. The headmaster agreed.

Someone at the table asked how Rawlings and his wife had met.

She said they had been childhood sweethearts. Rawlings, full of food at this stage, and now reaching for a dish of Chinese noodles, said, 'Nonsense. It took me nine years just to hold your hand. She was an Ashanti princess. While I was from the ghetto.' He looked up. 'A nobody.'

'Well,' she said, 'you did come to wash our car.'

He laughed, and the moment passed.

FOUR

The Forest King

HOUPHOUËT-BOIGNY had been the enduring president of the Ivory Coast, loved by the French, adored by his people: a man so enduring he could be called a king.

Richmond had heard a marvellous story from his aunt about the way Houphouët had prepared himself for his life of power. Houphouët, in this story, had had a consultation with a great shaman or witchdoctor. Following the advice of this remarkable man, Houphouët had had himself cut into little pieces, and these pieces had been boiled together with some magical herbs in a cooking pot. In that cooking pot at a critical moment the Houphouët pieces had come together and turned into a powerful snake that had to be wrestled to the ground by a trusted helper. The snake had then turned into Houphouët again. The story had a reliable witness: the trusted and powerful helper who had wrestled the snake to the ground. She was Richmond's aunt, and had been Nkrumah's cook, no less: Nkrumah the first president of independent Ghana, and one of the great men of modern Africa.

What Richmond had told me would have been told – in various versions – to tens of thousands in the country. It was not disrespectful, as might have been thought; it was by such supernatural or magical tales that the ruler's myth was kept alive among his people.

It was a tale for believers. I was not a believer. I fell at the first hurdle. In this fairytale the cutting up of the great man was too easy. He was like a worm, soft and uniform in texture; he could be sliced. No bones or muscle or delicate organs met the knife; there was no blinding spurt of blood. Richmond (who had a Danish ancestor) didn't look for that kind of detail. What was important for Richmond was that the witchdoctor's prescription had worked. Everywhere in Africa there was change, often bloody change. But Houphouët had ruled for life. Towards the end he had been challenged, but he had seen his challengers off. He had remained father of his people, a grand old man, *le vieux*.

He died at the age of eighty-eight. This was his official age; he was believed by many to be much older. His great age was further proof of his fetish-given power. He was said to have died on an important political anniversary. But no one in the country at large knew for sure. The private life of the ruler, the king, was always a mystery.

The royal compound was in the middle of the town of Yamoussoukro. This town was built around the site of Houphouët's natal village. A chief's village, but it would originally (before the French) have been close to bush. The compound was now surrounded by a high ochre-coloured wall nine miles long and was closed to ordinary visitors.

From the outside you could see something like a young wood behind the wall. Heaven knows what secret rituals, what sacrifices, served by heaven knows what secret priest-hoods, contrived to keep the king and his kingdom safe, at a time when nothing in Africa seemed solid.

Far away from the royal compound, at two different points in the new town which he had built, were mighty emblems of the imported faiths: a beautiful white mosque in the North African style, a style that had had to cross the Sahara to this far-off place in the wet forests of tropical Africa; and a cathedral that in its design paid homage to St Peter's. It was said to be higher than St Peter's (in spite of the pope's request that its dome might be shortened by a metre or two). This was more than cross-cultural town-building. Mosque and cathedral, growing out of no com-munities, might have seemed like a game in the desert, the whim of a rich ruler looking for foreign approval. But they were seriously meant. Religion mattered to Houphouët; it was what kept him afloat; he would have felt, almost, that he ruled because he was religious. It pleased him, in his expensive new town, to honour these two world faiths, even while yielding to the profounder African stirrings which might have been played out in private rituals, meant for the king alone, in the royal compound, beyond the moat with its sacred crocodiles, fed at great expense every day.

Richmond had said that Houphouët's magic had worked for him. And so it had. Power had stayed with him to the end. But even a king was only a man, and when his time had come Houphouët had died from prostate cancer.

Twenty-seven years before, when I had first gone to the Ivory Coast, I had been told by someone at the local university that when a great ruler died, his servants or slaves had to take care to run, because they might be buried with their master. The academic who told me this seemed to think it funny. He was an African who was proud of African traditions, but in his African way he thought domestic slaves were also funny. Telling me about the dangers to slaves at the time of the master's death, he had clapped his big palms together and then used them to make a swift rubbing gesture, a gesture of comedy, to indicate the slave's need for flight.

I heard this time, what I had not heard before, that there were servants of such extreme loyalty they would have wanted to die with their master. They would have thought of that death as a final service. But no one knew what had happened here at Houphouët's death. The ochre walls and the palace behind, with the wood or forest, kept their secret. From a foreign (but well-placed) source I heard that 'hundreds' had been killed at Houphouët's funeral – not necessarily slaves or servants, but people picked up outside, wanderers or vagrants who would not be missed.

There were still crocodiles in the moat or lake outside the palace wall. Houphouët had introduced those crocodiles, and in 1982 they were still sufficiently new for their feeding at dusk to be one of the sights of the town. A tall man with a red cap and a long white priestly gown came out of the palace gate and made his way between the rail outside the wall and the moat. He brought chopped-up meat in a plastic bucket, a number of trussed white chickens, and he carried a long thin knife. He ran the dark limber blade between the metal uprights of the rail at the edge of the water. It made a scraping, clacking sound. This was the signal to the crocodiles that it was feeding time, and they swam towards the two or three big rocks, like places for basking, that were just next to the rail and the white-gowned feeder.

The meat in the bucket was thrown to them; some of it went to the meat-eating turtles that could be seen swimming below the surface of the water. It was the turn then of the chickens. The spectators on the causeway between the public road and the palace, or at the water's edge between the rail and the palace wall, gave little gasps of horror. The crocodiles with their apparently smiling eyes snapped their jaws. It wasn't always a neat kill. The crocodile's jaws were too rigidly hinged; they couldn't swivel or turn; and the chickens appeared to escape. But not for long. A few more snaps of the jaws, a small adjustment of the body, and the chicken that had appeared to get away could be seen as a mash of white feathers in the maw of the crocodile.

In 1982 I had seen this ritual at sunset, the proper time. Now, twenty-seven years later, I went in the middle of the day; I couldn't wait for sunset. I remembered a planting of young coconut trees on both sides of the causeway across the lake. Coconut trees grow fast. I had expected those I had seen to be tall and beginning to be spindly. But they were not tall; perhaps the trees I had seen had been replaced; or perhaps the fetid water of the lake or moat had stunted their growth.

Perhaps the same fetid water had done away with the meat-eating turtles. I had seen them clearly in 1982, coming for their meat, swimming below the surface of the light-brown water, showing their underside, strong and silent and agile, more disturbing in a way than the crocodiles. Now in the dark water they were not to be seen. Perhaps it was this bad water that was going to do away with this ritual of Houphouët's kingship, slowly killing or choking the crocodiles that survived. (Though I was told later that crocodiles, rising to the surface to breathe, could survive fetid water.) There was a baby crocodile, pale, two or three feet long, away from the others, resting out of the water on a concrete pier of the causeway.

In ancient Egypt the crocodile was a sacred animal; most people here looked upon it as food. In Indian mythology the earth rests on a turtle's back. Some instinct, or the wisdom of some shaman, had led the old king to do honour to these creatures of ancient awe. But few people now, in 2009, were looking for the crocodiles in the water, though they were easy to see. Few people were present. Some young men and a strange young begging woman, possibly disturbed, passed by. The woman had a wild look in her eyes; she was more interested in the visitor than in the crocodiles. The young men were more interested in the silver helicopter which appeared over the town and seemed to be making for the presidential palace behind the ochre walls.

The guard on the causeway (he was there to keep unauthorised people away) said that the president was arriving that day, and of course he meant the new president that had come to the Ivory Coast after all the troubles that had befallen country since the death of Houphouët.

The Romans decreed godhood for quite a few of their early emperors. But the Romans, when they made Augustus a god, also had the good sense to create a school of priests to serve the new cult. These priests of Augustus would have been people of good social standing; that, rather than piety or priestly knowledge, would have been the most important requirement. The cult wouldn't have survived the turbulence of the next two centuries; and it would have disappeared with Christianity. I doubt whether the fact of its demise, the pointlessness of its once proud school of priests, would have been recorded.

It was possible now in the Ivory Coast to wonder how much longer a cult set up – over so many years and at such expense – by Houphouët would survive, and what form its forgetting would take.

In my hotel in Abidjan, the capital, there was a United Nations man who was doing work on epidemics. Epidemics were strange things, he said. In the beginning they swept everything before them; later, for no discernible reason, the virus or disease moderated. This had happened with syphilis. It was as though the virus feared that if it killed everybody it would destroy itself, since it would have no one to infect. Something like this seemed to have happened with Houphouët's crocodiles. They were no longer feared; people lived more easily with the idea of the thing, which as a result appeared to lose its power.

In any event the ritual could hardly survive its founder. It was built around his need. And it was as though with his death much of Houphouët's grandeur had disappeared into thin air. The airport still carried his name; so did the big orange-coloured stadium on the edge of the lagoon in Abidjan, and the stadium was also hung with a very big photograph of the man. But something like bad magic was about to befall that stadium. Some weeks after I left the Ivory Coast there was a calamity during the football match against Malawi. A wall fell (too many people perhaps); the police for some reason fired tear gas at the panicking crowd; and in the mêlée sixty-nine people died. It would not be easy for Houphouët's name to recover. Already, even before that tragedy, people were ready to speak less reverentially about the king and were ready at the same time to dismiss as Togolese the rituals that had once been used to perpetuate the rule of the crocodile master. (Houphouët's wife came from Togo.)

2

IN 1982, when the crocodiles and the meat-eating turtles were the draw in Yamoussoukro, the cathedral existed only in outline, with the dome (intended to be higher than the dome of St Peter's) only a few curving lines in metal. There was nothing more to see. Now the cathedral was what visitors were taken to Yamoussoukro to see. It was, indeed, a creation, beautiful and unexpected and staggering. It echoed St Peter's in its dome and its tall outside columns. In some accounts it had cost three hundred million dollars; in some it had cost four hundred million; and there were vain local people who said, boastfully, but without truth, that it had bankrupted the country.

The steps to the plinth were of white marble from Italy, and the floor there was a Roman design in coloured marble. Below the famous dome the strong tropical glare was softened by very tall French stained-glass windows in blue and purple that ran from the floor to the dome. At the far end was a copy of Bernini's baldaquin in St Peter's (which had itself been partly made from bronze impiously stripped from the ancient Roman Pantheon, a full fifteen hundred years after Hadrian's reconstruction of the burnt-out original). A notice asked pilgrims and visitors to be silent: we were in a house of God.

It was quite desolate outside. The columns of the porch framed extensive flat gardens: shrubs trimmed low to fill a European-style design. Various comparisons came to mind. It could have been a pastiche somewhere in the United States. For its costliness – and thoroughness – it could have been Houphouët's Taj Mahal.

The architect had left out a device whereby cleaners or their brooms could have got up to the coffered ceiling between the high columns of the porch. Cleaners couldn't get up, but tropical spiders could: they had begun to create noticeable brown webs up there. Elsewhere, between one column of the porch and the outer skin of the dome a fair-sized piece of stucco had fallen off, revealing the metal armature. Much complicated scaffolding would be needed before that could be put right; perhaps it never would be. It was possible that this was how it would be nibbled away, this piece of vainglory of the forest king. A woman guide said that on Sundays up to nine hundred people came for the services. This might have been so; but until the government moved the capital the hundred and fifty miles from Abidjan to Yamoussoukro (as was projected) there could be no rooted community in the forest town. Even then there would be much to do. Hidden from the cathedral and its gardens were moraines of uncollected garbage that lay in all the streets of the town: Africa reclaiming its own.

3

AS MUCH AS on his magic Houphouët's rule had depended on the support of the French. In 1982 there was a French army base amid the coconut trees near the airport; and in many places in the Ivory Coast there were French people helping to keep Houphouët's show on the road. The French were welcomed as investors and they were glad to come since they could repatriate ninety per cent of their profits. They ran the restaurants and they ran them well, giving the Ivory Coast its reputation for fine French food. There was an official word for these French guests who helped to create the illusion that this African state, unlike its neighbours, was on the move. The word was *co-opérants*; it can best be translated as 'helpers'.

Even if one knew nothing about political situation one could be worried about this French presence. It seemed that a crisis was being prepared, and after Houphouët's death the crisis came: a very involved business, as crises in small places tend to be, not easy for an outsider to disentangle. There was a many-sided civil war: people of the country against black immigrants from the neighbouring poorer countries, a tribal war with the French on one side, with the French then retaliating against hostile Africans, and finally Africans against the French, so that yet another aspect of Houphouët's legacy vanished. The day came in 2004 when gangs of black men roamed the streets of Abidjan looking for white people to kill.

There was, as it happened, a survivor of that day staying in the hotel. She was not white; she was of mixed descent, with an African mother and a French father; and she had a black husband. She had gone on that bad day in 2004 to fetch her children from school. A black crowd surrounded her car and pulled her out. Some instinct of self-preservation made her say she was Moroccan, and not half French. She looked Moroccan; perhaps she had been told that before, and now she said it to the crowd, and it saved her. Morocco, perhaps because of its good airline, popular with Africans, has a fair reputation in this part of Africa.

When she told the story she tapped a finger of her right hand on her pale left hand. She said, 'They were looking for white skin.'

She had lived all her life in the Ivory Coast. So the experience had undermined her in many ways. It had given her such severe 'palpitations' that her black husband, a diplomat, had taken her out of the country for some years. She was now back in the Ivory Coast, but the country still made her uneasy. She still feared the sight of a crowd of black men.

But black crowds couldn't now be avoided. One Sunday there was to be an African football championship match in Abidjan, in the great orange stadium, named for Houphouët, which lay between the hotel and the lagoon. The Ivory Coast was going to play Zambia. Entrance was free. The match was going to start at four in the afternoon, but from five on Sunday morning people had begun to gather. The stadium had various entrances, far and near. Soon the crowd at each entrance made an unmoving mass; perhaps they didn't move because the stadium wasn't open. They looked picturesque, something for a painter of crowds, an African Canaletto: a stippling of black faces, jeans, and tee shirts orange, white or red.

At some time in mid-morning a few people appeared on some of the uncovered seats of the stadium, to the left, which I could see from my hotel window. Those people were going to wait for six hours for the match. The seats would have been hot enough already, and the great heat of the day was to come. I expected the waiting crowd now to move slowly into the stadium, but it didn't happen like that. It wasn't possible from my hotel room to understand all the movements of the crowd. From time to time, as the start of the match drew near, the riot police charged sections of the crowd; it was like a game. The charged crowd ran away in various directions. The stippling effect broke up, and what had looked picturesque became frightening. And then, quite quickly, the crowd re-formed.

The 'Moroccan' lady had seen the crowds. Later she said, 'I *hate* football.'

The Ivory Coast lost to Zambia that Sunday. The local people couldn't be generous to the winners, after the hours of waiting, the heat, and the occasional trouble with the police. It was easy to understand their frustration. Football released great passions here. Houphouët's stadium was orange-coloured. Orange was the colour of the national side. Six weeks later, when Ivory Coast was playing Malawi, and winning, a wall in the stadium fell down and sixty-nine people died.

4

ABIDJAN had grown so much I had trouble thinking back to the town I had known in 1982. I had stayed then in the Forum Hotel. No one seemed to know about it now. I remembered an open field across the road where fat baobab trees grew. I remembered the lagoon, like the sea, outside one of the hotel's public rooms; in the heat of the afternoon the algae-covered water rocked and it was then like an undulating green carpet. I remembered a general feeling of openness. There was nothing like that now; all those memories seemed to have been swallowed up by time itself. Two days before I left, a taxi-driver, showing me the sights, took me to the Golf Hotel. It was set, stylishly, a little way from the busy road and the lagoon was at its back. It would have been the old Forum, re-made in the image of over-peopled Africa, with a new kind of staff and a new kind of clientele.

Houphouët, promoting his town of Yamoussoukro, had built an autoroute to it from Abidjan. A hundred and fifty miles, mainly bush: at the time it had seemed part of the vainglory and general wastefulness of Yamoussoukro. But the autoroute was now in use, beaten up in parts, a short stretch replaced by a red-dirt road (tree branches on the asphalt announcing the diversion), and it was now the main thoroughfare for heavy trucks from the north and the countries to the north, bringing supplies to Abidjan.

Between Abidjan and Yamoussoukro the land is ravaged. For a hundred and fifty miles the tropical woodland or forest has been cut down and replaced by patches of petty planting: banana, knotty cassava (introduced to Africa by the Portuguese): the subsistence food of people who are not yet a peasantry. They make scratchings in the bush; these scratchings may develop into a village of grass and mud and mats (for the roof), and that village might turn into something more durable, of concrete and tin.

The pressure on the land is great; the migrants never stop coming down from the poor and arid north. From the days of Houphouët and the French there is a myth of the blessedness of the lush Ivory Coast where no one need starve. Needs are small; there isn't the time or space to think of grandeur. But, in spite of the myth, it is possible that in that ravaged, once-forested land they will one day be hungry. For people to aim at grandeur they must have a picture of grandeur in their minds. Houphouët didn't provide this. His rhetorical buildings were part of the private magic that served him alone.

The land has suffered much. The Ivory Coast – land of ivory beside Ghana's land of gold – is now without the elephants that by their death provided the ivory of their tusks. There are two cruel elephant monuments in Abidjan – one of a female elephant with her calf (elephants are food in this part of Africa), and a tall awkward obelisk composed (wickedly) of elephant tusks alone. Many small hands got rid of the mighty elephants, and many little scratchings have surely destroyed the great forest.

In another direction – east of Abidjan, to Bingerville – the idea of landscape has been undone or certainly hidden by line upon line of inelegant small houses. I remembered the road to Bingerville as a road through country, almost wilderness. Now it belongs to the developers; and the wretchedness of Abidjan encroaches.

Bingerville is named for Binger, a French governor of the Ivory Coast. And there is so little of history and architecture here in this former French colony that Binger's house, said to be a great house, is promoted as one of the sights. It is far from being a great house. There are a score of grander public and private buildings in a small place like Trinidad, on the other side of the Atlantic; and Binger's house is now, more appropriately, an orphanage: Africa drowning in the fecundity of its people.

In Ghana, just next door, with the same kind of people and climate and vegetation, the British (as they did elsewhere in the empire) created a botanical garden, which still more or less stands, with a few local intrusions. Next to Binger's house there is said to be a botanical garden. On the outer wall, freshly distempered, an enormous sign, newly done over in fancifully shaded letters at least two feet high, says that there is a garden. All that is missing is the garden.

After two short lines of ancient and very fat bamboo clumps, dead and grey in the centre, then yellow, then streaky green – clearly from the original garden, and they still cast a pleasant shade, bamboo's great virtue in the tropics – after this there is nothing, only bush and a few mildewed concrete buildings. But the guides still want to show you the gardens and the plants.

When they give up they tell you that destruction came to the botanical gardens of Bingerville during the troubles, the many little wars that undid the country when Houphouët left it. So the developer's landscape that disfigures what might have been beautiful hills between Abidjan and Bingerville, and these tragic gardens might also be said to be part of the legacy of Houphouët, who allowed the French to keep the country going, while practising magic for himself, wasting the substance of his country, building religiously, like a pharaoh – Shelley's Ozymandias again.

The land is full of cruelty which is hard for the visitor to bear. From the desert countries to the north long-horned cattle are sent for slaughter here in big ramshackle trucks, cargoes of misery, that bump along the patched and at times defective autoroute to Abidjan, to the extensive abattoir area near the docks. And there in trampled and vile black earth these noble creatures, still with dignity, await their destiny in the smell of death, with sometimes a calf, all alone, without a mother, finding comfort of a sort in sleep, a little brown circle on the dirty ground, together with the beautiful goats and sheep assembled for killing. The ground around the abattoir goes on and on. When sights like this meet the eyes of simple people every day there can be no idea of humanity, no idea of grandeur.

5

IT WAS PART OF the wisdom of the country that nature here was bountiful and unfailing; it was what brought the immigrants. Part of the bounty of nature were the bats. For half an hour or so every day in the late afternoon the bats came, flying low, just outside the windows of taller build-ings. They speckled the sky. One million bats would have made a memorable show, but prodigal Nature provided four or five millions, at least. The bats flew in a circle over the city. They had no fixed destination. They roosted on trees, hanging upside down within the pale-pink protection of their wings, which they folded around themselves with an almost human gesture. The trees from which they hung were damaged at the top, half stripped.

Africans eat everything that Nature provides (except

when a particular animal is the totem of a tribe or clan). The local people liked eating these bats. The main trouble was in getting them down. Some people used slingshots, and then there was the trouble of cooking the creatures. The bats were tough (all that flying) and had to be cooked for hours before they became acceptable.

It might have been thought that with all that flying some hundreds of bats would have dropped dead every evening and fallen from the sky to a grateful people. But no one had seen such a thing, a bat dead on the ground. And I was told by someone (perhaps not an expert) that when bats had to die they did not show themselves, but hid away, being in this like cats, who could leave their houses and go away to die.

This, however, was a luxury few of the cats of the Ivory Coast could enjoy. No cats wandered the streets here. Cats were eaten; they were part of the bounty of Nature, and they could be reared to be killed. 'Like chickens,' the youngish man said, and the comparison amused him.

It was only on the last morning of my stay, on my way to the airport, that I found out what was the best way in the Ivory Coast of killing a cat or kitten. You put them in a sack of some sort, and then you dropped the sack in a pot of boiling water.

The thought of this everyday kitchen cruelty made everything else in the Ivory Coast seem unimportant.

Then, a few days later, when I was in Gabon, I learned more about the bats of Abidjan. They were fruit bats; they were also known as flying foxes. And they were not as innocent as they sounded. They, or their fleas, were carriers of the contagious Ebola virus. The victims bled helplessly till they died. No one knew for sure how the virus jumped from bat to man; but a good guess was that the virus was transmitted by the eating of the bat. So the darkening of the Abidjan sky at dusk was not only part of the visual drama of West Africa: it was like a plague waiting to fall on the men below.

FIVE

Children of the Old Forest

GUY ROSSATANGA-RIGNAULT, a lawyer and an academic, a former dean of the university of Gabon, said, 'The new religions, Islam and Christianity, are just on the top. Inside us is the forest.'

In another country it would have sounded too poetic and mystical, too imprecise, someone trying to cover up for a backward country. But Rossatanga wasn't like that; and in Gabon his words had meaning. Gabon, as big as Britain in area, with a population of less than two million, was an equatorial land of river and forest. It was hot; it steamed; it was malarial. From the air, as you came down to the airport, the shiny river-estuary and sea seemed about to overwhelm everything else. The forest near the capital was secondary, with plantings of oil palm that spoke of awful labour and heat. A little way inland the true forest began, primal and tall and tight. The tufted land, green with tints of the palest yellow, became hilly. The cloud shadows didn't fall flat here, as on the sea; they fell unevenly; and these jagged up-and-down shadows helped you to imagine the contours of the land below the forest canopy.

The French were unwilling colonists. They staked out their territory in the 1840s. Just thirty years later, after their defeat in the Franco-Prussian war, they felt they didn't have the resources, and wanted to call the whole expensive business off. They actually sent a ship to take their people away. The missionaries, though, refused to leave, and the colony survived. River traffic developed. The great French-Italian explorer Brazza, starting from the river Oguwé, shifting to a tributary, and then continuing on land, was within four days of sighting the mighty Congo River.

With the establishment of the colony there began the logging, the cutting down of the primal forest. It has never stopped, and yet after more than a century it doesn't really show. Perhaps it will soon. Thirty-year permits have been granted to the Chinese, the Malaysian, and the Japanese. They are more ruthless and better equipped than the people who went before, and at the end of their licences there will almost certainly be patches of desert in what was once forest. An international expert says that in a very short while thirty per cent of the forest of Gabon – the focus for centuries of Gabonese love and religious awe – will go. The good news, from the same expert, is that there may be some kind of international action (some form of subsidy, perhaps) that will make it worthwhile for the Gabonese to leave their forests standing. In the meantime, even with the areas of loss, the forests of Gabon are still one of the great sights of the world.

ROSSATANGA-RIGNAULT, an attractive man in his forties, was of mixed ancestry, as his double name suggested. His father was French, his mother African. He was educated in Gabon and in Paris. But, like many people of mixed ancestry here, he appeared to be embracing the African side of his inheritance. He didn't speak a great deal about his father; and he had married an African woman from the Ivory Coast. When he first came to see me he was at the end of his university day (he was a very busy man) and he was in his university clothes, a grey double-breasted suit. He was more relaxed the next time. He came with his two children and was informally dressed in a long West African gown decorated at the neck. This kind of gown was not Gabonese wear, and I imagined he was wearing it in tribute to his Ivory Coast wife. I thought the grey suit became him better.

When he was going to school Gabon was rich enough (from oil) to be a welfare state. His parents, as he said, had to pay only for the school bag. Everything else was free. There was even pocket money for the children when they got to the secondary stage. Every Wednesday the children lined up for a quinine tablet and milk to help the quinine down. Even the university education in Paris was free. And when Rossatanga married in Paris, the Gabon government paid for his wife's fare to Gabon, even though she was from the Ivory Coast.

He was a lawyer by profession and thought of himself as a political scientist. At the university of Gabon he also taught political anthropology. It was through these latter studies, no doubt, that he came to his poetic understanding of the place of the forest in the Gabonese mind.

It wasn't always like that. His mother was a civil servant and he was born in a hospital in the town. When he was three he was taken to the forest. It was a great opportunity to learn the ways of the forest, but he was too young to see it like that. The forest was frightening; it is frightening even now, although in the family house they have a generator. In the forest night falls very quickly. It is dark by seven; by eight you go to sleep; and you wake up at five. The darkness is dense. To understand the vision of the people of Gabon, you have to understand the forest.

'When darkness comes to the forest there is no sound. But at night there are different sounds or noises that come from animals hunting. The night plus the noises make up our mentality, because people are linked to everything in the forest. Thunder isn't just thunder, as it is for you. It is the voice of God: try to understand that. In our village the most terrifying creature is the owl. We are frightened of the owl because it is a manifestation of evil. If you are out walking and you see an owl it is a very bad omen. And this country of ours is a specific place. Our village is in the mouth of the river, and even if we take a car we will get nowhere, because of the water and the condition of the roads. It is a primeval area. The forest will always break out, always win. There is a place called Loango Lodge.

You should see it. It is heaven, an Eden. On the land you will see elephants. From the same place you will see whales and dolphins in the sea. When you see that place you will understand why I say that this land was not meant for humans. It is for the animals. It is very hard to survive in the forest. You cannot farm here. You might not have noticed it, but we have no cattle. Put these things together and you will understand why this country, which is half the size of France, has such a small population. Malaria, sleeping sickness, and the hot climate.'

The French, fine engineers though they were, never built roads here. There was too much rain, too much water; it washed everything away. The French concentrated on air travel. The first railway was built in 1981 by independent Gabon; it was very expensive, and it was done against the advice of the World Bank.

I asked Rossatanga, 'What is it like physically in the forest?'

He said with extraordinary passion, 'It is like a *wall*. At fifty feet you cannot see, as it is so dense and thick. Your vision is limited by the forest and everyone of us in the forest is *small*. I'll say it again: this land was not made for humans. You have to fight to survive. You don't know what will get you even in the river. It could be a croc, a water snake, or something living there. God knows what else is there.'

'How does this affect your belief?'

'We feel that everything has life, even trees. There is a mystical tree, a red tree. When we go to the forest we talk to it and tell it our problems. We also ask its permission to cut its branch or bark, and we tell the tree why we are taking its bark, why we are cutting it. You *must* tell the tree. All tribes have totems here, and that totem is taboo for them. They can never kill or harm their totem. They can never hunt it. It can be a crocodile, parrot, monkey, anything.'

Because the conditions of life are so hard, everyone in Gabon believes in the forest and in the principle of 'energy' that the forest exemplifies. This is the principle that keeps people going. To lose energy is to fade away. To revive is to get new energy from some source.

Rossatanga said, 'Every living thing is energy. Every one of us is like a battery. In our version of the world even the animals are batteries. That is why we believe there is no such thing as a natural death. If someone dies in the family we know that someone has taken his energy. To do that you have to kill the victim, be it man or animal. You kill and take their energy. We also go to the witchdoctor to take someone's energy. This is why it sometimes happens that people feel they have to do a ritual sacrifice. We are a matrilineal society. We take our mother's name, and our mother's elder brother is the big man in the family. He is so powerful that if a nephew dies people in the family suspect the uncle. They think that he wanted his nephew's energy.'

Rossatanga's first experience of the supernatural – linked to the overwhelmingness of the forest – occurred when he was five. It was in his grandmother's village, a traditional village, as he says. He had gone there for his circumcision rite. That was 'imperative', a rite of passage to manhood. Whatever formal – Christian – religion the family professed, there were these old African ways that had to be honoured and perhaps were more pressing than the formal outer faith.

One day during this visit to his grandmother's village he went with his mother to a 'plantation' – something much smaller than the English word: a family allotment, a vegetable patch. His mother was not familiar with the way, and when they were going back to the house they became lost. They came to a clearing. It was a cemetery, but they didn't know. There they saw something very strange: four monkeys sitting with red bands tied to their foreheads. Red is a powerful colour in Gabon. (Only three colours are known: red, black and white.) Eventually they found their way back to the house. His mother told the villagers what she had seen. The villagers said that what they had seen were not monkeys, but ghosts.

Rossatanga said, 'I wanted to get away from the village.'

But the supernatural began now to force itself on him. A long time afterwards he went to his mother's village with an American friend, the son of a foreign friend of his parents. This friend was prospecting for oil in Gabon. When they got to the village a man told them not to throw litter or in any way pollute the stream that ran by the village. A spirit or jinn lived there and didn't like the stream to be polluted. The American said it was black magic and nonsense and to prove his point he spat in the stream.

Rossatanga said, 'Ten minutes later there was no water there, and there was a hue and cry. The village was up in arms, we had to do a lot through the local traditional man to placate the jinn or spirit. We spent a lot of money, and after many ceremonies or rituals the water came back just as quickly as it had vanished.'

So in spite of his ancestry and his Paris education, his analytical mind, and in spite of his fierce rationality in other fields, Rossatanga had become a believer in the magic of the forest and, like other believers, had many stories to prove his point.

He said, 'There is another jinn of this sort in Lambaréné.' Famous as the site of the Schweitzer hospital. 'It lived in the river. You needed a ferry to cross that river and the government decided to build a bridge. The old people in the area warned the engineers about the jinn and told them they should ask the jinn's permission first. The engineers, who were Dutch, just laughed and carried on. Every day a worker died. People became very frightened, and even the engineers thought they should stop the work. They said they would bring an exorcist along with the local witchdoctor to placate the jinn. They went and brought a traditional doctor and he performed many rituals, and they were finally allowed to build the bridge. I believe these forest spirits are linked to the psyche of our people even if they live in the city. This is one reason why the American evangelical churches have been so successful here. They also invoke the Lord's spirit to remove the devil. This is like what we do when we go to the witchdoctor to remove the devil. The principle is the same. The common ground is the spirit.'

I asked him if he could define the religion of the forest more closely.

He said, in a precise academic way, 'We cannot call it a religion. It is a set of beliefs. We don't pray to God because in our understanding God is not accessible to humans. It [he meant the idea of God] has many other problems and has no time for humans.'

In forest belief the organic world, the world that mattered, was like a pyramid. 'The first level are the minerals and ore, the second level are the trees and flora, and the third level are the animals. The fourth level are the human beings.'

If it had stopped there it would have sounded like a version of the Elizabethan chain of being. But he went on, and it soon became clear that this concept was a local one.

He said, 'In the human beings you have divisions. Children are spiritually stronger than the middle-aged, who are useless and blind. The elderly, like the children, are spiritually strong because they are about to go to the new place. Children are strong because they have just come from the new place. They are pure and still have the sight. They can sense evil as they have an open mind. Sometimes they cry because they see too much, and then you have to take them to a strong traditional master. He places a stone on their forehead to stop the sight, but you have to be very careful, because too much of the stone can turn the child into an idiot. As for the old, they are special because they have power and they are close to the ancestors. Only the ancestors can intercede with God. You have to keep the bones and skull of your ancestor and feed it rum and talk to it when you are in trouble.'

This was what Rossatanga himself did. So in this matter at least he was not talking with the distance of the anthropologist.

He said, 'Before leaving the village I go and put alcohol and food on my mother's grave and my grandfather's grave.'

I liked him for saying that. Were there other ways of worshipping the ancestor?

He said, 'Every family has an elder who can talk to the ancestor. There is one man in every family chosen for the job. This elder keeps the bones and skull. The way to worship is through initiation. Initiation is a fundamental rite and practice.'

I had heard much about initiation. Everybody in Gabon talks about it, or so it seems. It requires a master, an all-night ceremony with dancing and drumming, and eating the bitter root of a hallucinogenic plant, the *eboga*. The rite is secret, and even at the end of my time in Gabon, I didn't feel I had begun to understand the idea or importance of initiation.

I wanted to know whether in this ritual of honouring the ancestor there was also contained the idea of virtue, the good life.

Rossatanga said, 'No. The ancestors are there only to

provide answers for your problems and give you what you want.' And about initiation he said, 'You have no say in the village or its matters until you are initiated. To be recognised as a man you have to be circumcised in the village. And that itself is a ritual. You take the child's foreskin and bury it in the ground. Then you plant a banana tree or sucker. This is the boy's banana, and you watch it grow. When it gives its first fruit there is a big ceremony, since the banana is a sexual symbol of the boy's manhood. The boy will eat the first banana, and the rest of the fruit is rubbed all over his body. No woman must be nearby or see this ceremony.'

I asked him, 'Are you saying that if you follow the various rituals you need not be afraid of the forest?'

'You remain afraid. Initiation and ritual only give you a path through the forest. You are not protected against others, women especially. Women are very important in this society. They are the real power. A woman may not exercise power, but she gives it to her son. We are a matrilineal society, and women give life. This country was not made for men. Women's bodies are stronger, and so they are witches. There are many ritual sacrifices where the eyes are removed and tongues torn out of living victims. Every day there is a ritual sacrifice. White skin is very prized here, and for that reason I cannot let my light-skinned children out in the evening.'

'What is the importance of the tongue?'

He said, 'They remove the tongue to get energy.'

'What do you think about that?'

'There is no name. It is too shocking.'

It was a relief to hear him say that. He had spoken of 'energy' in such a positive way I thought he might have been more accepting.

He said, 'Power is everything. It is always sought out. There is a lot of rural migration and so you have many forest people living in the cities. During elections you have to be very careful because of ritual sacrifice. You have to go every day to pick your children up from school. I was twenty-five when I did my Ph.D., and they think because I am a lawyer and successful and work late into the night I am a wizard and in a secret society. At night normal people sleep! They will think that you are a wizard too. And so far as the president is concerned, he is the king of kings of the wizards.'

'When the forest gets thinner, with the logging, will these forest ideas fade or change?'

'Maybe. But I'm not sure. People who have not gone to a village for twenty years still have the same mindset. It is still a forest mind. It is a challenge, and I'm not sure that we will win. You will see people here in Libreville splashing about in the sea. But, generally, Gabonese people will not go to the sea because it is not our domain.'

'Does this fatalism depress you?'

'It doesn't. I know a lot of educated people who go to the witchdoctor and spend a lot of money. This society works with this belief. All our music, painting, sculpture, everything is linked with the forest.'

2

IT WAS FROM Professor Gassiti that I first heard of the Gabonese miracle plant, the *eboga*. It was not especially rare, and it looked ordinary enough, with the spindly stem and the leaves of a kind of pepper plant. The root, suitably, was bitter. When the patient or aspirant, after due psychological preparation, ate this root it emptied his stomach and gave hallucinations. And (since we can hallucinate only about what we expect) local people could be sent on a dream journey to meet their ancestors in the other world. It also in this other world (since it took you behind the scenes, so to speak) showed you the other side of reality and revealed clearly, as in daylight, whoever might have sought to damage you with charms or witchcraft. Once you had this knowledge you could protect yourself.

The professor taught at the university and was a pharmacist in his own right, with a famous modern pharmacy in Libreville. He was also known as an expert on local medicine and traditional ways of healing. He compared this medicine to the Indian ayurveda. It was based on metals, animals, and above all on plants. It had a spiritual side; it literally dealt with the spirits. The plants were aromatic herbs from the forest collected by traditional healers.

He learned about traditional healing from his paternal grandfather and his ancestors who were healers. His grandmother's name meant 'the tree is medicine'. The whole family was inspired by this lady, but his main influence was his grandfather's cousin. She was a very famous healer. She healed many patients all over Gabon.

'I went to France for my studies. There I met a Gabonese man who told all the students there that they should acquire skills and go back to Gabon. He told me to become a pharmacist. Actually my elder brother was to have done it, but he did engineering instead. So I did pharmacy and plant specialisation. It was the time when everybody was talking about the *eboga* plant. It is a plant that is found in central Africa. In Gabon it is used to cure many things. It is now used as 'methadone' in the West. It is a substitute for heroin and morphine and is now used to help addicts to break their habit. It has fifteen substances in the roots. Since time immemorial *eboga* has been used in initiation rituals, and these initiation rituals are unique to Gabon. It can be called the Gabon patrimony. The first tribe to know of the *eboga* were the pigmies.' The small people of the forest, gradually worn down by the bigger people. 'They are the true masters of the forest. They know and distil every kind of poison in addition to the *eboga*, and they passed this knowledge on to the other tribes. Strange, to think of it. They were the true masters and now an American has a patent and is making millions from it.'

Every day, the professor said, there was an initiation in Gabon, and people went to the 'tradition houses' to eat *eboga* and enter the other world. There, in the other world, people saw what was wrong with themselves. In their trance-like state they met their ancestors and told of their problems. The ancestors would tell them how to break the charms that have befallen them, and they would return 'free'. Many foreigners, especially from the former Yugoslav territory of Slovenia, came to 'traditional houses' to be initiated.

The professor said, 'They, or we, are very superstitious as a race.'

And though the professor went to the ceremony with his friends, mainly in order to be with them, and though he had regard for the ceremony, he wanted to be free of it. He said, 'I prefer being in the domain of chemistry.' He was an elderly man with a round, humorous face.

SOONER THAN I expected, I was taken to an initiation, or that part of it which was not secret. It was in Libreville, in that district which was known as PK 12, Kilometre 12 — the kilometres being measured, I imagine, from some point on the Libreville coast.

I went with Nicole, a captain in the army. She had been appointed my bodyguard. In an extraordinary act of generosity the defence minister, who was also the president's son, had made me his guest in Gabon; and during all my time in the country I had this important protection. Nicole was well educated, had travelled, and was well connected.

After the Ivory Coast, Libreville, with its ocean drive and new official buildings, presented a smiling face; it was easy to believe that there had been an oil boom. But the road to PK 12, an outer area, undid that early impression. The lights were dim; in one place the narrow road was flooded, because of a burst water main; and traffic was difficult, especially at crossroads. Someone who was to meet us somewhere couldn't come, and though Nicole had reconnoitred the route in daylight, in the darkness houses and shops with their feeble, almost ghostly, fluorescent tubes looked alike, and we overshot the initiation house by a good kilometre. Habib, the driver (also in the army, and with a gun), began very slowly to take the big car back. We came upon two 'cruisers' full of white people. They went through a big gate in a high compound wall. They were clearly like us, people going to the initiation; and we followed them.

The compound wall concealed an initiation 'village'. It was the creation of a big, handsome Frenchman who had a Gabonese wife. The drumming was ceaseless; it was mingled with some kind of rough chanting and very deep shrieks, quite impressive. The Frenchman appeared to be asking Nicole too many questions. I thought he was checking on us; but later, at the end of the evening, when she was paying him money, I thought he had been letting Nicole know at the outset that there was to be a hefty payment for our party. Nicole knew the ways of Gabon in these near-spiritual matters and had come supplied with cash, which was more than I had done.

The 'village' and the 'initiation dance' were both productions for tourists or townspeople, to give them a taste of the *eboga* experience. So it wasn't the real thing. This was disappointing; but a moment's thought showed that it was wrong to be disappointed. What else could be expected in the capital? To see the real thing, assuming it existed, and was accessible to strangers, you would have to go far into the interior; and there you would be an intruder, which would have been disagreeable. And the drumming here – ceaseless – was real; the painted dancers were real: glimpses of them all the time in the thatched huts in the lower part of the yard: red, white and black the arresting colours of paint on bodies already beaded with perspiration.

Later, when he showed us into the initiation hut, before the dance, the Frenchman referred to his drummers and dancers as *artistes*; and that probably said it all. For all their passion and energy, they were performers. They did it every Saturday. It was a livelihood for everyone concerned. All the troupe, the Frenchman said, were members of his wife's family.

A little way in from the entrance a steep hillside led down to the sounds of the drums and the chanting. Steps had been cut into the hillside, and at the bottom there was a clearing of flattened earth, lit by kerosene lanterns and rolled-up palm leaves. This was where the dancing would take place. Around this area was a half-ring of tables and stools, for visitors. It was hot, with the lanterns and the burning palm leaves, and there was much moisture in the air; but there were no mosquitoes.

The drumming went on and on, together with the chanting and the shrieks that made for a kind of wild rhythm.

A woman, apparently a servant of the house, asked whether we would like to drink something. I asked for a cola drink. It came in an opened bottle. Habib, the driver, swift as a hawk, objected to that. The woman said, 'I have done nothing.'

When the Frenchman invited us to go to the initiation hut to see the artistes invoke their ancestors and the spirits, Nicole refused to go. She was a Christian and wanted no part of this spirit talk. The drumming and chanting might have been done only for tourists, but it agitated her. Working her lips, but not speaking loudly, she was saying 'Hail Mary' again and again, speaking her Christian charm against whatever charms were in play here, and unwittingly paying tribute to the power of African spirits.

The initiation hut was a low structure of mud and dry palm leaves. Palm leaves burned on the earthen floor, and the initiates, splendid in costume and paint, sat in a semi-circle around the fire. They were of various ages, from six to thirty. It was hot enough outside; the palm-leaf fire made the heat overpowering. The great heat, the drumming, the shouts and shrieks, the low roof, the feeling of an encroaching darkness, with an inability to see very clearly, made the scene hypnotic.

The initiates shouted (I believe), '*Bukowa! Bukowa!*' The Frenchman tried to instruct us in a response. But we needed a lot more time to learn, and we did the next best thing: we gave money. As so often on these occasions, it was enough.

The dancing, done sometimes with burning palm-leaf brands, was breathtaking. Energy seemed to come to the dancers from some external source, and we could imagine that it came from the *eboga* root. Habib, the driver, who took his bodyguard duty seriously, told me afterwards that there were times, during the dancing, and the waving about of brands, when he had become worried for me.

After the dancing there was to be dinner for those who wanted it. On a lower level (the hill was full of levels) we could see where tables had been laid with white tablecloths. There was, of course, a charge. And after the dinner there was to be, for a further fee, something connected with initiation. That sounded quite serious and I didn't think I should stay for it. One can be an observer only up to a point. Beyond that point one was an intruder (and there was the further worry about Nicole's Christian agitation).

We went back up the steep steps to the top of the hill. There the Frenchman met us and showed an *eboga* plant. Nicole paid him; it seemed to me in the darkness that she was paying him a fair sum.

The general who was Nicole's superior telephoned her as we were going back to the hotel. The traffic was easier than it had been earlier in the evening; but the weak fluorescent light still teased the sight. General Ibaba wanted to know about the evening. Nicole gave him a summary, but the general wanted to know about it in minute detail. We were in good hands.

Near the end of my time in Gabon, when we were far inland, in a village in the Lope national park, I witnessed another piece of African dancing. This was outside a chief's hall, which was a shed with traditional bark walls and an old corrugated-iron roof. Only the bark wall spoke of old forest ways. The shed was cleaned up in our presence, and a short stiff broom was applied to the uneven ground outside. The dancing came after a dinner carefully prepared and laid out on a table in the open air.

The drums were there but not as thrilling; the body paint was there on the dancers, but more perfunctory, a dab of white and a dab of red standing for something more complete; the originals of all the movements were there, but in a lesser, undeveloped way. There were a number of children among the dancers, but not many young people; there was little in this piece of bush in Lope to keep young people; the ambitious or the bored wanted to go to Libreville. Yet even with its thin chorus line (so to speak) this village performance was as genuine as could be. But I preferred the Frenchman's metropolitan creation in Libreville, and not only because its human material was richer, its dancers more accomplished. It used the same local materials, but it added style and finish, and I did not think it lacking in spirituality or feeling.

3

THE PIGMIES, the small people, were the first inhabitants of the forest, and they became its masters. They knew its multifarious plants, their healing or poisonous qualities. They were the first to learn of the hallucinogenic *eboga*. ('Hallucinogenic for you,' one professional Gabonese lady said unexpectedly. 'But for Africans it's their reality.' Opening up a whole vista of the relativity of perceptions, too

much of a quicksand for the short-term traveller to go into.)
Africa is a land of migrations, and it was the pigmies who
showed the later Bantu migrants the 'path' of the forest, the
philosophy of the forest.

Claudine felt passionately for the pigmies. She now lived
in the forest close to them.

She said, 'I thought it was awful that they were considered sub-human and low-value and had been herded into
reserves. That was why I wanted to know more about
them. We have no regard for them, but we go to them in
secret for healing. For initiation, barrenness, for sickness
the hospital cannot cure. Sometimes people step on a charm
hidden in the ground and they become ill. The hospital
cannot find out what's wrong with them, even with all their
modern amenities. So the sick person will go to the pigmy.
The pigmy will tell them who put the charm and where and
how. A person can become paralysed by stepping on a
charm. He loses feeling in his lower limbs. I have made
many photos of people who were injured by these mystical
weapons, and I have seen how they were healed.'

Her feeling for the pigmies and the 'path' made Claudine
use extraordinary and sometimes very moving language.

She said, 'The closer we come to the pigmies the more
we understand that the world has a soul and has a life. It
has energy. Pigmies are like our memories of the past. They
hold the knowledge of that world.'

The events of the second half of the nineteenth century
ripped the continent open. But the pigmies remained close

to the forest. They preserved their knowledge of the forest; in that knowledge lay their civilisation. Other tribes lost much of that knowledge.

'In spite of the relentless pressure of the outer world the pigmies retain their civilisation. They still have to kill an elephant to become 'a man'. A group of young initiates wear masks made of palm branches and they go hunting. It is a rite of passage.'

And then there were the charms – never far away in any consideration of the shifting reality that surrounds men.

Claudine said, 'In the mystical world' – 'mystical' was the word used for anything beyond rationality – 'you can make a charm from someone's leftover food to hurt that person. And that person will have to go fast to the pigmy for help. The pigmy will look into water or a mirror and he will see whether the victim will live or die. Or whether indeed the victim has already "crossed the river", as they say: has already died. There are two kinds of healer here. The small healer will deal only with malaria and influenza. Pigmies are very good with malaria. For bigger problems, like charms, you have to go to a master healer. He has been a disciple of a great man for many years. He has learned all the "tactics" of the spiritual world. When it comes to fighting the spirits you have to know the rules, or you can die, because the spirits are very strong.'

How was the pigmy healer or master rewarded?

Claudine said, 'They know about money now. But those who really know their work, the genuine healers, the real masters, will not want money because they feel it corrupts their gifts. They look upon their gift as something that has come to them from the ancestor. So you give the healer or the master whatever you want – cloth, alcohol, food or tobacco. He will not ask for it. You do not give money. He does not want it. I knew a person who went really mad. They took him to a pigmy master who treated him for three months, and he was healed. The man wanted to reward the master with anything and everything – car, house, a plot of land. He said he would do anything for the master. But the master wanted nothing. All he said to the man was, "Take my young daughter home with you. Adopt her and educate her in modern ways." The man did as the master asked. He brought the girl to Libreville and educated her and treated her like a close confidante. She is now a civil servant and is still very close to her people. You see, the master knew that the world had changed, and the pigmies would need their own people to be a bridge to the new world.'

Pigmy villages were small, from twenty to fifty people in all. At one time the pigmies lived in branch or leaf igloos, made afresh every evening. But now they follow Bantu ways and live in more permanent Bantu-style mud huts.

Claudine said, 'I don't think their culture has changed as a result. The outer form has changed, but the content is still the same.'

There were two important tribes in the south of Gabon. They had introduced the pigmy to the all-important initiation ceremony, and the pigmy in his turn had passed on his knowledge of plants, including the *eboga*, to them. Initiation (for men alone) was a necessary stage in divination, which was done here with water or with a mirror; and in this field the pigmy was the master. So you could say that the two cultures, Bantu and pigmy, had come together.

More important than divination was the gift of communication with your ancestors. This, too, could come only after initiation, and it was of great importance. It was only from your ancestor that you could find out about your position in society, your duties and your responsibility. For this you needed the skull and bones of your ancestor, and they had to be truly of your ancestor; you couldn't use the skull and bones of a ritual sacrifice. The skull and bones for this ritual had to come from an elder who, as he was dying, gave you permission to keep his bones as a relic.

In every family there was only one person, and he was an elder, who had the privilege of talking with the ancestors. It was this elder and his wife who kept the skull and bones; the wife's duty was to keep the skull and bones clean.

Claudine said, 'This *buitee* or ritual is only for men. Some tribes have included women now, but people are very unhappy about it.' She began to talk in a practical way about *eboga*-eating. 'It is very bitter. The mouth becomes numb. The body becomes numb, and every sensation is enhanced. In the real *buitee* the ancestor comes at three in the morning.' It occurred to me that at PK 12 I had heard something like this, but had thought of it only as a way of getting us to stay longer. Claudine said, 'The ancestor comes at three in the morning and speaks in an ancient tongue no one can understand. Only the third level of initiates can understand him. At that level the initiate can talk to the relics, and can also initiate other people. Women can be healed by *buitee*, but they cannot be initiated. Another thing: to be a healer you have to have an ancestor somewhere in your past who was a healer.'

Even with Claudine's knowledge of pigmy ways, and her love for them, it was hard to arrive at a human understanding of the pigmies, to see them as individuals. Perhaps they weren't.

I asked her, 'Are pigmies happy people?'

'They are happy and they are gentle, but they are a very wary race. They become tactile after a long time. They don't trust easily.'

'Do they still hunt?'

'They hunt at night now, and they have guns. Before they used to make traps.'

'Do you really like living in the forest?'

'Yes. Because my ancestors were savages.' She laughed, at the double irony of her words, which acknowledged what was said about Africans by people outside, and, within that, what was said about pigmies by the Bantu. She said, 'Life is simple in the forest. You have no urban stress. You bathe in the river. You eat from communal kitchens, and you go to sleep at seven. The forest is peaceful and tranquil and I can think about "myself". I am not afraid of the forest. I never think of the dangers there, because you radiate energy. Animals can smell negative waves of fear and then they attack. It is here, in the forest, that I understood that the forest talks to us. It asks us questions, and it feeds us. It is the beginning and the end, and that is why pigmies, who understand this, are the masters.'

I wanted to know about death: how do pigmies deal with it?

'Pigmies believe in nature. They believe they come from the earth, and that is why they do not want to pollute it with the dead. They do not bury the dead. When a master dies they wrap him in a mat and put him under a big tree. They leave him there to rot, and no one will go to that place. They will not hunt or forage there. When decomposition is complete they put the bones in a grave, and they will quarantine that area. They cannot understand Christianity.'

'What do they find especially hard about it?'

'They fail to see why Jesus should have all the power. For them power has to be distributed among many chiefs.'

'How long do they live?'

'The average span is fifty years. Life is short because civilisation has introduced many diseases that were not known to them. Alcoholism, HIV.'

'How dark is the forest?'

'During the day light filters through the canopy and it is full of shadows. At night it is pitch dark. I think of it as a "locked" darkness. It is important, too, to remember that the canopy absorbs pollution. This is why we must preserve the forest.'

4

FROM THE AIR the depredation of the loggers hardly shows. The forest seems whole and tight and eternal. At ground level it's another story. There are the logging roads; the rains wash the loosened earth into the rivers, and the fish suffer. For anyone who feels a mystical bond with the old forest there is pain. Mme Ondo, a high civil servant, and a very elegant lady, felt that pain acutely. She was of mixed ancestry, but her heart was all African.

She said, 'We were told that we would plant a tree for every tree we cut, but it is not so. It sickens my heart that we don't follow that principle. When I see a truck full of logs, I don't see trees or wood. I see murdered people. They are not logs for me, but dead people. The trees are creatures just like us. Trees live longer than human beings, and they give us everything, even oxygen. We need to learn a lot from trees.'

Mme Ondo was elegant, but that elegance was not a simple matter of inheritance. It came from deep within her. Her mother was a peasant, and so was her mother's mother.

'I used to help on the small farms they worked on, and I used to go with my mother to the forest. I was brought up by an aunt and uncle. Once, when I was eight, they took me to the forest and left me alone in an encampment while they went fishing in the big river. I was alone in the night, and I was afraid because I kept thinking of the stories of the anaconda snake that comes at night looking for children. In the morning I was very glad to eat the fish they had caught, but at night it was a different story.'

Later she became attuned to the beauty of the forest.

'The positive side is that it is very cool. There is a great calm. The birds sing, and there is great beauty in the trees. And if you see the small path twisting and turning like a snake in the forest you think of the image of the absolute. The search for the truth comes from the forest. I adore the forest, and even if I spend years abroad I have to come back and rush to the forest. I need the thick forest to feel alive.'

'Will the philosophy of the people change with the thinning of the forest?'

'It will change us completely, because we are all tied to the forest. We need the logs to develop the economy of Gabon, but we need a policy of reforestation to be followed very strictly. You have to remember even then that a primeval forest is very different from a planted forest. Even if you leave the young saplings to grow around the trees you have felled, it still affects the flora and fauna and the animals. The animals disappear.'

The loggers crack the forest open, build the tracks, and leave it ready for the poachers, who turn up now with AK-47s and other Kalashnikovs which, on animals in the opened-up forest, have the equivalent of the killing power of fly-spray on flies and insects in a small room.

Mme Ondo had an African heart; but within that, and even with her mixed ancestry, she considered herself culturally of the Fang tribe. The Fangs (pronounced in the

French way, without the final 'g') are one of the big tribes of Gabon. The French-American traveller Du Chaillu (1831–1903) went among them in the 1850s and (though suspect in other ways) left detailed drawings of the Fangs, their hairstyles, their filed teeth, their musical instruments and their iron tools. He said the Fangs were cannibals. This (rather than their extraordinary skills as metal-workers) gave them a special notoriety in the nineteenth century, always on the look-out for the more sensational side of Africa.

Mme Ondo said, 'Fangs were never cannibals. But we don't know what is done in the mystical ceremonies. They may eat or not eat people. We don't know. It was the colonial way to denigrate the Fangs because they saw the Fangs as fierce and warlike. The Fangs were coming from the north-east of Africa. They were told that their land was by the sea. The legends said that they were to go to a place where the sun set in the sea. In order to do that, they had to pass through many tribes and territories, and they had to be warriors and fierce to reach here, where the sun sank in the sea.'

It was on this great migration that the Fangs met the pigmies.

'The Fangs despised the pigmy, but they were taught about the forest by the very pigmy they despised. The pigmy is master of the forest and knows all the remedies needed for the many diseases that are found in it. Also, the pigmy is master of traditional healing.' It was interesting how this emphasis on disease and healing came up again and again: suggesting that the forest, spiritual healer though it might be, good for the soul, was always felt in folk imagination to be at the same time a place of illness, a place in constant need of medical or magical attention.

Mme Ondo said, 'Even though the Fangs hated the pigmies for their size and smallness, they needed him to run and fetch in the forest. To survive in the forest they needed the pigmy. The forest is a very big struggle. The Fangs' struggle with the forest, their penetration of it, is sung in their oral history. They have a legend called *Odʒaboga*. It tells of the Fangs and the forest. The legend says that when they came here they saw a big tree, the *fromager* or cheese tree.'

I had heard the name for the first time in the Ivory Coast, and had understood that the truly beautiful tree, grey-trunked, lofty, with a few well-balanced branches, noticeable even in the high forest, was used by the French to make boxes for certain kinds of French cheese. I imagine the wood of the *fromager* was neutral in aroma and taste.

In the Fang legend the migrating Fangs spent years digging into the trunk of the *fromager* that barred their way to the great forest. They tunnelled and tunnelled.

Mme Ondo said, 'The tree they dug into is called *adʒap*, and it is in the oral history. There it is the symbol of the immortal country and is sacred. The entire universe sees this tree. It is on top of a mountain and has wide lateral branches. Well, the Fangs succeeded in digging through the trunk, but then the tree collapsed and took them into a ravine, where a giant snake appeared and took them to the other side of the forest. That is where the legend ends.'

Mme Ondo had been initiated into Fang rites. Silence was the first law of initiation, she said; and she wished to say nothing of her initiation. She was willing to talk more about the forest, the medicine and plants that fight illness, and make it possible to deal with the jinn and spirits of the forest. These spirits and jinn can heal the human body. The Fangs have a religion that they practise in grottoes deep in the forest; women have to stay away from these places.

'You dig a hole and put the bones of the elder or master-healer in it. Then you get a special wooden statue. These statues were made long ago by traditional priests. Nowadays they are sought after as antiques and are very expensive. You put the wooden statue on the bones in the hole. The priest will then be able to speak to the buried person, who is an ancestor or elder. There will be a religious service, and the Fangs who gather there will be in a trance-like state. They eat a plant very similar to the *eboga*. This plant is called *alane* and is very bitter. The priest asks first for forgiveness for his sins and the sins of the initiates.'

In this account by Mme Ondo, the asking for forgiveness by the priest seemed to me to have been borrowed from Christianity. But I did not raise the point with her; I did not wish to divert her.

Mme Ondo said, 'Only the priest can talk to the statue of the elder, because we know only the elder can talk to God. We cannot talk to God; we are impure. The elder will intercede for us and give us what we seek. Then we do the rituals. We sacrifice a sheep without horns.'

If, as I felt, some tinge of Christianity had crept into Fang ritual, it was also true, as Mme Ondo said, that Christianity had done away with many Fang rites and rituals. In Fang legend, the tribe had to look for a land where the sun sank into the sea. They found that land in Gabon. What the legend had no means of saying was that, as soon as the French had staked out their colony in the 1840s, Christian missionaries, American and French, were going to be active, undermining (and in the north suppressing) old Fang life in unforeseen ways.

Mme Ondo said, 'Here when an old person dies we say a library has burnt down.'

I had heard that said in the Ivory Coast in 1983. The words had been reverentially attributed to a wise old Ivorian, Ahmadou Hampaté Ba, then said to be very ill in hospital and close to death; the words had clearly passed into folk memory.

But Mme Ondo also thought that certain traditions, certain ways of belief, especially those that had been enshrined in oral tradition, would survive. 'Here certain traditions have become institutionalised over generations and cannot be lost. I agree that if a master of a forge dies, and does not pass the iron-smelting knowledge to his apprentice, the knowledge of the forge will die. But traditional rites like initiation and those connected with the oral tradition have preserved their knowledge.'

I asked, 'How do the Fang re-charge?'

'The Fang masters do astral journeys. It is a common phenomenon, as it is for the yogis of India. They can double and be in two places at the same time. When they return we feed them raw eggs and offer animal sacrifices for them. Witches and wizards can also do this astral journey, and they can sometimes fail to come back. They are found dead in the morning. Or they turn into owls, bats and flames that you see in the forest in the night. Daylight stops them re-entering their bodies. Only a very strong wizard can do it, but he will become very ill. Then the traditional priest will have to perform many rituals and sacrifices to cure him.'

DOUBLES, astral journeys, the fragility and yet the enduringness of ritual, the idea of energy, the wonder of the forest: the themes recurred. And yet there were things that surprised me.

Ernest, a museum curator, a Christian, said, 'Our life is bound with the forest. Every initiation is related to the forest. The relationship between the people and the forest is seen in the ritual. You went to see it at PK 12. The harp, or what we call the *gombi*, is crucial. In the strings of the harp are the intestines of our first ancestor, the first men who lived in the forest. It is the main instrument in the initiation ceremony, and it was the first religion of the forest.'

I thought back to the occasion: the night, the heat, the blazing rolled-up palm-leaf brands, the drumming, the painted figures, the shouts. I remembered now, at the very edge of the dancing area, a man at a harp, leaning with infinite tenderness over his instrument, as though anxious in the din to catch every vibration from the strings. He was, I thought, like G. F. Watts's blindfolded figure of Hope insecurely atop the world. In the roar of the dancing yard I saw him as a minor figure, contributing little. I noticed him and then I didn't look at him. It was shocking to me now to understand, what nearly everyone there would have understood, what the strings of the harp stood for.

5

I HAD HEARD so much about the splendour of the forest that, before I went to the Lope national park, I allowed myself to play with Hansel-and-Gretel ideas of what I might find. I imagined myself sleeping in the narrowest of clearings between mighty trees, among whose buttressed roots small, friendly people moved in and out of their small mud huts: pigmies. I imagined a wonderfully clean forest floor, spotted with soft sunlight falling through a high forest canopy.

Of course it wasn't like that. For a hundred and sixty years, ever since the beginning of the colony, Lope (not a Spanish or Portuguese name, but African, the name of a brisk little local river) had been a station on the great river Oguwé. Since the 1980s there has been a railway service from Libreville; and Lope, with about a thousand people, was now in part a railway town, with the houses, near the railway station, of railway workers.

I had been told that the railway had been built with great difficulty over the watery land. The aluminium coaches looked a little tarnished, the effect no doubt of tropical sun and rain. But the train as a whole looked solid enough, the gravel embankment high and true; the French locomotive was smooth and powerful, the wheels remarkably quiet; and after thirteen years of punishing use the air-conditioning still worked beautifully.

The forest came slowly, broken in the beginning by little clearings and peasant dwellings, sometimes by small settlements. Absolute forest didn't seem to come at all; but perhaps a little distance from the track there had always been absolute forest; and it had to be remembered that the track had been laid on what would have been original, untouched forest. In this and in other apparently small ways the forest was being nibbled away. Where the logging companies were at work the forest had been battered in a big way. At certain places you could see the heavy, long trucks bringing the straight, ancient logs (Mme Ondo's dead bodies) to the railway. I had been told that the railway had been built to meet the need of the logging companies rather than the need of travellers. That might have been so; but certain events have unexpected consequences; and it was now agreed by everyone that the railway had tied the country together. But equally there could be no doubt that where the railway had come, people and town would come as well, and the forest would begin to melt away.

The land began to be broken: gullies, ravines, chasms, all forested, all requiring to be bridged, all adding to the cost of this great engineering venture in the middle of the equatorial forest. And then we were running beside the Oguwé itself and its many side waters, so to speak: it was wonderful to be brought so close to the mighty river, and the glimpses big and small of its ancillary power: the spectacular view continuing dizzyingly for mile after mile, far too much to see, to take in, to understand.

The train set us down at Lope. We were able, a while later, to see the high aluminium coaches leaving. For Mme Ondo a twisting path in the forest was an image of the absolute. For me, bred on old Westerns, the sight of the sturdy departing train spoke of a horrible kind of solitude.

The Oguwé ran through Lope. It was a kind of Nile here, with islets and rocks and isolated trees. It was in a wide valley and was muddier than the Nile in Uganda. It roared over unseen rocks. Beyond that roar, on the other side, rose gentle hills, strangely light green (I had been looking forward to forest), strangely like savannah or parkland, with contrasting accumulations of dark and deep forest in clefts in the hills and on the riverbank. About these accumulations were what looked like many smaller green splashes of vegetation: they looked superficial, easy to scrape off, but it was the great forest, ever seeking to re-colonise the land and extend its domain. The oldest forest, a few thousand years old, was beside the riverbank; that of course was where the water was, and from the other bank (where I was) it looked logical enough.

The pale-green colour of the savannah appeared to underlie everything, like the priming on a canvas. It made the landscape look tamer than it was, a place where tourists might come in buses and where teas might be served.

There was a further surprise: in this land, scraped clean and green in so many places, the separate clumps of forest marked the site of old, even ancient, villages. For this reason UNESCO had designated Lope as a heritage site. Between seven hundred and fourteen hundred years ago the villages were abandoned, for an unknown reason, and never reclaimed. So in spite of its apparent tameness the land held a mystery.

My guide was Kate White. She had spent many years in Lope as a researcher, in conditions of remoteness where I don't think I would have lasted for a month.

It was necessary to people the landscape with Africans — such as one could still see — to begin to understand its drama: the land discovered and settled many centuries ago; the villages built, the trees planted; in some places the remains of kilns surviving where the vanished people had smelted iron ore into iron, using charcoal and local bellows in a difficult method the mid-nineteenth-century traveller Du Chaillu was still to see; and then, after centuries of success, centuries of mastering the land, because of some unknown calamity everything abandoned, only the village trees left growing, with no further record of the presence of men until our own time.

The places where smelting was done still showed as bare patches on the hillside. There were many of them in one place. You could – and it seemed a privilege, a link to the remote past – still pick up shiny flakes of ancient, burnt-out charcoal, and bits of half-smelted ore.

The roads of Lope were country roads, rough and red, much cut up by rain and raging water. They required patience and a strong back, even in a four-wheel-drive.

Some small trees beside the road had been half broken by elephants, and we were told that the elephants of the equatorial forest were a metre shorter than the African elephants of more open spaces. Lope was a national park and elephants here were to some extent protected. But elsewhere in Gabon elephants were under threat; the very size that made them fearful creatures before the age of the gun now made them hopelessly vulnerable. Local people liked to eat elephant meat, and there was again a Chinese market for ivory. The loggers opened up the forest; the poachers moved in. Some of the logging companies were themselves Chinese, able now, far from home, fully to express the Chinese hatred for the earth.

Local people liked what they called, in their manly way, 'bush meat'. With modern guns they were now able to kill for trade as well, sending carcases to Libreville. In a government magazine I read that a million animals – clearly a random figure – were killed in Gabon every year. Since people in places like Lope hunted all the time, the real figure would be much higher. Africans, like the French and the Chinese and the Vietnamese, ate everything, not only elephants and dogs and cats, but everything else with life. Everything with life was, you might say, fair game. The eating of bush meat had become a cultural matter; it was not to be questioned. The forest, with its apparently endless supply of bush meat, was like a free supermarket, open to everyone.

In this dependence on bush meat, the easy bounty of the forest, might perhaps be found a reason for the failure of the people here to develop a serious agriculture, which might have created another kind of civilisation, another kind of man, better able to take the outside world on, better able to move in all directions. But that was only one side of the story. Guy Rossatanga-Rignault had said that the sleeping sickness and malaria and the great heat had made the keeping of cattle an impossibility in Gabon. Perhaps, then, as he had said in his inimitable way, the land was not made for men; it was only for animals.

The problem remained: why had the villages disappeared? Had the people eaten out the forest? Had they been compelled to go deeper and deeper into the forest? Had it become harder to drag the carcases back to the villages? Had the villages then begun to starve? The current theory, according to Kate White, was they had been laid low by the Ebola virus, brought to them by the fruit bats, themselves an African delicacy.

6

IN LOPE I got to know Mobiet, a white American of thirty-seven. He had been educated at a private university (his parents had paid), and he had come with the Peace Corps to Gabon eleven years before. He had been on some kind of spiritual quest, and had stayed. He had been dissatisfied with the United States and his restless life there. In Gabon he had done the *eboga* initiation; it had met some need. He had married a Gabonese woman and they had three children. For some years, after the Peace Corps, he had done paid research; but now, with three children to look after, and the years ticking by, he had begun for the first time to think more seriously about money and a proper job.

For the time being he was a free-lance. To be a free-lance in a place like Gabon, and especially in an out-of-the-way place like Lope, must have been a hard row to hoe. He sold African carvings, but I don't imagine there would have been much of a market here; and I suppose it was as a free-lance that he had been attached to our party.

He had come to Gabon with the Peace Corps as an agricultural expert. That was an exaggeration, to put it charitably, and in the beginning it worried him; all he had done in the United States was to work for a while in a plant nursery. In the end it occurred to him to tell local people that he had come to learn about their agriculture.

He liked to tell about his first day in the village. Some

people took him to the house where he was to live. A man fell in behind them, and when they entered the house the man behind them began to shout, 'Get out! Get out!' It was unnerving, but the man behind them – the owner of the house, as was soon apparent – was not shouting at Mobiet. He was shouting at people who were in the house, and these people – no doubt unsatisfactory tenants – picked up their scattered things and left. The next morning the house-owner came back to take Mobiet to the local guardhouse. He wanted Mobiet to tell the people there why he was in the village. The guardhouse was where the local men hung out. The head of the guardhouse and the village watch was a kind of chief, and Mobiet had the time to notice that he was weaving a mat.

Mobiet looked about him. To his right was a sharp, towering granite rock, and a little distance away was the deep forest. The air was fresh. It was more beautiful than Mobiet had imagined; at the same time, because it was so unlike anything he had known, he was fearful. Some of the houses were of mud, and some were of concrete with a thatched roof. He thought with alarm: 'Am I going to stay here for *two* years?'

That was when he decided to abandon the Peace Corps line and to tell people he had come to learn about the kind of agriculture they did.

He learned the hard way. It was a Fang village. He cut and slashed with the men, learned to hunt and set traps and do what they were doing. It was punishing; he had never before done such hard physical work. The women worked on the planting allotments, which were generally smallish, about a hundred metres square.

There was a woman in the village who had befriended the previous Peace Corps volunteer. Now she befriended Mobiet. She lived just across the road from Mobiet. She was thirty, just a few years older than Mobiet, and had eight children. He valued her friendship and the many things she taught him about village life. She taught him, for instance, about the standing of various people in the village, which he had not always appreciated. She got him used to the absence of privacy (the children coming into a house all the time, to stare at him and to touch his things). She also taught him about everyday things, like ants, that can take over a house, and about simple skin lesions that can become infected. It was a platonic friendship; he thought of her as a mother and a guide; he failed to see that the woman's husband was becoming jealous, and the husband's brothers and other people in the village were looking at the friendship as a kind of insult to the family.

When he found out he became enraged. He thought he should tell the Peace Corps that they had sent him to a bad village and they should send him somewhere else. The best way for him to do that would have been to go to Libreville. Libreville wasn't far away in terms of miles, but the forestry companies didn't maintain their roads: it took eight hours on truly dreadful logging tracks to get to Libreville. So Mobiet postponed and postponed the journey.

Then something terrible happened in his bad village.

He was in his house one lunchtime. He had prepared his lunch, such as it was: rice, peas, tomato paste and sardines. He wasn't a cook; he cooked only because he had to. A toddler from the family across the road came into his house, a little girl of two and a half. It was the custom in the village to share food. So he gave the little girl some of his rice. She ate it and went back to her house. Next morning he heard screaming and wailing from the little girl's house. He went to look. Some village boys outside the house told him that the little girl he had given rice to the previous day had been poisoned. Her aunt had poisoned her. Mobiet knew the aunt. She was a strong and intelligent woman, and was mad. Half the family were making a coffin; the rest of the family were tying up the aunt. Mobiet thought it was something for the police. The family said no; they would deal with the matter in their own way. Mobiet heard later that the aunt was dead.

It was about this time that Mobiet's woman friend decided to leave her husband and go to Libreville. She asked Mobiet for money for the trip, and he, in all innocence, gave it to her. Mobiet would visit her from time to time, and it was during one of these visits that Mobiet met the woman he would marry. She was his mother's neighbour. What he liked about this woman was her calm. Two years after meeting her he married her.

Closer to her now, he understood that his wife was not well. He found out that she had been 'spiritually persecuted' by her family. And it was through this search for his wife's mental health that Mobiet became started on his own spiritual quest. Looking for a cure for his wife, they went to traditional healers. They did not help. She was pregnant at the time, and wanted urgently to be well. It was urgent for him too. He had left the Peace Corps and was looking for jobs.

Help, though, was at hand for them both, in the form of a young new healer. Mobiet's wife decided, at the urging of this new healer, to go to the forest to be with the pigmies and to be with her new healer. This was a time of great anxiety for Mobiet. He would ask himself, 'What is wrong with this woman I love? Will she come back?' He meant: come back from the pigmies, come back to health. And some time later his wife came back from the pigmies, completely cured. As a result of this he went deeper and deeper into the spiritual side of things. He had always had a spiritual inclination, even in the United States, and even before he went to university; he never took the 'power structures' around him for granted; he sought to understand them.

Mobiet became initiated, the local *eboga* initiation, when his son was two.

He said, 'I was comfortable with my wife and I wanted to know my spiritual essence. I wanted to know how to direct my energy. When I decided I wanted to be initiated I went to the same traditional healer who had healed my wife. I thought of him as my spiritual father. It was a test for both of us, a test for me, and a test for my spiritual father. He was afraid to initiate. It was his first time too. Honestly speaking, I was always interested in *eboga*. I knew that I would do the voyage. I wanted to do that journey when I was ready for it. You go on a long journey, and you have to be prepared for it, because you risk going to a place where the spirits are dead. You see your ancestors and you can be pulled in different directions. I had seen the country initiations, but they don't tell you all. After initiation you don't fear death. I fear it only because I have not prepared my family to live without me. I am not afraid of losing my essence. I pray I live a long time and see my children grow, but you need to go beyond yourself.'

I asked Mobiet to describe his spiritual father: not only his spiritual qualities, but also his appearance.

'He is a strong man. He is a soldier, very lean and muscular and very well defined. I know that if things go to hell, and we are in real trouble, I want to be with him, because he is so resourceful. He has only been educated to the fifth or sixth class in primary school, and is a sculptor. I was the first person he initiated. He was still a young healer then, learning his craft, and now he has learnt a lot more. He inherited it from his father. There are other ways to become a healer, but that involves the black arts.'

Initiation had worked for him.

'It makes me listen to my inner voice. It confirms the existence of God and it makes me move in tune with my dreams. And you meditate.'

7

MOBIET HAD arranged a special afternoon excursion for us. I suppose it was the kind of thing he did as a free-lance in Lope. And it was special: he was going to take us to see the ancestral bones of a tribe. This wasn't the kind of thing you could see every day. It involved a journey by road to the new village of the tribe – after the death of a chief a village shifted: usually to the other bank of the river – and after that road journey, a trip by river, by dug-out (with perhaps an outboard motor), in the company of the tribal chief, to the site of the old village where the sacred old bones were kept.

The road journey took longer than I expected (Mobiet hadn't been all that precise); and the very length of that journey led me to believe that we were going to a landing stage on the river. It wasn't like that. We came to a village. Mobiet looked up his friends. That took a little time, and then we picked our way past a couple of wood huts, not to the landing stage, as I had hoped, but to a stretch of tallish grass bounded, discouragingly, by bush. I had trouble with the tall grass; it wrapped itself around my shoes. After a while my nervy, frail legs began to give out; and they gave out completely when I saw some barrels, taller than the tall grass, barring the way in the distance.

A pretty little sign said *Débarcadère 500 metres*. I suppose it was meant to be friendly, but it broke my spirit. I felt we had already walked that distance. I had given it all my zest.

I thought about what I might have to walk at the other end, before I could see the bones; and I doubted whether I would have it in me to walk a thousand metres on the way back. The trouble was that I had done a fair amount of walking (for me) in the morning, in the great forest, following in the sodden tracks of an elephant. It had exhausted me; but Mobiet thought, as he said, it was a demonstration of what I could do.

He had invested much in this trip to see the bones. He thought now that I could be wheeled in a wheelbarrow to the riverbank. A barrow miraculously appeared, but it was an African job, heavily rusted, and not sturdy, sagging below my weight when, leaning back far too much, I tried unsuccessfully to sit in it.

It was the village chief himself, small and wiry, who put an end to the wheelbarrow absurdity. He appeared, walking easily in the tall grass, coming up from the river, holding a clutch of iron tools, hammer, mattock, saw, which were amazingly like those Du Chaillu drew for his book. He clearly had put in a lot of effort into getting the bones ready for our visit, and he was more disappointed than Mobiet. I had missed seeing the sirens in the river, he said. They were white women, and they were well worth seeing; they protected the river and they didn't like intruders; he had gone to some trouble to placate them for our sake.

So I had let everybody down. It had taken some of the savour for the village out of the rest of the programme – the dinner, and the initiation dance afterwards – which Mobiet had prepared.

But I had not let Nicole, my bodyguard, down. She was a Christian, but she had the old Gabonese anxiety about water, an inauspicious element. The talk about the white sirens at the bottom of the river wouldn't have pleased her at all; and she had been praying and praying, against hope for much of the time, that the river trip wouldn't take place. Now, miraculously, her prayers had been answered, giving her, I suppose, yet another proof of the power of prayer.

I began to walk back to the road. I went around the wood huts at the front of the yard, asked the surprised women at their washing-up stands to forgive me, and crossed the road.

UNLESS YOU knew him, and if you were looking for something regal or chief-like in the man, you would have missed the chief. He talked easily, he had good manners, but there was nothing chief-like about him. The simple wood houses of his family – two or three separate houses: I assumed they were the houses of his family – were like those of the women on the other side of the road.

There he was now, working in his yard with others of his family, shirt falling away from his strong but bony chest, to put the place straight for dinner. There were chairs – white plastic of a familiar design, capable of being stacked – for the visitors in his chief's hall, a low rough building with a roof of old corrugated iron and traditional bark walls. He had the white chairs put in a line and invited us to sit. He was sorry not to have had the dignity of showing us the sirens in the river and the bones of the elder; he complained, but only a little; and thereafter his manners and formality did not fail.

He was a traditional healer in Lope. He was also a retired police officer. So to be a chief was not, as I had half imagined, to hold down a hereditary honour. A chief here was more a kind of civil servant, someone appointed by the government. His father had been a maker of dug-outs. He had also been a healer in the traditional way, and an initiator. The religious side of his father's attainments (a healer had to have healing in his ancestry) could be said to be the chief's true inheritance.

I wondered whether he was finding it hard nowadays to keep up the old traditions.

He said, 'The first difficulty is the park itself.' The Lope national park. 'The park took away all our sacred places in the forest. When the park was created they said that the village would have a protected zone. That zone for the village was not respected. The second difficulty is the increase of evangelical churches.' Nicole belonged to an evangelical church, but she kept quiet. 'They keep calling us devil-worshippers and pagans, and their propaganda has worked. In reality our religion respects God more than these churches.'

There had been Protestant and Catholic churches here; but these evangelical churches – the local people called them the rock-and-roll churches – appeared in the 1990s. About the influence of the evangelical churches he said two different things. He said at first they were a threat to the traditional religion; and then he said that the young people of the village were in his church. He had initiated them himself. I thought it sounded as though he was exaggerating the evangelical threat. But he said he wasn't. The influence of the rock-and-roll churches was growing.

He said, 'I was baptised and confirmed, but I decided that the traditional religion was strong in me, and I wanted to come back to it. In our initiation the fundamental belief is that there is only one God.'

He was sixty-four or sixty-five. He was born on the day in 1944 when a Frenchman came to the village to do a census; so it was easy for him to remember when he was born. The people of his tribe had always lived where they lived, on the riverside. They moved to the other bank only when a great chief died.

'We wanted to take you where our great ancestral king is, and where the siren is, a white woman. But you were not able to get to the riverbank.'

'Have you seen her?'

'The siren? Many times. You don't need to be initiated to see her. You go to the riverbank and make a prayer to her, and offer her a sacrifice, and ask her for fish. If she is happy with you she will grant your wish, and sometimes she will appear.'

'Has she always been in the river?'

'I don't know.'

'How did you become chief?'

'I was a civil servant and more qualified. I became a chief in 1987. But they may remove me, or I may quit. It is a government appointment. I am responsible for two villages, and I am a master initiator.'

'How did you become an initiator?'

'I was born into it. My grandfather was a master initiator. When I was born he put the red paste from the padouk wood on me, and said I would follow him. I went to school and had a life, but the traditional religion was always in me.'

'Are you preparing someone to take your place?'

'Not as yet. I am still strong and powerful and not ready to go. When you appoint someone the religion leaves you. You are ready to go and it leaves you. It is semi-mystical. You cross the river. The person you appoint cannot escape his fate, no matter where he goes or what he does.'

'Is this the pigmy religion?'

'The pigmy is master of this particular religion. I trained with them. I speak their language and so it was easy for me.'

'Where did you train?'

'In a village called Okouka, forty kilometres from here. My grandfather had gone south on an old walking road and he had captured two pigmies. He owned them. The pigmies have power, and we keep them just like you keep a pet. You can do anything you like with your pet, but there is something in the pet that you don't have. We kept them and we pitied them. We gave them food, and soon they knew that we were not bad for them, and so many more came and we worked together. They gave us their knowledge. But the pigmies who kept their tradition have died. There is only one left today in this area. Young pigmies are not interested in their inheritance. They have been won over by modern ways and now are drunks. In the old days no pigmy drank like this. Now they all want alcohol and modern things.'

I asked the nostalgic old chief about the forest. Was he worried about its future?

'I am afraid for it. This village is not my ancestral village any more. It has become the world's property. *You* have as much right here as I have, although it is *my* forest. Deforestation brings its own problems. The *mwabi* tree has gone. It was very important in traditional medicine, together with python fat.'

'Do you think deforestation will go on and on? Can you imagine a time when there is no forest around you here?'

'It depends on the state. As far as the forest going, I don't think it can happen here. We are a cradle of peace, unlike Ivory Coast. If the forest goes, there will be global consequences.'

8

THE SUN was going down. For the dinner (and, later, the initiation dance) the chairs were moved out of the chief's hall and placed in a row on the uneven ground in the open, the row continuing the line of the bark wall, so that we on the chairs looked across the chief's small yard, the scene of the dancing to come, to where a detectable extra growth of bush and young trees, low and broken, marked the limit of the chief's ground. We could just about see the side wall of the neighbouring hut. On our side of the boundary there ran, from the front of the yard to the back, and down the side of the chief's hall, an unmarked way. People were going down this way all the time, in ones and twos, gathering in the half-obscured greenery at the end — the green room, it might be said, the country version of the Libreville Frenchman's palm-thatched hut — for the chief's dance.

Women from the houses in the chief's yard began laying out the dinner. They brought a table, covered it with a white oilcloth, shiny and patterned, and began laying out food, dish after laden dish in very good ware: plantains, sweet potatoes, fish and other things. It was a metropolitan entertainment; perhaps Mobiet had suggested the style.

The food — the smell, the knocking of the dishes — brought out the house dog. He was of the local mixed breed, brown and white, small but in good shape, deep-chested. Perhaps he was a hunting dog, with a fixed place in the family scheme. He was perfectly secure in his yard; he lay down at the back of the white chairs, confident that he was going to get what he was going to get.

The same couldn't be said of the second dog who appeared. He might have been of the same family as the house dog. He had the height, but was altogether more shrunken and ribby. Good treatment would have filled him out, but for some reason he was not cherished. He was of paler colour, as though he had missed some necessary nourishment since birth. His nervousness showed in his eyes, and the trembling of his tail.

The house dog growled when the newcomer came, but not too aggressively. Perhaps that was one of the things he did for the house: warning other dogs off. A woman who had helped with putting out the dinner dishes noticed the intruder and made as if to throw something at him. Without waiting he ran to the back of the chief's hall. And then in no time he was back, in an ache of worry about the food. It was the way he spent his life.

I asked Kate White whether it would be bad manners to give him some of the food from my plate. She said it would be all right, and I gave the dog some of my food. The house dog noted this and was strangely accepting; he didn't growl. It seemed that as a house dog he did what was expected of him.

The assembly point or 'green room' at the back of the chief's yard became busy. The evening's dancers, many of them absolute children, had been rounded up – the chief was clearly a man of authority – and were being marked and dabbed with paint. Some older men, too, came. They were drummers, very serious, and their drums were un-usually slender and long, like small cannon. They lit a fire in the open space in front of us, and heated the goatskins of their drums until they were satisfied with the tone.

One of them broke off from this important business to ask Nicole, 'I like you. What about it?' When she reported this she said it was the Bantu way; in these matters they could be direct.

The chief said to me, 'You see how the young people come. They aren't all in Libreville. You see how we maintain our traditions.'

It became dark enough for the palm-branch torches, very romantic. A spark from one of the torches fell on the back of my hand and the burn-mark stayed for days.

The boys stood in a line in the mouth of the chief's village hall, the girls and one or two women in a line outside. Two by two, then, they left where they were and did their turn; that was the limit of the invention; it was not much better when the wiry old chief himself did a turn. I had the feeling that he had shouted and done his turn to pep things up and to encourage the others. But it didn't work. Something was missing; perhaps we, the audience, were foreign and wrong; perhaps we didn't inspire the drummers or the dancers.

MOBIET WAS disappointed. He said, 'They could have shown you a lot more. Those chaps playing the drums know a lot about the initiation ritual.'

He suggested that I had discouraged them by not going down to the river and not seeing the bones of the tribal elder. They couldn't give of their best after I had let them down.

He was nevertheless punctilious about thanking people in the village for what they had done. The afternoon had been his show; he felt the failure keenly.

In the car, going back, we talked some more about initiation. He said his wife had done the special woman's initiation, but there were things in it they couldn't talk about.

What things? Sorcery?

He said, 'I believe that there are people who use their negative energy to harm people. Negative emotions do harm. Sometimes they use material objects to make sure that the harm is done. It begins with meditation, and people will call it black arts, but I would not call it that because that is racist.'

'Have you talked about this to other people? Your parents?'

'Part of the spiritual path is enlightening others, but not in an evangelical way. As for my parents, I did try, but it did not work. I do films and I show them in the USA. My parents are in the audience and they have not asked me any questions. So I will wait until the time is ripe.'

'Do you think you will lose your spiritual life in the USA?'

'No. That is inside me. What I will miss is the forest, and the leaves, and the ritual sides of the ceremony. They are very important. I have to go back for a better future for my children, but I want them to have a taste of their mother's country. Gabon has been part of my destiny, but I don't know the whole story yet.'

'What do you feel about the forest now?'

'I always knew that plants were living beings, but now I know that they are conscious beings. They have spirits, and there is so much diversity in them. They have special and many chemical properties that can be used if we talk to them. I know that if you analyse all the plants of Gabon you cannot activate the healing process unless you know the language of the plants. To know that language you have to know the religion that comes with initiation.'

9

ON THE WAY BACK to Libreville we stopped at Lambaréné, the place connected with Dr Schweitzer. We had gone from Libreville to Lope by train and we were coming back by helicopter, courtesy of the army and the minister of defence.

Until I had got to Gabon I had not associated the country with Dr Schweitzer. When I thought about him I had thought of a vague tropical African space. Now it was here, next to the helicopter landing ground, and my first thought was of the overwhelmingness of water and heat, the nearness to nothing that was close to one, and how hard it would be to spend the best part of one's middle life here. Lambaréné was a narrow island, some fifteen miles long, in the Oguwé river. After the disturbance of the helicopter blade, sending dust noisily into the nearby bush, there was, as it seemed to me, something like the equivalent disturbance of the official welcome. Everyone welcoming the guest of the minister of defence seemed touched by the urgency of the helicopter; everyone – the representatives of different layers of local government, the officials of the

Schweitzer hospital – seemed anxious to say what he had to say right off. It made for some breathless moments. I had been hoping for a period of quiet in which I might expose myself to the genius of the place (using that word in its classical sense), letting the place speak for itself, and arriving through that at some private idea of the man we had come to honour.

It wasn't like that. The place felt cleansed of the presence of Dr Schweitzer, in spite of the long low-eaved hospital building, with the two rooms at one end that had been the doctor's. There was a lacklustre piano (the second of the two pianos that the doctor had had sent out to Lambaréné, we were told), with opened sheet music unnecessarily in place (for the actuality, no doubt) forty-four years after the doctor's death, the exposed music sheet brown from the harsh light of the broad Oguwé. There was a bookcase with some of the doctor's books: not books he had owned and read, but Asian translations (for which no true home had been found) of some of the doctor's own books, part of the unimportant detritus of a writer's life. In the next room was the doctor's narrow bed with a mosquito curtain. On a table were technical-looking relics, including a microscope. There were photographs, not easy to look at. It was possible that the real relics were elsewhere, and we were looking only at things that could be spared.

When I was a boy in Trinidad, on the other side of the Atlantic, I used to think that the light and heat had burned away the history of the place. You couldn't feel that bush or sea had a history. To have a sense of history you needed buildings, architecture; and history came to the place – you seemed to see the change occurring – in Marine Square in the centre of the old Spanish town, and the few ambitious buildings of the British period. Here at Lambaréné there was no architecture, only nondescript tropical buildings, in ochre-coloured distemper, of no distinctive style, that seemed to have eaten up the past.

While we looked, the young woman who was the official guide recited the dates of Dr Schweitzer's life: it was part of the continuing hubbub of our welcome.

In spite of that microscope on the table it was well known that Dr Schweitzer was more of a missionary than a doctor. The medical degree he had taken was the abridged one missionaries took; so that in Africa he was a little like the barefoot doctors the Chinese created for China much later in the century. When he and Lambaréné became famous more qualified doctors came out, attracted by the idea of service which he appeared to exemplify.

Dr Schweitzer came out to Gabon in 1915. The French colony had been established more than sixty years before, and missionary activity, both American and French, Presbyterian and Roman Catholic, had been going on for almost all that time.

The English traveller Mary Kingsley came to Gabon in 1893 and 1895. Her famous book, *Travels in West Africa*, was published by the house of Macmillan in 1897. (This was the year in which Somerset Maugham published his first novel: it gives a kind of context.)

Mary Kingsley describes a busy river life in Gabon, with

traders and missionaries. Dr Schweitzer, when he came to Gabon twenty years later, in 1915, would not have had to live the life of Robinson Crusoe. Mission life by this time would already have been formalised. African children would have been trained in housework; the missionary whose energy was low needed only conduct a service in his church, which might be next door to his house.

Mary Kingsley writes especially about Dr Nassau, a very early missionary from the American Presbyterian mission. He had been working among Africans for forty years when Mary Kingsley met him. She is full of praise for him; and he is clearly an unusual man, of high intellect, full of energy, and wise about the ways and beliefs of Africans. The subject of African religion interests Mary Kingsley, too. She consults Dr Nassau at length about what she calls 'fetish', which is her portmanteau word for African belief, and she gives the subject five chapters in her book, a hundred pages.

Set beside Mary Kingsley and Dr Nassau, Dr Schweitzer doesn't shine. Among Africans his reputation, which has lasted down to our own time, is that of a man who was 'harsh' to Africans and was not interested in their culture. This perhaps is the true mystery of the man: not his ability in 1915 to turn his back on the civilisation of the time (though the 1914 war might have been a factor), but the – almost heroic – idea of his own righteousness that enabled him to live apart in Africa for all that time: the ideal of the missionary taken to its limit, the man less interested in serving men than in beguiling them.

Early on her travels Mary Kingsley saw the ruins of the first mission house Dr Nassau built on the upper Oguwé. It was on one side of a ravine, and in front of it, 'as an illustration of the transitory nature of European life in West Africa', was the grave of Mrs Nassau. The four or five lines about this — the ruined mission house above the grave — make a telling point about dedication and loss and the swift growth of bush.

Quite different is the cluster of granite crosses beside the Lambaréné hospital building. The crosses are close together. They seem not to leave room for anyone else. These are the Schweitzer family graves. They speak more of possession and triumph than tragedy. Nearby is a caged, depressed-looking pelican, padding about on trampled mud. Dr Schweitzer had a pet pelican; and this unhappy pelican, flying nowhere, diving nowhere, is kept in his memory.

It became time to get back in the helicopter and leave. Some schoolchildren had been mustered in the afternoon sun for this farewell, and there were photographers. The boy closest to me, living deep in his imagination, blind to everything else, began to shadow-box for the photographers, and they, not seeing him, clicked away.

SIX

Private Monuments, Private Wastelands

IT WAS THE South African winter. In the high land around Johannesburg the air was dry and the grass was brown; outside the airport the jacaranda trees (as they had been identified to me) had turned yellow. Nothing of tropical Africa here, it seemed; the colours were like the winter-bitten colours of places far to the north, Iran, perhaps, or Castile. The straight lines of the industrial buildings on the way to the great city belonged to a culture of science and money, the style of another continent, another civilisation. The African workers at the roadside, at first exotic in this setting, gradually began to fit (though the extraordinary light gave a deeper tint and an extra shine to their blackness).

Two days later, in central Johannesburg, I saw what had befallen a section of the post-apartheid town. The white people, nervous of what the end of apartheid was going to bring, had left, just like that, and Africans had moved in, not local people, but footloose people from the countries round about, Mozambique, Somalia, the Congo and Zimbabwe. The government of free South Africa, in a fit of African-ness, had thrown open its borders to these people, and they were living in their own way in this corner of the too big and too solid and unyielding city: reducing great buildings and great highways to slum, or at any rate to a kind of half-life, in a way that would have been hard to imagine while the buildings served their original purpose. At road level solid-glass panes had been kicked in, and all the way up an office block (or perhaps an apartment block) there were lines of poor washing.

It is a saying of the extraordinary South African writer Rian Malan (born 1954), seeking always without rhetoric or falsity, and in an almost religious way, for an illumination to the racial pain of his country, that in Africa the white people built themselves a moonbase for their civilisation; when that crumbles there is nothing for black or white.

Forty years before, in Rwanda, on the shore of Lake Kivu, I had seen a much simpler Belgian holiday settlement surrendered to forest and people of the forest. The forest people, welcoming ready-made roof and walls and solid floors, ready-made shelter, had moved in, but had then grown unhappy: they didn't like the rectangular spaces of the Belgian houses, and they had sought gradually to shrink these spaces to the more familiar circular spaces of their huts. Some years later, in the Congo itself, I had seen whole residential areas of the town once called Stanleyville, now called Kisangani, swallowed up by forest, with here and here a bleached signboard from its earlier life showing (though the plan of the streets had already become indecipherable).

This area of Johannesburg, speaking of science, style and architecture (speaking as much of learning and dedication as the mysterious textbook Joseph Conrad found in a hut on the bank of the Congo), had the effect on me of the bush of Kisangani. It sent my mind back to other places of dereliction and ruin I had seen: the wartime rubble of East Berlin kept as a monument in the communist days. But it seemed easier even in the bad days for that part of East Berlin to be rebuilt than it would be for the half-life of this part of Johannesburg to be restored to something like its original meaning. Where would one begin? One would have to begin with the idea of the city, the idea of civilisation; and already, before one had even begun, one would be swamped by protest.

There were further discoveries to be made within that new slum. A sturdy old warehouse had been give over to new merchandise, which would have been like a parody of what had been here. It was a market of witchdoctors' goods, and it was extensive. These were the *muti* goods that witchdoctors required their customers to get, to be used by the witchdoctor as he pleased, usually to make medicines, which the unfortunate bewitched man or woman had to drink. The least offensive of these magical goods were the wreaths of herbs which could be used to fumigate a room or house to make life uncomfortable for a bad spirit. Higher up in the scale of seriousness were roots with earth clinging to them; perhaps they were used for purges: the purge is a recurring theme of African magic.

And then we were in the realm of awfulness: animal body parts laid out neatly on a kind of platform. The hawker was sitting on a low stool beside his goods. The goods themselves were stored in the market; people like the hawker didn't have to drag everything away at the end of the day and bring it all back in the morning; municipal regulation helped the *muti* market. He was a skilled hand at arranging this kind of display, our hawker; he could set disparate things side by side, a jaw, a rib, and make them appear to be related or part of a series. In the top left-hand corner of his display were three horse heads with fur still on the heads, suggesting that these pieces, given pride of place among his goods (and clearly precious), had at one time come fresh from the slaughter-house. They would not have been easy to come by. A most grievous kind of bewitching would have lain on the man who had been asked by the witchdoctor to go and get a horse head. It would have been an expensive piece of magic. (But perhaps not as expensive as the white woman's breasts that, according to the police, someone had been offering as *muti*.)

I would have liked to get a price for the horse head, but I was nervous of asking. I had asked many questions already and had exhausted my credit with the hawker. He was beginning to look cantankerous. He was proud of his stock and the way he laid it out. Every day he would have had idlers like me, visitors, tourists, coming and asking about the purpose of this and that, without any intention of buying, just wasting a dealer's time, and expecting to be taken seriously.

In addition to the horse heads there were a number of heads of deer, split down the middle with a single blow from a sharp knife or axe, the way in a cocoa estate, at harvest time, a cocoa pod, held in the left hand, might be split by a machete held in the right. The neatness and speed were necessary so that the brain of the poor animal could be taken away from the cranium and hawked about; and it was done so quickly that the thin-muzzled heads were still dainty and undamaged, and could be offered for sale in the market, with eyes that continued to look alive and interested and unafraid.

The smell was abominable. In addition to body parts spread out flat on the hawker's platform there were stomach parts that were hung out on display lines, like pieces of fabric, so that the expert in body parts might choose or examine what he wanted. These display parts were white or whitish, without colour; they had gathered dust.

The hawker had two guinea pigs in a cage. They were tormented by the smell of death and huddled together, finding a fleeting comfort in the warmth and life of the other. The hawker, noticing my worry, called out that they were his pets. It was his joke. The guinea pigs, when they were sold, would be ritually slaughtered, with a knife to the heart, very painful, but the favoured way, and their fresh blood drunk, at the witchdoctor's direction, part of the sacrifice.

I thought it all awful, a great disappointment. The people of South Africa had had a big struggle. I expected that a big struggle would have created bigger people, people whose magical practices might point the way ahead to something profounder. It was impossible for any rational person to feel that any virtue could come from the remains of these poor animals. As it was impossible later to feel that any succour the local diviners offered could put right the great hurt that the big city and its ancillary too-stringent townships inflicted on the people who lived in them. There was nothing here of the beauty I had found in Nigeria among the Yoruba people, with their cult, as it seemed to me, of the natural world; nothing here like the Gabonese idea of energy which was linked to the idea and wonder of the mighty forests. Here was only the simplest kind of magic which ended with itself, and from which nothing could grow.

Yet only a couple of hours before, at the Apartheid Museum, I had been dealing with another kind of African pain. The two Africas were separate; I could not bring them together. That was how it was here when you began to look: you swung from one Africa to another. And moving in this way from one set of ideas to another, you came to a feeling that its politics and history had conspired to make the people of South Africa simple.

Not far away from the *muti*-market was the street of diviners. Spaces were very small; the counter and the bench for customers took up most of the consulting room. In the first shop there was a very thin woman who had come to get some medicine for her baby girl – clearly some trouble with Aids, but I didn't want to ask. She gave the healer a hundred rand and the healer came back very soon with forty rand and some herb or herb dust in a piece of newspaper, with which the thin woman was pathetically pleased, thinking she had bought health for her baby. Across the road was another consulting room. Space again was a problem, and it was dark. There were two candlesticks. The diviner squatted low, made us throw bones, just as we had done some months before in Nigeria, in a space just as cramped, and she interpreted the signs for us.

Police cars were parked outside. Our driver went and talked to them. He said when he came back that the police were on the track of dangerous criminals and they had come here hoping to get protective *muti*.

2

IN THE Apartheid Museum one wall was engraved with the names of some of the repressive racial acts that had helped to keep the state in order. There was no longer apartheid, but it had lasted long enough – thirty-six years – for people to be made by the intrusive laws. Fatima, our guide and arranger, had been made by the laws. Someone less remarkable would have been crushed. Fatima had literary ambitions; this idea of nobility helped her to keep her soul. She also had an idea of other cultures outside – in the beginning she dreamed of the Islamic world – and though this Islamic dream was misguided, it also in the end helped her.

She told us when we met that she was 'coloured'. This was a South African word, it could mean someone of mixed race in a purely descriptive way. It had another meaning as well, and then it was loaded with unspoken insult. It came from the remote past and it implied that an ancestor was a Bushman: the equivalent here of what a pigmy was in Gabon, physically negligible, but also to be considered the first man, full of wisdom about trees and plants and poisons. In the 'Origins Centre' at Witwatersrand University they endlessly ran short films (scratchy and loud from being run over and over again) about Bushmen singing and dancing and hunting the magnificent eland, which they poisoned and killed in a terrible way.

On her mother's side there was a great-grandfather who was English. Her great-grandmother was Xhosa. She claimed to be of mixed race (already the fantasy created by apartheid legislation), but Fatima saw photographs of the lady and thought she was very much a Xhosa woman. Fatima's paternal grandfather was very black, but the family spoke Afrikaans and hated dark skin; and when Fatima went to visit them they took her to the hairdresser and had the kinks in her wiry hair straightened out so that she could look white.

So she grew up as 'just a coloured girl', without any identity. The Xhosa girls at school all had identities, and she had nothing. She grew up in a coloured community. She had Muslim neighbours and she saw they had feasts and rituals and a complete Muslim identity; and it was no doubt to grasp at this identity that when she was twenty she married a Muslim cleric. She was very pleased to have done that, feeding off the religion from the source, as it were. She began to 'cover up'; she started with a head scarf, and soon she was all covered, except for the face and hands. She did this on her own, but then her husband made more and more demands. He didn't like her sitting in taxis with other men; he didn't like her shaking hands with them. He threatened to divorce her. Her job as a reporter became impossible; her dream of an Islamic identity fell to the ground. It had already taken a knock when she went to Durban and tried to attach herself to the Indian community there. They weren't easy; they wanted to know her family name, her village; invariably, at the end of this inquisition, when they understood that she was coloured, they dropped her. She read a lot about Islam; she got to know more than the Indians and Muslims who quizzed her; it didn't help. She went on the pilgrimage to Mecca, but felt nothing; she saw only the restrictions on her as a woman.

She began to look then for a black identity, but it was hard. Her coloured background again got in the way; the blacks rejected her as someone without a country or culture. So the whole South African journey for her was a discovery of pain: from her coloured beginnings to the Islamic dream, to the Indians of Durban, to the blacks of the townships. There were townships in Durban but they were near the airport and she didn't see them. She saw them properly only when she came to Johannesburg and began to work with the blacks. It was only then that she understood the great pain and, with that, the deception, for Africans, of political freedom and the end of apartheid.

Fatima said, 'I see that the blacks here reach out more than the white South Africans. They, the whites, want the blacks to be "there", not near them. They cannot reach out or forgive, and they want a distance from the black. They are full of preconceived ideas, like Soweto is dangerous and that a black boy friend is bad.'

I had wanted, when I began this book, to stay away from politics and race, to look below those themes for the core of African belief. But rather like Fatima looking for identity, I felt stymied in South Africa and saw that here race was all in all; that race ran as deep as religion elsewhere.

3

THE Apartheid Museum was my introduction to the South African idea of the monument. I found it moving; but there was something grander at the end of the Johannesburg–Pretoria road. This was the Afrikaner monument celebrating the Great Trek of the Boers from the Cape Colony to the interior in the first half of the nineteenth century. They trekked to be free of the British. They took all their goods and animals with them; and they went with ox-carts. It would have been slow and hard. The trekkers didn't always know what they were up against. The Africans were unfriendly; many of the trekkers died. Fatima, at school, had to study the Great Trek; all the skirmishes on the way became battles, and all these battles had to be committed to memory. Yet, in a further twist of cruelty, she was not permitted to visit the monument.

The monument, which is of brown granite, is at the top of a hill. From the road it shows as a bump on the hill. Nothing free standing, no heroic, larger-than-life sculpture. You approach it from the garden at the back, looking up to its great height, and you climb up to the main level. At the entrance there is a green bronze statue of a stern woman, larger than life, her head covered, protecting two clinging children. This is a strange sentimental touch, out of keeping with the 1930s Germanic weight of the monument, which (like so many art-deco buildings) is a little like a magnified 1930s radio or radiogram. There is a symbolic perimeter wall here which seems to protect the monument. It is made up of a circular laager of sixty-four ox-carts done in low relief. The number is important. That number of ox-carts made up the laager when the trekkers were attacked by the Zulus on 16 December 1838. The Zulus were badly defeated, and it is that victory, of Blood River, that the monument celebrates.

Inside, past the teak door, the monument is circular and cool and beautiful, lit by four tall arched windows, one on each side. Within four uprights these windows have granite mullions that, strangely, create an Islamic pattern. At eye-level, on the circular wall, are twenty-seven sculptured plaques in low relief marking the stations and defeats and victories of the Trek. It should be said at once that the Africans in these sculptures are not caricatured. They are shown nude, more or less, and for that reason look more heroic than the Trekkers, who are in full nineteenth-century clothes, which do not work as well in sculpture as nude bodies do.

All this would be impressive, but there is more. Below the floor of the main hall there are further levels where artefacts connected with the Trek are displayed. Work on the monument was inaugurated on 16 December 1938, the centenary of the battle of Blood River, and the monument was formally opened, in the presence of a crowd of 250,000, on 16 December 1949 by D. F. Malan, in the first full year of the apartheid policy he and his Nationalist government had laid down for South Africa. It was an Afrikaner monument, a monument of African defeat, and it is easy to understand why Fatima and people like her were not allowed to visit the monument.

The architect, Gerard Moerdijk, said he had built a monument that would last a thousand years. He should have been more careful. It is too easy in a place as fragmented as South Africa to see what one wants to see and to commit oneself to building on sand. Times of course have changed. Moerdijk's Afrikaner monument has become a national monument, part of the national patrimony, and is allowed to live on. But no one can really be sure what the future will bring.

4

RIAN MALAN introduced me to the writing of the Afrikaner writer Herman Charles Bosman. Just before I left he gave me a copy of *Mafeking Road*, one of the writer's four collections of stories. It was a South African publication and gave no indication of the writer's career and dates. I felt as a result that I was reading blind. I had only a quote from Roy Campbell to hold on to, and he had died many years ago. Bosman's talent was a humbling one. He writes about simple or retarded country people, near the end of the nineteenth century, and the stories build up, add to one another. They create a community, and the simple manner of the writer can take him far, to many moods. He can do comedy; the same simple voice can create great beauty. There is a story about a leopard who appears to the narrator, sniffs menacingly almost up to his face, but then behaves almost like a dog. The narrator begins to boast about his leopard. His neighbours don't believe him. One day the narrator sees the leopard sleeping like a dog on the road, with crossed paws. A closer look reveals the gash caused by a Mauser rifle on the animal's chest. The Mauser is the weapon of choice in the village. The narrator's boasting, and the cruelty of his oafish neighbours, have brought about the death of the magical creature.

The biggest story in the collection is about a mimic trek. The great trek from the Cape is part of the folk wisdom of these simple people; in their imagination it is something that's open to them all to attempt. It takes very little now, at the end of the Boer war, which has been lost, to persuade them that they are about to be oppressed by the British where they are and they should trek to freedom, to Namibia, German South-west Africa, where they will find Germanic people more like themselves. But this trek will be across the terrible Namib desert. Not many of them know about the desert and how to find water in the desert. But their folly makes light of the trouble to come.

They load up the ox-wagons, like the earlier trekkers, and start; the calamities follow almost at once. There are no false leads in Bosman's writing. After the first watering of the cattle the water runs out. Later a muddy hole is found, but the poor tormented cattle sink to their knees, get no water, and find it hard to rise. In their delirium the trekkers, after only a couple of days, persuade themselves that the crossing of the desert is almost done. One morning they find that their African servants have deserted; this is like a death sentence for the group. Detail adds to detail: Bosman's understated style rises wonderfully to the pain and majesty of its terrible subject. Some of the would-be trekkers decide to go back, but in a strange twist (though it is now clear to everyone that the trek across the desert is a horrible mistake) the people who seek to go back lose their moral authority; they have let the side down. One man, the first promoter of the trek, goes mad. He presses on and is later – when the survivors go back and can count the missing – found dead by Bechuana African trackers.

I have bracketed Bosman's stories and the Voortrekker

Monument because they share an ambiguity. The ambiguity lies in the subject. The Voortrekker Monument is not only about the Great Trek. It is also about African defeat and African pain. The Monument is a work of art; it aims high. It took eleven years to build and in the early 1940s cost close to 400,000 pounds. Everything about it is thoroughly considered; yet it is brought low by its subject.

Something like this can be said about Bosman's stories. They are beautifully done, but their underlying subject is unstated. These people are not only simple country people, but out of their simpleness, their lack of imagination, they will bring untold pain to the Africans among them. It might be said that Bosman plays fair, that in his quiet way he leaves nothing out, and the reader is free to interpret everything. It may be that Bosman is too quiet, in his way. Rian Malan thought he could be compared to Mark Twain. And there is something there. The comparison has to be with Huck Finn's frightening, absurd father, a wonderful comic creation. But there is nothing as full-blooded as that in Bosman; that full-bloodedness is outside his range, which is more delicate.

5

A TRULY great man travelled in the 1890s from Durban to Johannesburg to Pretoria. His journey, in part a modern version (by rail and stage coach) of the Great Trek, was a kind of Calvary; it altered his life and set him on the path of his life's work; but that work was in India rather than South Africa, and there is no monument to him in Johannesburg or Pretoria. The traveller was Mohandas Gandhi, and the story of his Calvary is like this. He came to South Africa in 1893. He was only twenty-four, and though, because of family connections, he had come out as a lawyer for a wealthy Indian Muslim businessman, he had hardly any experience.

He had appeared in court only once, in Bombay, in an absurd thirty-rupee (two pounds) affair in the Small Causes Court. Nothing could have been pettier, but for Gandhi it was a fiasco. When the case was called Gandhi got up. He should have questioned the people on the other side. But he became very shy and he could think of nothing to say. All he could do was to sit down again and ask for the case to be transferred (for fifty-one rupees) to Mr Patel, one of the lawyers at the lawyers' table. Mr Patel dealt briskly with the matter, and no doubt got his fee; but Gandhi was too mortified to find out whether his former client (a woman) had won or lost. It seemed after this that all he could do as a lawyer was to avoid the court and draft memorials.

It was a livelihood of a sort, but then there came the South African offer from a Gandhi family friend. A year in South Africa, first-class return fare, a wage of £105, everything found. Gandhi had the wit to see that with these terms he was going out more as a servant than a lawyer. He also would have seen that the business folk were getting a lawyer cheap. But he didn't mind; he liked the idea of the adventure, and he didn't haggle.

In the beginning it was like adventure: a slow sea journey: Lamu, Mombasa, Mozambique, and then Durban. There he met his employer, and the employer told him he was going to be a white elephant for the firm, since there wasn't much for him to do. Gandhi discovered that the legal case hinged on accounts. He bought a book and began to study it, and he soon knew as much as he needed.

After eight days a first-class ticket to Pretoria (in the north) was bought for him. His employer thought that Gandhi should have a five-shilling ticket for bedding. Gandhi preferred to save the money, and thought that this obstinacy and meanness brought on everything – though it is hard to see why he should have thought so. And so began the Calvary. Every stop on the way – Maritzburg, Charlestown, Standerton: every name remembered thirty years later when Gandhi was writing his autobiography (though not all of them survive in the modern atlas) – was full of shame and fear and insult, such bad treatment, such violence, that he wondered whether he would arrive in one piece.

At Maritzburg the railway attendant asked if Gandhi required bedding. He said, 'I have one with me.' And though he doesn't say, he believes this started the trouble. Two officials came, and then a third, and it was this third who told him he should move to the van compartment. When Gandhi refused, and said they would have to remove him, the official called a police constable; the constable pushed him and his luggage away. Gandhi settled down to waiting through the night. It was very cold. He had an overcoat in his luggage, but thought that if he asked for it he would be insulted. He did a lot of heart-searching that night. Should he go back to India? Should he stay and fight? Should he go on to Pretoria and not mind? He thought he should stay and fight the disease of prejudice, suffering in the process if he had to. At the end of this heart-searching he decided to take the next available train to Pretoria.

If that was all about him in a crisis he would not be Gandhi. But he was already Gandhi – in addition to everything else, a man of forms, a man of the law, with faith in the law (not yet faith in the faith), and the next morning he sent a long telegram to the general manager of the railway. The train he boarded (with the bedding ticket he had refused at Maritzburg) took him to Charlestown. The Calvary continued there. There was no railway between Charlestown and Johannesburg in those days; there was only a stage coach, and the man in charge of it was an absolute thug. He tormented Gandhi, not allowing him to sit inside, and then requiring him to sit not on the box beside the driver but on the footboard. He knocked Gandhi about so badly that the other passengers objected.

The coach stopped for the night in the small village of Standerton (not on any biggish map now). There were Indians there, sent by Gandhi's employer to receive Gandhi. So there was protection, and Gandhi used the lull to write a full letter to the agent of the coach company. He got an encouraging reply: the coach from Standerton would be bigger, and the thuggish leader would not be on it. The Indians who were looking after him took him to the coach in the evening, found him a good seat, and so, at last, he reached Johannesburg safely. To do the final leg of the journey, to Pretoria, in the style he insisted on as a lawyer – first class – he took the precaution of writing a note to the station master telling him who and what he was, going in person to buy the ticket (one sovereign) and wearing a frock-coat and necktie (there is a photograph of Gandhi in South Africa in this garb, and if we assume that his wardrobe was limited, it is possible that this photograph shows Gandhi as he went to the Johannesburg ticket office). And then, as so often happens when we prepare too much for trouble, there was none. The man in the ticket office was not South African. He was from Holland, and he was all courtesy and friendship.

Gandhi at this stage believed in the British Empire. He believed that Indians in South Africa were discriminated against because they were politically indifferent, made no representations and were not organised. When the legal work that had brought him to South Africa was done (he persuaded the parties in dispute to accept arbitration), he prepared to go back to India. He went to Durban to wait for a ship. While he was there he saw an item in the local newspaper about the Indian Franchise: there was before the Natal legislature a bill that sought to disenfranchise the Indians of the province. Gandhi was shocked, but the rich Indian businessmen he spoke to knew nothing about it, and were not too concerned. That was even more shocking; and what they decided to do after a little discussion was to shift the burden of protest to Gandhi.

So Gandhi postponed his return to India. It happened like that again and again; his vision of Indian disabilities widened; Gandhi's one year in South Africa stretched in the end to twenty years. He had been very young and untrained, absurdly shy, only a lawyer who could draft memorials, when he came to South Africa; he was in middle life when he left, the lawyer subsumed in the mahatma, his political tools perfected: civil disobedience, the fast, his own spirituality.

It had all begun to happen on that terrible journey from Durban to Maritzburg to Charlestown to Standerton to Johannesburg to Pretoria. In forty-eight hours his shyness fell away like a garment; young as he was, he became a leader of men. Many Europeans, German Jews especially, helped him in Johannesburg. This would have been a revelation to him. His cause was Indian and local; this outside encouragement would have made him less parochial, and opened him up to the world, politically and in religious matters. When he wrote later of Johannesburg it was with love. Though it has to be said that Gandhi had trouble with Africans; he found it hard to see them, to fit them into his world picture.

Even at that moment of crisis on the Charlestown coach he can find a cruel word, *Hottentot*, for the coach-leader's African servant sitting beside the coach-driver. It is a strange word to come out of Gandhi's mouth, when he is complaining of race prejudice. But there may be an explanation. Gandhi was dictating his autobiography in Gujarati to his Gujarati secretary, Mahadev Desai. Desai did the translation into English, and it is possible that *Hottentot* is the dictionary English word, a kind of synonym, that Desai alighted on.

6

YOU CAN BE some time in Johannesburg – the great avenues, the motor-car showrooms, the parks – without seeing the townships. You know they are in the background, of course – so much has been written about them – but still the first township you see can be quite startling: the little houses of brick or concrete, one like the other, the straight rows, the small yards, the treelessness. When you are far enough away in bad areas the houses or huts become the merest shacks of old corrugated-iron sheets, roughly daubed with a number, for the purposes of identification alone. It is amazing that people can live and thrive in such dwellings, but they do, and they make one think of Oscar Wilde: 'One can survive anything except death.'

When life was done there was the road to the cemetery at Avalon, named as if in jest after the cemetery of King Arthur's knights: acre upon acre of low tombstones that appeared to repeat the pattern of the petty houses, completing in this way the cycle of life and death. Saturday was the great day for funerals here. The motor-cars going there flashed their hazard lights, to tell people that they were on solemn business and required priority. It required only a flick of a switch to put on hazard lights, but the effect of the rich-looking cars, the merging traffic lanes and the dancing lights was so jolly that one had the idea that the drivers, out of their Saturday joy, were playing with the switches as they drove.

Walls on the way to the cemetery were painted with the names of undertakers. Death was big business here; it never failed; every Saturday brought fresh customers. In the openness of Avalon, below the high bright sky you could see the dark-suited groups of men and the women in red and white whose presence marked the spots of fresh graves and funerals. The soil was red and stony. Sometimes – I suppose it depended on the stylishness and the charges of the undertakers – a little tent (flat-roofed, without walls) had been put up not far from the grave, and below this tent (and not really in shade) were women connected with the dead person. These women sat on chairs and some of them wore blankets. The blanket here, Fatima said, was a ceremonial garb, a development from the flayed skin of the sacrificed cow, which was sometimes used to wrap around the corpse to keep it warm.

The new graves were close together, the earth mounds almost touching, and each grave was marked with a provisional identifying slab, to be replaced in time, I supposed, with a proper tombstone. Many of the slabs were for young people, perhaps carried away by the HIV pandemic, a further twist in the chronicle of pain of these people.

Considering the extent of Avalon, the abundant grief it represented, I thought of what Fatima (and others) had told me: that without apartheid, there was no further cause for South Africa in the world, nothing for its writers to explore, nothing to attract attention, no true motive for loss or tragedy. Was there not some deeper, more universal motif, apart from the obviousness of apartheid? Something that continued pure, and of itself alone? It seemed unlikely. D. H. Lawrence (to take a name at random) could get away from the coal pits of Nottinghamshire; but he had the rest of England to contemplate (though he remained a provincial at heart), and then he had the rest of the world. That couldn't be said of South African writers: they remained bound to their wheel of fire.

I asked Fatima whether she thought people might change.

She said, 'The present government wants people to move away, but the people don't want to. People sound the same as they did before, and the grievances of apartheid are kept alive so as to fob off responsibility. When you have no better answer you will use that. It supports our film industry: "Once we were black . . ."'

I wanted to know what she felt in Avalon, seeing the blankets on the women, and the mourners dancing on the graves. What I was seeing was new to me, and I thought that for other people as well there must have been something more immediate and personal than thoughts of apartheid.

She said, in her remarkable open way, 'It reminds me of

my past. It makes me think of my grandmother who wore the white-and-red uniform. It also reminds me that even if you are a Christian you will sacrifice an ox for the ancestors. In some places they sacrifice the ox or cow and wrap the body in the skin for burial. The animal has to scream so that the ancestors hear it, but I cannot do it. I could not even watch my own goat being sacrificed when I did the pilgrimage.'

And that idea of the cow being made to bellow in death was so painful that I thought of the way they killed cats in the Ivory Coast, putting them in a sack and then dumping the sack in boiling water. And just as that Ivory Coast way of preparing cats for table made everything else in the country seem unimportant, so that sacrificial way with cattle darkened everything else here.

7

TO BE BLACK in South Africa was to be an inheritor, or at any rate to have that possibility. To be white and sensitive was to wonder about one's place in the new scheme of things, and almost immediately, when a situation was too difficult, to start dealing in ideas that were perhaps too large for the brutal subject of survival.

Colin lived with a feeling of fear. He said, 'It is extremely difficult to voice anything without looking over your shoulder. There is a complete absence of discourse. I feel I am unable to speak and I am reacting endlessly to a situation without being able to take a step back and thinking about the situation or my reactions. I took another look at humanism in the hope of finding something to clutch at. You can have Africans contributing to humanism, but you cannot have African humanism. But you can't say that. I live with fear and the paralysis it brings. The suffocation is very present. I look back and I think of the 80s, and the struggle to do the right. I persisted in the struggle because I came from a family full of conflicts. Now it is only a memory, but that memory sustains me.'

The conflicts in Colin's family came from his divided ancestry. He was half English and half Afrikaner. He had a grandmother who talked a lot about the British concentration camps during the Boer war. He understood the Afrikaner rage about the camps; at the same time, through his father, he had a feeling for British liberalism. When he was twelve Colin was sent to stay with an uncle in a small country town. In those towns segregation was not as severe as in other places, and Colin became friendly with a black boy, Franz, of his own age. This friendship was very important in his, Colin's, intellectual development. Colin said of it, 'I saw Franz and me and our connection as a humanist moment in time.' And Colin could talk like that because he was completely serious.

He talked to Franz about the city, and Franz in return showed him Nature, the desert and the forest and grasshoppers. One day Franz was stung by bees. Colin pulled the dead bees out of his hair: the memory was fresh all these years later.

The time came for Colin to go back to his family. He thought that he and Franz should write to each other. But that wasn't possible. Franz, though, had a favour to ask: he wanted Colin to post him a dictionary and an atlas. White schoolchildren were given these things as a matter of course; black children weren't. And it happened that Colin had the money to buy those books for Franz.

For the fear that continued to nag him, and perhaps also for his unfulfilled humanist yearnings, Colin now consoled himself with nature and his work and – unexpectedly – his cat's 'very intense personal relationship with me'.

I felt, though, that in Africa, where cats and animals generally are given such a hard time, even in a protected place like the Kruger Park, Colin's relationship with his cat might open up a whole new area of pain. Colin himself told this story:

'Some time ago there was a major football championship match in the stadium here. Some time during the match someone threw a black cat in the midst of the rival team. Of course, the cat was killed, and the rival team was up in arms, saying that there was magic and an evil spell put on them. I keep thinking about it, and the only rational answer I have is that the proximity between animals and animism itself allows such brutal behaviour. Also, you have to understand that while all societies have metaphors which dilute the emotion connected with what is unpleasant, or with frustration or anger, here in South Africa the distance between metaphor and reality is very little. During the elections the ANC and its rival call each other cockroaches, snakes and dogs. You can get into real trouble very quickly here, using metaphors, and during intense debates where animal metaphors are used, real blood will flow. This is very frightening and depressing for me.'

In 1987 Colin went to Paris for the first time. He was 'blown away'. Some things he could relate to, but there were things he could not understand at all. Still, the experience gave him a new way of looking.

He said, 'We will have to go through a very violent post-colonial period to become human. You don't have to go to a university to become an intellectual. There are organic traditions here too. Biko called it *buntu*, and it is the idea that you are a person because of another person. It gives the wish to aspire. My hope lies in the aspiration, not in the flaws all around us — though the idea of aspiring can bring its own flaws.'

He couldn't escape conscription into the South African army. He was sent to Angola and there he had to guard refugee camps. The camps had black women and children, coloured women, and some blonde white women and children – Portuguese families who had been abandoned by their men.

'It was in this camp, while we were wearing the hated uniform, that I realised that men have a moral choice to do what they do. There were men who raped, exploited and did terrible things, and there were also men, like me, who made a small group who tried to make things better for these women, who were ready to do anything to protect their children. I saw moral shades in this army. There was, and is, a moral choice always. But I feel that being white is a debt you can't pay even if you fought in the struggle.'

8

I ASKED Phillip whether there could be an idea of possibility in the society. I thought it was an important idea both for the society and the individual.

He said, 'In my view the idea of possibility has to do with humanity. In my own small way I think that our transition from apartheid to democracy through the Truth and Reconciliation Commission has provided the sense of humanity to some extent. It may have been flawed in some ways or not enough, but at least we did not have a civil war like Zimbabwe, where they wanted to get rid of the whites. This brings a sense of possibility.'

He worked professionally with a mixed group. 'I don't feel that because I am not black I don't have possibility here. In a strange way it is and is not a disaster area. Maybe it's like being in denial. Yet in another way I am trying to do what I can do as a South African for my country. I also know that I live with the constant dilemma of: should I go or stay? Sometimes I even wonder if this is a carry-over or part of my Jewish ancestry. My mother's ancestors came in the 1900s to escape the Eastern European pogroms. There was a big Jewish community here pre-1994, and there was a dramatic drop in this community after '94. It was really a dramatic drop. Many left and went abroad. When I feel there is no hope, seeing the crime, corruption and general decay, I feel I am behaving like the white whingers. But I always have this at the back of my head: should I go?'

This freedom to move out was like a privilege. Colin didn't have this privilege.

Phillip said, 'When Zuma [the new, 2009 president, a Zulu] came into power and had all this rape and arms-corruption controversy and tribal air all around him there was another exodus. I thought that even though I did not like Zuma I would stay, because maybe it is a good thing. Maybe he will connect us to the populist movement in the country.'

Unlike Colin, he saw no philosophical side to his predicament.

'Part of me says it was bound to happen. Maybe I'm making excuses, but the people here have suffered so much as "inferiors" that this inverted black racism has to happen in order to heal in the long run. I believe it may take another generation to develop a philosophical resolution to our predicament. And that can only happen if our educational system improves. That is a big "if" here.'

It was a universal complaint. Poor African education (no dictionaries for Franz, and no atlases) was part of the apparatus of apartheid; fifteen years later its effects were still being felt right through the society.

Phillip said, 'At the moment American consumerism is consuming us – malls, long streets, and cars to drive everywhere. It is very ironic. I have become more reclusive because I don't like what I see in the city. There is a climate of fear, and I have seen what it is to live in a city without fear. When I go to Europe I see what a big city can be – small shops, people walking, a street culture. Not everyone is in a mall and they are not driving everywhere. I still try to walk into town some days, because I cannot live in a car all day, and if I cannot do this then I will have to leave. There is a move to reclaim our city and areas in it where the whites simply moved out. They moved because of fear.'

9

JOSEPH WAS said to be a Zulu traditionalist. I thought I should go to see him, to connect again with some of the earlier religious inquiries I had made elsewhere for this book. I had no idea what to expect. He lived in a low concrete house in what looked like a pacific mixed area. That was ordinary enough, but he had guard dogs in a wire enclosure, like rich people, and there were young men in his back yard (many plastic chairs there) and in the street outside his house. These young men were his followers: Joseph was famous and well-to-do, and the people who were his followers tried to walk as he did and tried to talk as he did. A certain amount of what passed for political and cultural thought in the townships came from Joseph. He was in his thirties. He knew his reputation. He talked a lot, always provocatively. The upholstered chairs in his sitting room looked a little rumpled; they had been much used that day. A middle-aged woman secretary sat at a computer with her back to the room; she was working out or tabulating Joseph's appointments. He was in demand.

He said that whites owned most of the media, and he spoke the well-known fact like one who had earned the right to speak it. He went on to say that foreign media had no regard for local traditions. This was much more the kind of thing he was expected to say; and having got there, he became easier, and his speech flowed. He knew, what foreigners didn't always know, that when you were working in an area you had to ask permission of the local chief, and when it was given you had to make a gift to the chief: a bottle of brandy and 200 rand. And when you had done your work you couldn't just go away. If the chief wanted you to stay for a farewell feast, you had to do it. White and Indian producers didn't understand this, and they created problems. Sometimes as a result the chief fined them, and this fine had to be paid. It was an African tradition, and it covered many mistakes – getting a girl pregnant, stealing someone's goods, getting drunk and abusing an elder. In this way you completely by-pass the white man's law. It was the African way.

Quite abruptly, then, he broke off and asked me, 'Where do you come from?'

I said, 'Trinidad.'

And he was completely thrown.

I said, 'Near Jamaica.'

He said, 'Bob Marley.' And then, reflectively, he said, 'The slave trade.'

I said, 'Yes.'

'Has Britain apologised for the slave trade?'

I said, 'It was a long time ago, and many nations were involved.'

He dropped the conversational mode and began to make a speech, clearly one he had made many times before, that nothing was known of African stories or history or traditions. All African children, on the other hand, knew about Cinderella and pixies and Western soaps and Western history. This made them 'confused'.

He said, 'We have anglicised our children and we feed them selective information which is always lauding the West. Do you know that people here have forgotten their own funeral songs? They bring big ghetto-blasters and play a CD at the grave or wake. If you tell them that Christianity and Islam were part of our colonisation, they get very mad. Even when they go for a white wedding and walk up the aisle, all that is part of our colonisation. The twenty-first-birthday party is not African. We have lost all our traditions and we are doing the wrong thing.'

People talked against polygamy. That irritated him. He was a product of polygamy and had no problems with it. In Africa the gender ratio was one man to thirteen women. 'It was part of the African wealth. Our wealth was land, women, cattle, crops and children. To be an elder we had to have these, and now all that is gone.'

He did the talking; he raised the topics. And very soon he was talking about Christianity and contrasting it with the traditional African beliefs which he said were his own.

He said, 'I am a modern man.' He meant a modern

African man, someone who had shed much colonial baggage; he used certain words in his own way. He said, 'I am not a Christian. My mother was a priest and my father was also in the church, but they could not give me an identity. Only when I went out and found my ancestors did I get a feeling that I belonged somewhere. The old ways summoned me and I found peace. We have many Christian churches here and they all straddle and suffocate our African identity.'

It was possible, putting everything together, to understand why he was thought to be a Zulu traditionalist, and why he had such a hold on the young. A poorly educated person from the township, knowing no history and having hardly any idea of his place in the world, would be given something to hold on to, and Joseph's special style would make it attractive.

He was fierce about the need to sacrifice cows and goats in the traditional way; the animal rights people had to stay away. 'They make a noise only when low- or middle-income people do it. You should see when a big wig does it. He does not hide it, and everyone comes in cars, limos and helicopters to be part of the ritual. When we slaughter a goat we have to stab it in the side many times to get the bad omen to go. Look at my body. It is full of scars. It is not child abuse. A witchdoctor came and cut me with a razor blade and then rubbed and filled the cut with the ashes of a snake. It is our way. And I must, as a traditional man, cut or slaughter a cow in our way. Why do you want the animal to be slaughtered in another way which you think is more humane? First of all, the animal which is to be sacrificed belongs to the ancestor, and so it has to alert the ancestor by crying out loud. I am sick of black people censoring or condemning our culture. They are doing it because they are so diluted. They do not know who they are and what the rituals mean. I question Christianity right down to its roots. Who are they to say that we must do these things in a hygienic way? We will arrive there ourselves. Do we go and film their circumcisions? Why do they come here and pay poor people to allow them to film their sacred rituals? They, the Christians, created apartheid and they enslaved my people despite the Bible. I practise the old ways. I go to the townships to slaughter the animal, and if the ritual is very complicated then I will go to my ancestral village. I have my shrines and I worship there.'

He had a pair of rusting handcuffs on the wall behind him. Rusting, but not very old: I was sure they were there as a conversation piece, a token of the slavery he liked to talk about. He said he had bought the cuffs in a junk-shop. He took them down from the wall and began to play with them, as though he had made them harmless. He asked me, 'Are these things older than you?' I examined the question, fearing a trap, but could find none, and then I said I didn't know. It must have been the correct reply, because he gave up the subject and sought to re-affix the cuffs to the wall.

He continued to talk, making a leap from the cuffs to the fast-food chains of Johannesburg. He wondered why they didn't do African fast food. He had exhausted his proper subjects and was now only speaking at random. The fast-food people and everybody else came to Africa only to make money, he said, and as a result Africa was 'a quagmire of wars'. In the old days there used to be tribal wars, but they burnt themselves out very quickly. Now, when there was no tradition, and people had no idea where they came from, they had very little regard for the tombs of their kings, and things were generally deplorable. The ancient graves of the Zulu kings – buried in a sitting position and wrapped in a cowskin – were neglected.

He said, 'I really feel we have paid a great deal for our freedom. Mandela let us down. He let the white people keep their wealth and lifestyle and walk into democracy. Rainbow nation is rubbish. Black people are still called kaffirs, and coloured people are nowhere. They have no heroes and are called "woolly hair". They had to endure the pencil test.'

It was becoming too random and glib. I felt it was time to go. He followed me into the yard.

He said, 'I've always wanted to do this.'

I had no idea what he meant; and then he held the car door open for me. His followers – in jeans and tee shirt – were relaxed in the traffic-less street, in a cool mid-afternoon light. They could see us through the open gate; but he was so secure in their affection he could afford to do this clowning with the car door.

10

ON MY FIRST trip to Soweto (or through Soweto) I had seen the Mandela house, from the front and the side, and then, as the road had climbed, from the top. It had seemed to me impressive. It wasn't small. It was in dark-red brick, with a fence of the same material, and it had an outer rock garden. This garden was an oddity in Soweto, and its purpose was no doubt to give additional privacy and protection to the people of the house.

Now an appointment had been made with Winnie Mandela, and on this Monday morning we were able to enter the Mandela yard from the front, through one of the two big gates. There were five or six security men in dark suits.

In the entrance to the house were many artefacts and photographs. They were laid out on the floor, as they might have been laid out on a display table. They partially blocked the doorway to what was furnished like a dining room. The photographs looked personal; they were of the family. The artefacts looked like official gifts. There were a surprising number of Indian pieces among them: modern versions of Indian deities, with faces and bodies much influenced by photographs and the cinema, all done with an artificial bronze-seeming finish. Among the photographs were big ones of Nelson Mandela, some in colour. He didn't live in the house, but one felt that his was the guiding presence; and the house felt bereft of its master.

Just beyond the dining room was a big room with upholstered chairs: the sitting room, clearly. A sliding glass door was open, and a cool winter wind blew in. The glass door looked out on to the inside of the rock garden, where some men were weeding and some were using water-hoses. Without this watering the garden would have been dry, like the rest of Johannesburg.

We sat with the man who had arranged the meeting, and this simple act of waiting gave a regal touch to Mrs Mandela when she appeared, quite modest, soft in body, in a grey trouser suit, with her famous wig and with pearls around her neck and wrists. It was hard not to be affected by her, seeing her close, a woman whom one had seen in countless photographs, and in varying moods, a woman to some extent by-passed now by the great events that had come to South Africa.

She was still full of political passion, still close to the fears she felt in the bad times.

'You have no idea what the name Mandela meant. It meant imprisonment and interrogation. This was a period where people vanished or were killed by the security forces for being members of the ANC. The greatest danger was that the leadership would perish in prison, and that people would get disheartened and lose faith. So I exposed myself, and did it quite deliberately. I had by then lost all fear. When you undergo every possible humiliation or torture there is nothing left. You lose all fear. One night they just came and threw all my things in a van, and I was banished to a desolate place for nine years.'

She used the banishment and the remoteness to recruit people and to send them out of the country for training.

It was in Soweto in 1976 that the revolution became critical. 'This is where it began, and I still live here. I cannot dream of leaving my people and going to live in a grand suburb.'

She was referring obliquely to the larger-than-life statue of Mandela that had been put up in a rich Johannesburg square. She thought it was a 'foolish' statue; and the day I went to see it two white children were playing on the chunky feet.

She said, 'You must remember that the Mandela who went in' – went in: went to jail – 'was a revolutionary, and the Mandela who came out was preaching peace and compromise. In fact, the statue should have been here in Soweto, where it all began and where he lived. The way to dilute a person is to commercialise him, and they have. The man who went to prison would not have allowed this commercialisation or being a brand name for a Foundation. My grandchildren are deeply hurt by all this commercialisation, and it is an albatross round their necks.'

The greater hurt was the 'compromised' freedom that had come to South Africa. 'I feel that we were short-changed. It was a freedom based on compromises and concessions, and that is what Mandela accepted. Black economic empowerment is a joke. It was a white confidence measure made up by local white capitalists. They took malleable blacks and made them partners. But those who had struggled and had given blood were left with nothing.

They are still in shacks: no electricity, no sanitation, and no chance of an education.'

When she spoke Mandela's name she didn't use the first name, Nelson; and she had two distinct ways of enunciating the name Mandela. Mandela the revolutionary was pronounced in one way; the later Mandela was pronounced in another way.

She said, 'I felt very bad when he went to get the Nobel Prize with his jailer De Klerk. Why did he go with the oppressor in tow? De Klerk had done nothing to release Mandela. Time dictated that it was necessary to release him, and there was always the promise of great violence to come if things had carried on as before.'

We talked about the Truth and Reconciliation Commission. This was meant to heal the racial divisions in the country, but Winnie Mandela (and others) were scornful. She thought it was especially hard for black people, who had suffered so much, to appear before that Commission and condemn themselves for resisting.

She said, 'It should be an individual process and not forced on a society. I think it is a terrible insult to women and men who sacrificed their lives for removing apartheid. They had to go and account for their actions. Not many people know what it was like living under that regime day in and day out. What they forget is that for over four decades black people had lived as non-people. The abnormality of racism had become a normal reality for them. The Truth and Reconciliation Commission was not a realistic idea. It opened up wounds that could not heal. You learned about atrocities and the method and means of your loved one's death. How and where they were killed. What was done to them and their bodies. How can you forgive or forget something like that? Bishop Tutu came up with this fairytale-like concept. When Tutu came to see me I said I was not going to say sorry so that everyone should feel good, and in my case I was not the least bit sorry for what I did. I told him that he and the other Commissioners were only sitting there in my living room because of people like me. It was our struggle, what we had done and had been ready to do, that gave us this freedom. Tutu turned all this into some sort of religious confession, and he should know that people who come to church and confess readily go out and do exactly the same. So much for confession, but then peace throws up heroes like Tutu.'

It occurred to me then, thinking of her long life and all that she had lived through, to ask how much had survived in her of her tribal Xhosa culture.

I was astonished by her reply, and her passion.

She said, 'I am defined by my culture and I know that I am from Xhosa land. I know that I am an African, and we know what to do from our grandmothers. The advent of European culture has affected our people, but our men still go to initiation schools. In my case it is a personal choice, and I will give you an example. If something is not going well for my children or grandchildren, I will go home to the graves of my ancestors and ask them for their help. We believe that the ancestor works with God.'

When she was a girl she thought she would like to be a

doctor. But she didn't know what it meant, and the ambition fell away. 'Now you have affluent blacks who send their children to posh white schools. They want their children to have the kind of education they dreamt about, and why not?'

So she was content?

'When I see my grandchildren I feel like a billionaire. There is nothing like it. But then when I am alone in my bedroom I think about being in death row and the long solitary confinement they put you in to break your spirit. The brain recalls everything.'

NOT FAR FROM this house of Winnie Mandela's there was a monument or memorial which I had been told I should see. It was the memorial to Hector Pieterson, a twelve-year-old schoolboy who, with nineteen others, had been shot dead in June 1976 during a protest in Soweto against the imposition of Afrikaans as the medium of instruction in township schools. This would have been part of the great 1976 uprising in Soweto, the tide-turner Winnie Mandela had talked about.

At the back of the memorial was a stall selling animal skins. I was sorry to see it. I thought this trade had been outlawed in South Africa; the zebra skin seemed very white, as though it had been washed in bleach or some fierce detergent.

The memorial itself was an affair of dry-walling and water slipping into a pool: the standard metaphors of this kind of memorial. It would have meant nothing without the blown-up newspaper photograph of the death of Hector Pieterson: the dead or dying boy being carried in the arms of a young man, his distraught sister walking beside them. As it happened, she was there that morning, talking to a group of overseas visitors; and when she was done with them she came to us, a woman in middle life, thirty-three years older than in the photograph, ready to re-live the incidents of that day.

Even with the animal skins in the background it was intensely moving; and yet the memorial seemed a passing thing, wasteful of space; the photograph, its centrepiece, seemed destined to fade; and I wondered how much longer this memorial to real pain would last. It was only seven years old, and had already been vandalised more than once by local children, to whom its architectural metaphors meant nothing. Elsewhere in Soweto, outside a café, the newspaper photograph had been rendered quite effectively in sculpture, without comment; that seemed more likely to last.

11

IN SOUTH AFRICA, with its many groups, its many passions, its abiding tensions, the visitor, seeking a necessary point of rest, moves from group to group, saying, rather like a Zen student: 'Not this, not this.' It is the method in small of Rian Malan's great book, *My Traitor's Heart*; but the division in his heart – an Afrikaner for nine generations – is the basic and bloody division between black and white.

The book begins with a brief and incomplete account of an eighteenth-century ancestor who, in defiance of law and custom, runs away with a slave woman. When this ancestor reappears he has no slave woman beside him; more than that, he has become a complete white leader. The writer can give no reason; the records give none; there is no story of the life of the ancestor with his slave lover. The whole thing is a mystery; and *My Traitor's Heart* suggests, but only suggests, that the writer's waverings have this quality of old mystery.

This unusual back-and-forth method, of autobiography and reportage, works because Rian Malan is a master of landscape and a master of narrative, with a gift of living language that bubbles up from a full heart and an active mind. But a book is a book; it has narrative needs. The back-and-forth method will not take a book through to the end; it needs some kind of resolution. The reader has to be sent away with a feeling of purpose, of something achieved. Rian Malan is enough of a writer to understand this. The bulk of the book took two years to write; but the last few pages took six months. Language wouldn't have been a problem; the writer's worry would have been the resolution of the material he has laid out, as big a problem in his book as in real life.

When we talked about things he said, 'This is a history of victims. There are no real heroes aside from Mandela, who suffered nobly. There is no one who will spell it out. Apartheid is over, and you have the abyss before you, and the only thing that will get you out is work, work, and work.' He was not an admirer of Winnie Mandela's; but I thought this idea of work (which was also Joseph Conrad's) would have coincided with hers. (From *Heart of Darkness*: 'Their talk, however, was the talk of sordid buccaneers: it was reckless without hardihood, greedy without audacity, and cruel without courage; there was not an atom of foresight or of serious intention in the whole batch of them, and they did not seem aware these things are wanted for the work of the world.')

Rian Malan said, 'I am obsessed with what came after apartheid. One legacy of apartheid is that this is the only country where the economy works and there are solid skyscrapers on the skyline. The rest of Africa is such a mess. If these African countries want to see how it works they should look at South Africa.'

So *My Traitor's Heart* ends with a parable (the author actually uses the word). It is the story of a white (or English) couple who seek through a life of work and sacrifice in a desolate and heartbreaking landscape to get to the heart of Africa (if it can be put like that). Nothing in Rian Malan is straight, however, and this parable of apparent triumph is actually a story of a tragedy, of two wasted lives; but Rian Malan, while acknowledging that, in his unbending way rises above his story, and suggests that this might be a way ahead for white South Africa: a place where whites have no guarantees.

The couple in his parable are Neil and Creina Alcock. They move to a piece of church land on the boundary of white South Africa and they begin to practise there the simple, machineless agriculture that might attract Africans. It is a terrible piece of land. It will never – like parts of white farmland – look like central California. It is rocky and arid, and is liable to repeated drought that can wipe out the work of years. The land carries too many people. It is also full of borderland hate: white for black, and all the unreasoning hate – often blazing up into full-scale war – that the Zulu factions have for one another. Still, Neil and Creina work this unpromising land until the church (fighting its own war, and unhappy with Creina for giving birth-control pills to African women) asks them to leave. They have the good fortune to get a piece of land, sixty miles away, from a South African corporation, and they continue their work there.

Their first idea had been to start a cattle co-operative. Pasturage could then be controlled by segments in this badly eroded land and the grass could revive. But there was a tradition of cattle-rustling among the Zulus; hundreds of unprotected cattle would be a standing provocation. So the idea of the cattle co-operative was laid aside, and Neil and Creina looked instead to develop a self-sustaining agricultural project. The river would provide water; there would be experimental solar cookers and methane-digesters. The project was housed in eleven Zulu-style huts, mud and stone and thatch. Neil and Creina were living on fifty dollars a month. Visitors began to come, some to spend a night in a hut, and it began to look as though the difficult project was taking off.

It seemed at one time that the danger to Neil would

[323]

come from white farmers on the other side of the border. They thought that Neil was giving his Africans too much encouragement, especially during times of drought when he cut down fences on the border and sent the cattle and goats of Africans to feed on the lusher grass on the other side. But, in fact, Neil seemed to have enjoyed some degree of licence as a madman on both sides of the border. And the danger, when it came, was from a random source that no one could have predicted: a factional Zulu war that had almost no cause, and was principally an expression of the Zulu love of fighting.

And, final, dreadful irony, it was because he had agreed to try to end a little Zulu war that he was killed. He was killed in an ambush by warriors from one side. He was driving his microbus to a peace meeting. The warriors, rising from behind boulders at the side of the road, aimed at him, the peace-maker. He was hit in the neck; he opened the microbus door and fell out on the road, dead.

Life became very hard for Creina. A widow in Africa is nothing, and Creina lost all the authority she had enjoyed as Neil's wife. Young starveling boys she had taken in and nurtured now turned against her, began to steal from her. They stole her cassette, her typewriter. They stole the money, two thousand dollars, she had put aside to pay farm women for their beadwork; this was an important part of the farm's income. Now that there wasn't the money to pay the women she had to pay them in instalments out of her seventy-five dollars a month wages. It was easy to steal from Creina; there were no locks on her doors. And it got worse. One man falsely accused her of killing eight of his goats. He wanted money for his goats; otherwise he was going to kill her. People she knew pleaded with her to leave the farm, but she didn't.

She told Rian Malan, 'If you're really going to live in Africa, you have to be able to look at it and say, "This is the way of love, down this road: look at it hard. This is where it is going to lead you." '

This is the resolution of this marvellous book. It is not easy to accept. Creina is so much finer than the louts who exploit her. Perhaps the problem is that 'love' is not defined. Without that definition it is hard to follow Creina when she tells Rian Malan, 'I think you will know what I mean if I tell you love is worth nothing until it has been tested by its own defeat.' It may even be that in this parable the writer is finding a way of saying something quite difficult: that after apartheid a resolution is not really possible until the people who wish to impose themselves on Africa violate some essential part of their being.

March 2008–September 2009